CU00659958

THE CHRONICLE OF
HENRY OF LIVONIA

RECORDS OF WESTERN CIVILIZATION

RECORDS OF WESTERN CIVILIZATION

The Art of Courtly Love, by Andreas Capellanus. Translated with an introduction and notes by John Jay Parry.

The Correspondence of Pope Gregory VII: Selected Letters from the Registrum. Translated with an introduction by Ephraim Emerton.

Medieval Handbooks of Penance: The Principal Libri Poenitentiales and Selections from Related Documents. Translated by John T. McNeill and Helena M. Gamer.

Macrobius: Commentary on The Dream of Scipio. Translated with an introduction by William Harris Stahl.

Medieval Trade in the Mediterranean World: Illustrative Documents. Translated with introductions and notes by Robert S. Lopez and Irving W. Raymond, with a foreword and bibliography by Olivia Remie Constable.

The Cosmographia *of Bernardus Silvestris.* Translated with an introduction by Winthrop Wetherbee.

Heresies of the High Middle Ages. Translated and annotated by Walker L. Wakefield and Austin P. Evans.

The Didascalicon *of Hugh of Saint Victor: A Medieval Guide to the Arts.* Translated with an introduction by Jerome Taylor.

Martianus Capella and the Seven Liberal Arts.
Vol. I: *The Quadrivium of Martianus Capella: Latin Traditions in the Mathematical Sciences*, by William Harris Stahl with Richard Johnson and E. L. Burge.
Vol. II: *The Marriage of Philology and Mercury*, by Martianus Capella. Translated by William Harris Stahl and Richard Johnson with E. L. Burge.

The See of Peter, by James T. Shotwell and Louise Ropes Loomis.

Two Renaissance Book Hunters: The Letters of Poggius Bracciolini to Nicolaus de Niccolis. Translated and annotated by Phyllis Walter Goodhart Gordan.

Guillaume d'Orange: Four Twelfth-Century Epics. Translated with an introduction by Joan M. Ferrante.

Visions of the End: Apocalyptic Traditions in the Middle Ages, by Bernard McGinn, with a new preface and expanded bibliography.

The Letters of Saint Boniface. Translated by Ephraim Emerton, with a new introduction and bibliography by Thomas F. X. Noble.

Imperial Lives and Letters of the Eleventh Century. Translated by Theodor E. Mommsen and Karl F. Morrison, with a historical introduction and new suggested readings by Karl F. Morrison.

An Arab-Syrian Gentleman and Warrior in the Period of the Crusades: Memoirs of Usāmah ibn-Munqidh. Translated by Philip K. Hitti, with a new foreword by Richard W. Bulliet.

De expugnatione Lyxbonensi (The Conquest of Lisbon). Edited and translated by Charles Wendell David, with a new foreword and bibliography by Jonathan Phillips.

Defensor pacis. Translated with an introduction by Alan Gewirth, with an afterword and updated bibliography by Cary J. Nederman.

History of the Archbishops of Hamburg-Bremen. Translated with an introduction and notes by Francis J. Tschan, with a new introduction and bibliography by Timothy Reuter.

The Two Cities: A Chronicle of Universal History to the Year 1146, by Otto, Bishop of Freising. Translated in full with an introduction and notes by Charles Christopher Mierow, with a foreword and updated bibliography by Karl F. Morrison.

THE CHRONICLE *of* HENRY OF LIVONIA

HENRICUS LETTUS

TRANSLATED WITH A NEW INTRODUCTION AND NOTES BY
James A. Brundage

COLUMBIA UNIVERSITY PRESS
NEW YORK

Columbia University Press
Publishers Since 1893
New York   Chichester, West Sussex

Copyright © University of Wisconsin Press, 1961
New introduction, notes, and bibliography © 2003 Columbia University Press
All rights reserved

Library of Congress Cataloging-in-Publication Data
Henricus, de Lettis, ca. 1187–ca. 1259.
[Origines Livoniae sacrae et civilis. English]
The chronicle of Henry of Livonia / Henricus Lettus ; translated with
a new introduction and notes by James A. Brundage.
    p. cm. — (Records of Western civilization)
Originally published: Madison : University of Wisconsin Press, 1961.
With new introd.
Includes bibliographical references and index.
ISBN 978-0-231-12888-9 (cloth : alk. paper)—ISBN 978-0-231-12889-6 (pbk. : alk. paper)
  1. Livonia—History. I. Brundage, James A. II. Title. III. Series.

DK500.L57H4613 2003
947.98'02—dc22

                                              2003062458

Columbia University Press books are printed on permanent and durable
acid-free paper.
Printed in the United States of America

RECORDS OF WESTERN CIVILIZATION is a series published under the auspices of the Interdepartmental Committee on Medieval and Renaissance Studies of the Columbia University Graduate School. The Western Records are, in fact, a new incarnation of a venerable series, the Columbia Records of Civilization, which, for more than half a century, published sources and studies concerning great literary and historical landmarks. Many of the volumes of that series retain value, especially for their translations into English of primary sources, and the Medieval and Renaissance Studies Committee is pleased to cooperate with Columbia University Press in reissuing a selection of those works in paperback editions, especially suited for classroom use, and in limited clothbound editions.

Committee for the Records of Western Civilization

Caroline Walker Bynum
Joan M. Ferrante
Carmela Vircillo Franklin
Robert Hanning
Robert Somerville, editor

Piæ Memoriæ
M. T. B.
nunc diis manibus
dedicat auctor

Contents

Abbreviations

LUB   *Liv-, Esth- und Kurlandische Urkundenbuch nebst Regesten*, ed. Friedrich Georg von Bunge

MGH   *Monumenta Germaniae Historica*
      SS   *Scriptores*
      SSRG   *Scriptores rerum germanicarum*

PL   *Patrologiae cursus completus . . . series Latina.* Ed. J. P. Migne, 1841–1864

Introduction to

the 2003 Edition

[I]

For Latin Christians during the closing decades of the twelfth century, the East was the golden land of opportunity. Shortly before the beginning of the century, crusading forces from the West had conquered Jerusalem, and the political, military, and commercial outposts that they and their successors had built in the Levant soon became powers to be reckoned with. In Europe itself, Western soldiers, missionaries, merchants, hunters, and peasants had, for nearly two hundred years, since the time of Otto the Great (r. 951–973), been pushing at Western Christendom's eastern frontiers on the Elbe River. The Slavic peoples whom they encountered there offered tantalizingly ripe prospects for conversion, commerce, and colonization. A few years after the turn of the thirteenth century, other Western armies would establish outposts of Latin

Note: This new introduction is meant to replace my original 1961 introduction to Henry's *Chronicle*. The older piece is also reprinted in this volume.

xi

Christendom in southeastern Europe when they attacked, overcame, and partitioned the Byzantine Empire.

The political, social, and religious geography of Central and Eastern Europe went through dramatic changes during the century between 1140 and 1240. In 1140, Germany's eastern frontier still lay along the Elbe valley. East of the river, Slavic chiefs and kings ruled an assortment of rival ethnic groups who depended for their survival primarily upon a relatively crude agricultural technology, supplemented by hunting, fishing, and a modest trade in furs and amber. By 1240 all this had changed. The Elbe by that point was no longer the frontier; it now lay in the middle of the German kingdom.

The opening of the trans-Elbe regions to permanent German settlement occurred rapidly in the aftermath of the crusade of 1147 against the Wends, a Slavic people living in what would soon be called the north German plains. St. Bernard of Clairvaux (1090–1153) envisioned this Wendish crusade as a campaign for the expansion of Christendom and instructed the crusaders that they were to wipe out either the Slavs or their religion.[1] Although the 1147 expedition, which formed part of the broader crusading enterprise known as the Second Crusade, achieved only modest success, it inaugurated a century of conquest and colonization in Eastern and Central Europe.[2] By the middle of the thirteenth century, successors of the 1147 crusaders had occupied the region east of the Elbe River and had driven any pagan Slavs who survived their on-

1. Bernard of Clairvaux, *Epist.* 457, in his *Opera*, ed. Jean Leclercq et al., 8 vols. (Rome: Editiones Cistercienses, 1957–77), 8:433; Friedrich Lotter, *Die Konzeption des Wendenkreuzzugs: Ideengeschichtliche, kirchrechtliche, und historisch-politische Voraussetzungen der Missionierung von Elb- und Ostseeslawen um die Mitte des 12. Jahrhunderts*, Vorträge und Forschungen, Sonderband 23 (Sigmaringen: Jan Thorbecke, 1977), 10–12.

2. Eric Christiansen, *The Northern Crusades: The Baltic and the Catholic Frontier, 1100–1525* (London: Macmillan, 1980), 48–69; and Edgar N. Johnson, "The German Crusade on the Baltic," in *A History of the Crusades*, ed. Kenneth M. Setton et al., 6 vols. (Madison: University of Wisconsin Press, 1969–1989), 3:545–56, provide excellent brief accounts of the campaigns in 1147 and following against the Slavs.

slaught farther eastward, beyond the Oder River valley. Meanwhile Christian colonists from Germany and the Low Countries had begun to establish permanent settlements in the newly won territories.[3] During the decade following the crusade against the Wends, merchants from Lübeck and other German, Swedish, and Danish ports began to call regularly at harbors along the eastern coast of the Baltic Sea.[4] There they traded with the indigenous peoples—Estonians and Karelians, who spoke Finnic languages; Kuronians, Lettgallians, Semgallians, who are sometimes collectively called Letts; and Livonians and Lithuanians, all of whom spoke Baltic languages. With these various peoples, the Western merchants exchanged silver (rarely gold), fine textiles, and other luxury goods in return for honey, beeswax, leather, dried fish, amber, and furs. This commerce was brisk and profitable, although the hazards were considerable. Added to the unavoidable natural risks of sea travel, the Wild East was rife with human dangers—piracy at sea and banditry on land were constant perils, and when disputes arose, few governments in the region were well equipped to enforce commercial agreements by peaceful means.

The growth of German commercial involvement in the eastern Baltic quickly led to efforts to create permanent trading posts. Enterprising merchants wanted to construct secure strongholds along the Baltic coasts and river valleys where they could build warehouses to store their goods and snug houses for themselves so that they could stay over winter in

---

3. On the Second Crusade as a whole, see Giles Constable, "The Second Crusade as Seen by Contemporaries," *Traditio* 9 (1953): 213–79; Hans Eberhard Mayer, *The Crusades*, 2d ed., trans. John Gillingham (Oxford: Oxford University Press, 1988), 93–106; and Jonathan Riley-Smith, *The Crusades: A Short History* (London: Athlone Press, 1987), 93–104.

4. *Livländische Reimchronik*, ed. Leo Mayer (Hildesheim: Georg Olms, 1963), ll. 127–228; English translation by Jerry C. Smith and William L. Urban, *The Livonian Rhymed Chronicle*, 2d. ed, (Chicago: Lithuanian Research and Studies Center, 2001), 3–4.

reasonable ease and safety, rather than facing the recurrent discomfort and risk of sailing out from their home bases every spring, followed by another voyage back when autumn came. Creating settlements of this sort inevitably entailed complications. Construction itself required importing skilled craftsmen—mainly carpenters and masons—although less-expert laborers might be recruited from among the indigenous peoples. Even though few merchants survived for long without being able and equipped to protect themselves, they also needed trained soldiers to guard their outposts while they were away about their business. They needed, in short, to colonize by bringing in a small permanent population to build, maintain, and protect the settlements that they envisioned.

Western ambitions in the eastern Baltic were not solely commercial. Political and religious leaders, too, were eager to grasp the opportunities that they saw in the region. The Baltic and Finnic heathens that religious authorities learned about from merchants and sailors in their congregations struck the clergy as a fertile field crying out for conversion to Christianity. Temporal rulers in Germany, Denmark, and Sweden likewise saw the eastern Baltic as a promising area, a power vacuum where they might readily increase their own power, wealth, and prestige. Commercial interests soon converged with those of popes and kings, bishops and dukes. Toward the end of the twelfth century a full-scale German conquest of the Baltic coastal plains began.[5]

The early stages of this conquest are known to us primarily from the chronicle of Henricus de Lettis, usually known in English as Henry of Livonia. Henry's chronicle provides the only surviving evidence for many episodes in the early stages of Western Christendom's expansion into the eastern Baltic.

5. Manfred Hellmann, "Die Anfänge christlicher Mission in den Baltischen Länder," in *Studien über die Anfänge der Mission in Livland*, ed. Manfred Hellmann, Vorträge und Forschungen, Sonderband 37 (Sigmaringen: Jan Thorbecke, 1989), 7–14.

His chronicle likewise provides a vivid record of the experiences and impressions of a contemporary witness who was personally involved in this vast movement. Henry was a shrewd observer. He often describes sights he had seen and sounds he had heard, as well as the personal appearance and quirks of many of the people he encountered. His chronicle is a very human document. A later verse narrative, the *Livländische Reimchronik*, corroborates much of Henry's version of events and provides additional information about some episodes.[6] Documentary records of the events that Henry's chronicle deals with in the eastern Baltic during the period between 1180 and 1226 are relatively sparse.[7] Without Henry's narrative, much of the history of the early stages of the German conquest and settlement in this region would be irretrievably lost.

Henry's version of events centers around the role of the church in the German advance into the eastern Baltic. His chronicle opens with an anecdote about Meinhard, a canon-regular in the Augustinian community at Segeberg, in Holstein. During the winter of 1180, Henry tells us, after listening to the stories told by merchants and sailors who had traveled up the Dvina River[8] about their adventures among the pagan Livonians and Letts with whom they traded, Meinhard felt called to convert those peoples to Christianity. Although he was already elderly, "with venerable gray hair," according to Henry, Meinhard set out for Livonia in the following spring.[9] When he reached the German trading posts

6. Alan V. Murray, "The Structure, Genre, and Intended Audience of the *Livonian Rhymed Chronicle*," in *Crusade and Conversion on the Baltic Frontier, 1150–1500*, ed. Alan V. Murray (Aldershot: Ashgate, 2001), 235–51.

7. The fundamental collection of documentary records is *Liv-, Esth-, und Curländisches Urkundenbuch nebst Regesten*, ed. Friedrich Georg von Bunge, 14 vols. (Reval: Kluge und Ströhm, 1853–1859; Riga: N. Kymmel [imprint varies] 1867–1910); hereafter cited as LUB.

8. Known in German as the Düna, in Latvian as the Daugava, and in Estonian as the Väina River.

9. *Chronicle* I.2. Meinhard was by no means the first Christian missionary to the eastern Baltic, but the labors of his predecessors had failed to produce any

on the banks of the Dvina, Meinhard stationed himself among the merchants' booths and preached to any natives who happened by. As time passed, his labors began to meet with modest success. In or about 1184, Meinhard and a few converts erected a church in the village of Uexküll (called Ikšķile in Latvian), where he baptized a few Livonian catechumens.[10] During the following winter, after a band of Lithuanians attacked the Livonians, Meinhard offered the local inhabitants a bargain. If they would accept Christian baptism, Meinhard would arrange for construction of a stone fortress at Uexküll to protect them from future attacks. The Livonians, who knew a good bargain when they heard one, accepted his offer. Meinhard then secured the services of stonemasons from the island of Gotland and directed them to build the promised fortress as well as a stone church on the banks of the Dvina.[11] When construction was completed, however, the Livonians reneged on their part of the agreement. Some of the baptized Livonians relapsed into paganism, and the remainder refused to accept the sacrament. Meinhard had a similar experience with the people of Holm, a nearby island in the Dvina. There he also built a castle, after receiving assurances that the inhabitants wished to be baptized, only to have nearly all his prospective converts reject baptism.[12]

Meinhard returned to Bremen in 1186, where he reported

---

lasting results; see William L. Urban, *The Baltic Crusade*, 2d ed. (Chicago: Lithuanian Research and Studies Center, 1994), 33–34, 42n 24; Hellman, "Anfänge," 14–18.

10. 1184 seems the most likely date, since about two years elapsed between the building of the church and Meinhard's consecration as bishop of Uexküll in 1186; Albert Hauck, *Kirchengeschichte Deutschlands*, 8th ed., 5 vols. (Berlin: Akademie Verlag, 1954), 4:654; Leonid Arbusow, *Grundriss der Geschichte Liv-, Est- und Kurlands* (Riga: Jonck und Poliewsky, 1908), 8–9; Urban, *Baltic Crusade*, 36; Hellmann, "Anfänge," 23–28.

11. See Carsten Selch Jensen, "The Nature of the Early Missionary Activities and Crusades in Livonia, 1185–1201," in *Medieval Spirituality in Scandinavia and Europe*, ed. Lars Bisgaard et al., Odense University Studies in History and Social Sciences, vol. 234 (Odense: Odense University Press, 2001), 126; Jensen reproduces a sketch of an archaeological reconstruction of this fort and attached church.

12. *Chronicle* I.6–7.

the accomplishments and disappointments of his mission to his ecclesiastical superior, Archbishop Hartwig II (r. 1185–1207). Hartwig, like many of his predecessors in the see of Bremen, harbored ambitions of creating an ecclesiastical empire in northern Europe, and he seized upon Meinard's Livonian mission as an opportunity to advance this project. With the consent of his cathedral chapter, Archbishop Hartwig consecrated Meinhard as bishop of Uexküll and urged him to go back to Livonia to carry on the good work.[13]

Meinhard's return to his Livonian outpost with a small group of fellow priests proved intensely disappointing. The Livonians of Holm attacked him and tried to drive him out of the country. Many of his recent converts jumped en masse into the Dvina to try to wash off the baptismal waters. Meinhard and his companions soon became virtual prisoners of the Livonians. Theodoric of Treiden, a Cistercian monk who was one of Meinhard's associates, was able to slip away by subterfuge, and he carried an appeal to the papacy for assistance. Pope Celestine III (r. 1191–1198) responded by authorizing him to recruit additional missionaries and granted Meinhard and his helpers in the Livonian mission an indulgence.[14] Beyond that the pope was unable to furnish further help. Amid these dispiriting circumstances, Meinhard died in 1196.

As soon as he learned of the death, Archbishop Hartwig

13. *Chronicle* I.8. The new Livonian bishopric became a suffragan of the archbishopric of Bremen; see LUB 1:10–11, no. 9–10; *Regesta pontificum romanorum ab condita ecclesia ad annum post Christum natum MCXCVIII*, ed. Philip Jaffé, rev. S. Loewenfeld, F. Kaltenbrunner, P. Ewald, 2 vols. (Leipzig: Veit, 1885–1888; reprint, Graz: Akademische Druck- u. Verlagsanstalt, 1956), nos. 16325 and 16328; Arbusow, *Grundriss*, 9.

14. *Chronicle* I.12–14; LUB 1:11–13, no. 11; *Regesta*, ed. Jaffé–Loewenfeld, 16991. The policy enunciated in this letter became part of the general law of the Western church, and Raymond of Penyafort included an excerpt from it in the *Decretales Gregorii IX* at X: 5.6.11. It is part of the *Corpus iuris canonici*, ed. Emil Friedberg, 2 vols. (Leipzig: B. Tauchnitz, 1879; reprint, Graz: Akademische Druck- u. Verlagsanstalt, 1959), vol. 2. For an explanation of the canonistic citation system used here see my *Medieval Canon Law* (London: Longman, 1995), 190–202. Likewise, on Raymond and the compilation of the Gregorian *Decretals*, see op. cit., 55, 196–97, 222–23.

named Berthold, the abbot of the Cistercian monastery of Loccum, to take Meinhard's place as bishop of Uexküll. Berthold at first resisted the appointment, perhaps because he was reluctant to be abruptly pulled out of the familiar and peaceful routines of monastic life and thrust into the hardships and dangers of missionary life. Hartwig, who was eager to set out on his own journey to the Holy Land, pressed Berthold to accept the assignment and finally prevailed. He quickly consecrated Berthold as bishop in 1197 and sent him on his way in the late spring or early summer of that year.[15]

Upon arriving at Uexküll, Berthold attempted to win over the local worthies with smooth words and blandishments. After a group of them attempted to kill him while he was consecrating a cemetery at Holm, Berthold had second thoughts about this strategy.[16] He surreptitiously sailed back to Saxony and set about raising an army. He persuaded the pope to promise that soldiers who enlisted in his expedition would receive the much-prized privileges of crusaders, a shrewd move that no doubt greatly facilitated recruitment.[17]

Berthold returned to Livonia in the summer of 1198, accompanied this time by a small but well-equipped army of veteran knights and infantry. He peremptorily demanded that the Livonians accept baptism as they had promised. The Livonians flatly refused. After a brief standoff, fighting broke out between the bishop's troops and the Livonians. In the

15. Bernd Ulrich Hucker, "Der Zisterzienserabt Berthold, Bischof von Livland, und der erste Livlandkreuzzug," in *Studien über die Anfänge,* ed. Manfred Hellmann, Vorträge und Forschungen, Sonderband 37 (Sigmaringen: Jan Thorbecke, 1989) 39–64.

16. Jensen, in "The Nature of Early Missionary Activities," speculates that Berthold at first brought no armed forces with him to Livonia because he relied for military support upon soldiers that Theodoric of Treiden had recruited in Germany. Those forces, as it turned out, were diverted to another campaign in Wierland.

17. *Chronicle* II.3; the crusading bull that Henry mentions has apparently not survived. On the indulgence and other privileges of crusaders see my *Medieval Canon Law and the Crusader* (Madison: University of Wisconsin Press, 1969), 138–90.

heat of battle on 24 July, after Berthold was wounded by an enemy lance, enraged Livonians swarmed around him and tore him to pieces, limb from limb. The German forces retaliated with a ruthless campaign of terror, slaughtering the inhabitants of the countryside indiscriminately, burning their fields and dwellings, until at length the Livonian leaders capitulated. A hundred and fifty were baptized in two days. Their leaders agreed to welcome missionaries into their forts and promised to pay taxes for the support of the priests. Reassured, the army returned to Germany.[18]

As soon as the German forces set sail down the Dvina, the new "converts" again dove into the river to wash off their baptism. When they discovered a wooden carving that they supposed must represent the Saxon god, the Livonians flung it into the wake of the departing fleet. Within a month they had managed to make life so miserable for the few missionaries who had remained behind that they had to seek refuge in the fortress on the island of Holm. Some of the Livonians wanted to drive the German merchants out of the country as well, but well-placed bribes to their elders soon put a stop to that.[19]

Bleak as the future of the Livonian mission must have seemed during the winter of 1198, its prospects improved immeasurably in the spring of 1199 when Archbishop Hartwig named his nephew, Albert von Buxhövden, a canon of the cathedral of Bremen, as the third bishop of Uexküll and consecrated him on or about 1 March 1199.[20] Able, energetic, ambitious, proud, hard-headed, and relentless, Albert's combination of virtues and vices made him one of the most successful ecclesiastical diplomats and empire builders of his generation. He set out to create an ecclesiastical empire in

18. *Chronicle* II.4–6.
19. *Chronicle* II.8–10.
20. On the date of Albert's consecration, see Bauer's introduction to his edition of the *Chronicle*: Henricus de Lettis, *Chronicon Livoniae*, ed. Leonid Arbusow, rev. Albert Bauer. MGH, SSRG (Hannover: Hahn, 1955), xxviii–xxix.

Livonia for himself and the archbishopric of Bremen. Unlike the saintly Bishop Meinhard, Bishop Albert came to Livonia to conquer, not to preach.[21] Bishop Albert is the central figure in Henry's chronicle. He clearly admired Albert enormously, although occasional passages seem to suggest that he may have harbored a few cautious reservations.[22] Albert's preparations for his first voyage to Livonia show that he planned for conquest from the outset. Before he departed, he recruited an army of Saxon crusaders and made sure that his political position was impregnable by securing approval of his designs from the Danish king, the archbishop of Lund, the German king, Philip of Swabia (r. 1198–1208), and Pope Innocent III (r. 1198–1216).[23]

The forces that Albert brought to Livonia in this and subsequent years varied in size and composition, but they were invariably vested with the privileges of crusaders.[24] He recruited his first army in 1199 mainly from Saxony and Westphalia but also persuaded several hundred hardened Frisian

21. For Albert's family and background, see especially Gisela Gnegel-Waitschies, *Bischof Albert von Riga: Ein Bremer Domherr als Kirchenfürst, 1199–1229* (Hamburg: August Friedrich Velmede, 1958), 22–44. Jensen, in "The Nature of the Early Missionary Activities," 136–37, speculates that, contrary to the usual interpretation of the evidence, Bishop Albert's pontificate may not have marked an abrupt change in policy and that the two missionary bishops who preceded him had military forces available for protection.

22. In three chapters of the *Chronicle* (chaps. III.1, IX.1, and X.1), Henry calculated the year on the basis of Bishop Albert's pontificate, which probably commenced on or about 28 March 1199. Although Henry apparently regarded 25 March as the first day of the calendar year, he commenced most chapters in his narrative at the point when the Baltic ice was sufficiently broken up to make maritime operations safe, generally around 1 April, and thus very close to the anniversary of Albert's consecration; see R. Holtzmann, "Studien zu Heinrich von Lettland," *Neues Archiv der Gesellschaft für ältere Deutsche Geschichtskunde* 43 (1920): 183–205; and Bauer's introduction to his edition of the *Chronicle*: Henricus de Lettis, *Chronicon Livoniae*, xxx–xxxi.

23. *Chronicle* III.2–5; LUB 1:13–18, no. 12–13; *Regesta pontificum Romanum inde ab anno post Christum natum MCXCVIII ad annum MCCCIV*, ed. August Potthast, 2 vols. (Berlin: Rudolf de Decker, 1874–1879; reprint, Graz: Akademische Druck-u. Verlagsanstalt, 1957), no. 842; Urban, *Baltic Crusade*, 50–52; Gnegel-Waitschies, *Bischof Albert von Riga*, 51–55.

24. LUB 1:18–20, no. 14; *Regesta*, ed. Potthast, no. 2299.

warriors to join his expedition. They sailed from Lübeck but called at Gotland along the way, where Albert recruited additional volunteers for his crusade. Albert repeated a similar pattern year after year. Most of his crusaders served for only one or two years at a time, then returned home. Albert consequently needed to return annually to Germany to replenish his forces.

Bishop Albert soon realized that something more dependable than these ever-changing levies of short-term volunteers was necessary for the sort of permanent conquest and colonization that he envisioned.[25] In 1202, at the initiative of Theodoric of Treiden, now abbot of the recently founded Cistercian monastery of Dünamünde (Daugavgriva), Albert created a new military religious order, modeled on the established order of the Knights Templar. This was the Order of Sword-Bearers, also known as the Brothers of the Militia of Christ or the Livonian Brothers of the Sword.[26] This order's purpose was to provide a standing army for the German colony that Albert and his coworkers were building in the eastern Baltic. The order was under the bishop's command and formed the permanent nucleus of his armed forces, supplemented by the levies of short-term volunteers from the West. The order's members also furnished him with an army of occupation in the newly conquered regions.

Conquest was further consolidated by the establishment of religious communities of Cistercian monks and Augustinian canons. Members of these communities combined the functions of missionaries and civil administrators in the occupied territories. Following each successful campaign, the bishop appointed magistrates to take charge of the Livonian villages

25. Thus, e.g., *Chronicle* III.2; IV.1; V.1; VI.1; VII.1; etc.

26. In *Chronicle* VI.6, Henry refers to Abbot Theodoric as the founder of the order. Other sources, including a rescript of Pope Innocent III, credit Bishop Albert with its foundation; see LUB 1:18–20, 22–23, no. 14, 16; *Regesta*, ed. Potthast, nos. 2299, 4104. See also Friedrich Benninghoven, *Der Orden der Schwertbrüder: Fratres milicie Christi de Livonia*, vol. 9 of *Ostmitteleuropa in Vergangenheit und Gegenwart* (Cologne: Böhlau, 1965), 39–40.

that his troops had won and parish priests to baptize the surviving natives, instruct them in the mysteries of their new Catholic faith, and minister to their spiritual needs. Bishop Albert also kept in mind the commercial interests of the German merchants who accompanied his armies. In 1200, the year after his arrival, Albert founded the city of Riga on the site of an earlier Livonian port.[27] Here he built a cathedral dedicated to the Blessed Virgin Mary, houses for himself and his chapter, a headquarters for the Brothers of the Sword, barracks for the annual levies of soldiers, and warehouses for the merchants. Here, too, were cast the bells of the new cathedral, bells that could not only summon the faithful to worship, but also call the citizens to arms and celebrate the widening and tightening of the German grip on the land.[28]

By 1208, Bishop Albert had the machinery of his new principality working smoothly. Most of the Livonians and Letts had by this time been compelled by force and fear to "accept the Christian name," as Henry so accurately put it. The bishop's missionary and military activities now began to turn northward, toward Estonia. The fourth book of Henry's chronicle records these campaigns in all their savage ferocity.[29] The very repetitiveness of the chronicler's account year after year testifies to the systematic strategy that had by this time been worked out for the Christianization and subjugation of the Baltic peoples.

The process began with military expeditions against one after another of the Estonians' fortified strongholds. The Germans, armed with a superior military technology, overran them, village by village. The armor,[30] the siege machinery,[31] and even the musical instruments[32] of the Germans gave the invaders a decisive edge over their opponents. The Estonians

27. *Chronicle* IV.5–7; VI.1–5; Urban, *Baltic Crusade,* 54; Gnegel-Waitschies, *Bischof Albert,* 56–58.
28. *Chronicle* XIV.5.
29. *Chronicle* XII.6–XXX.6.
30. E.g., *Chronicle* IX.3; XIV.5.
31. E.g., *Chronicle* VII.7; X.12; XI.9; XXVIII.5.
32. E.g., *Chronicle* XII.6; XV.3; XXVIII.5 and 6.

tried in vain to organize an effective resistance. They called for help from the Russian princes of Polozk, Pskov, Novgorod, and Smolensk, all in vain. Neither the Russians nor the Estonians were able to stem the German advance. Without more efficient organization and considerable upgrading of their armament, the Estonians had little hope of halting the Saxon invaders. The Russians, for their part, were too much taken up with their own domestic quarrels and with fighting off the Tatar invasions to divert significant forces to take on the Germans.[33]

Competition between Latin and Russian Orthodox missionaries for the religious allegiance of the Baltic peoples further complicated the situation.[34] Orthodox missionaries had not shown notable zeal in converting Baltic populations under Russian rule to Christianity. As Henry noted, "It is, indeed, the custom of the Russian kings not to subject whatever people they defeat to the Christian faith, but rather to force them to pay tribute and money to themselves."[35] The Germans, by contrast insisted upon baptizing all of the peoples that they conquered in the Baltic area. In the face of the expansion of German colonies, Russian influence in the Baltic region steadily diminished. The Saxon bishop and his men defeated the Russian princes of Gerzike (in Latvian, Jersika) and Kokenhusen (in Latvian, Koknese) and destroyed their principalities.[36] Only after Bishop Albert had been dead a dozen years would a Russian army under the Duke of Novgorod, Alexander Nevsky (ca. 1220–1263), defeat a sizable army of German knights in the well-known battle of 1242 on the ice of Lake Peipus (Chudskoe ozero in Russian; Peipsi Järv in Latvian).[37]

33. *Chronicle*, XXV.2; XXVI.1; Urban, *Baltic Crusade*, 138–40.
34. On this, see especially A. M. Ammann, *Kirchenpolitische Wandlungen im Ostbaltikum bis zum Tode Alexander Newskis*, vol. 105 of *Orientalia Christiana Analecta* (Rome: Pont. Institutum orientalium studiorum, 1936).
35. *Chronicle* XVI.2.
36. *Chronicle* XI.8; XIII.1, 4.
37. Urban, *Baltic Crusade*, 197–99; Christiansen, *Northern Crusades*, 128–30; Benninghoven, *Der Orden der Schwertbrüder*, 379–82.

Danish and Swedish rulers also attempted to stake claims in the Baltic territories where Bishop Albert was building his empire. Of the two, the Danes were the more serious rivals to the bishop's ambitions. A lively, often acrimonious contest between Saxon and Danish interests continued until Henry the Black, Count of Schwerin, captured the Danish king, Waldemar II (1202–1241) in 1223. Despite this, however, Danish forces managed to retain control of northern Estonia.[38] Religious conversion of the population was a primary goal of the crusades in the Baltic. Crusades in this region, unlike those in the Holy Land, were missionary enterprises from the outset.[39] Baptism of the survivors routinely followed military conquest. Baptism, the sacrament of initiation into the Christian church, also symbolized surrender to German domination. Crusading armies in the Baltic accordingly demanded that everyone brought under their rule be baptized according to the rites and ceremonies followed in Saxony.[40]

Baptism also entailed subjection to the canon law of the Christian church.[41] The most immediate and obvious consequences of this were that the new converts now had to observe Christian marriage rules and, in addition, owed tithes to their new ecclesiastical overlords.[42] Both requirements were sources of resentment. The church's laws concerning marriage created serious problems for the practice of formalizing social and political bonds through consanguineous marriage alliances, as well as other traditional marriage practices among the Baltic peoples.[43] Bishop Albert dispatched Abbot Theod-

38. Urban, *Baltic Crusade*, 140–46; Christiansen, *Northern Crusades*, 106–9.
39. On the contrast between the two, see especially Benjamin Z. Kedar, *Crusade and Mission: European Approaches Toward the Muslims* (Princeton, N.J.: Princeton University Press, 1984).
40. *Chronicle* XXIV.5–6.
41. *Chronicle* XVIII.7; XXIII.3.
42. *Decretum Gratiani* C. 13 q. 1 c. 1 and d.p.c. 1; C. 16 q. 1 d.p.c. 44, c. 45, 55, 57, and passim, in *Corpus iuris canonici*, ed. Friedberg, vol. 1.
43. See my "Christian Marriage in Thirteenth-Century Livonia," *Journal of Baltic Studies* 4 (1973): 313–20; reprint, with original pagination, in Brundage, *The Crusades, Holy War, and Canon Law* (Aldershot: Variorum, 1991), no. XVIII.

oric in 1201 to consult with Pope Innocent III about these problems.[44] Theodoric prevailed upon the pope to issue a series of rulings in the decretal letter *Deus qui ecclesiam*, which resolved some of the most pressing of these difficulties.[45] The tithe, a 10 percent tax on most kinds of personal income, supplied the revenue necessary to sustain the building and maintenance of churches and to support the clergy, matters in which Henry took a strong personal interest.[46]

Popes and councils had traditionally insisted that baptism be administered to adults only after they had been instructed in the elements of Christian belief and practice and had accepted those teachings of their own free will.[47] The practice on the Baltic frontier was different: baptism came first, instruction and acceptance might (or might not) follow. Priests regularly accompanied the crusading armies. Among their principal duties was administering baptism to the survivors in the conquered settlements.[48] Priests gradually settled in the conquered villages, established parishes, built churches, and ministered to the converts. One such priest was the chronicler Henry.

[II]

Henry scattered bits of personal information throughout his chronicle. Although Latvian writers have occasionally claimed

44. *Chronicle* IV.6.

45. LUB 1:15–18, no. 13, prints the text of this decretal, but dates it erroneously to 1199. *Regesta*, ed. Potthast, no. 1323 provides the correct date, 19 April 1201. Significant portions of it also appear in the *Decretales Gregorii IX* at X 3.1.11, 4.19.9, and 5.38.8, in *Corpus iuris canonici*, ed. Friedberg. An improved text appears in *Senās Latvijas Vēstures Avoti*, ed. A. Švabe, 2 vols. (Riga: Latvijas Vēstures Institūta Apgaādiens, 1937), 1:23–24, no. 33.

46. *Chronicle* XI.3; XV.5; XVI.4–5; XXI.6; XXVIII.8–9; and XXIX.3.

47. See the authorities cited in, e.g., the *Decretum Gratiani* D. 4 de cons. c. 54, 58–60, 93, in *Corpus iuris canonici*, ed. Friedberg, vol. 1.

48. Thus, e.g., *Chronicle* IV.3; X.14; XVI.4; XIX.4, 8; XXI.5, 6; XXIV.5; and XXX.4,5.

that he was a Livonian or Lettish priest educated in Germany,[49] the preponderance of the evidence strongly suggests that he was one of the clerics who came to Livonia from somewhere in northern Germany.[50] Throughout his chronicle Henry identifies with the German conquerors, notably when he uses the first person pronoun to recount the actions of the German forces during episodes to which he was evidently an eyewitness in 1219.[51]

Everything that we know about Henry's life and character must be deduced from remarks in his chronicle, which clearly reflects its author's personal experiences as one of Bishop Albert's parish priests. Henry must have been born sometime in the last quarter of the twelfth century, perhaps around 1188, probably in Saxony. He was educated in Germany, very likely at the monastery of Segeberg in Holstein, to which he refers frequently.[52] Wherever he went to school, he received a thorough grounding in Latin.[53] His prose echoes the language of the Vulgate Bible and the Latin liturgy on nearly every page. While he occasionally quotes from or alludes to classical Latin authors,[54] Henry refers to biblical and liturgical sources far more often.[55] Some passages in his chronicle resemble a patchwork quilt, pieced together from phrases and figures taken from the Vulgate and the Latin liturgy.

Henry may have made his first acquaintance with the Baltic

49. Alfred Bilmanis, *A History of Latvia* (Princeton, N.J.: Princeton University Press, 1951), 55; Arnolds Spekke, *History of Latvia*, trans. H. Kundzins et al. (Stockholm: M. Goppers, 1951), 129.

50. In addition to Bauer's introduction to his edition of Henry's *Chronicle* (Henricus de Lettis, *Chronicon Livoniae*), v–ix, see also Paul Johansen, "Die Chronik als Biographie: Heinrich von Lettlands Lebensgang und Weltanschauung," *Jahrbücher für Geschichte Osteuropas* n.s. 1 (1953): 1–24.

51. *Chronicle* XXIII.9.

52. *Chronicle* I.2; VI.3; IX.6; X.7

53. On his technical competence as a Latinist, see esp. Leonid Arbusow, *Colores rhetorici* (Göttingen: Vandenhoeck & Ruprecht, 1948).

54. Among them Cicero (I.2; II.5), Horace (X.3), Ovid (X.17; XXX.5), and above all Vergil (IX.1; X.3; XII.2; XIX.1; XXIX.8).

55. Leonid Arbusow, "Das entlehnte Sprachgut in Heinrichs 'Chronicon Livoniae,'" *Deutsches Archiv für Erforschung des Mittelalters* 8 (1951): 107–34.

languages while he was at school. Certainly he was employed as an interpreter in Livonia, and, if he was schooled at Segeberg, he could well have come into contact there with boys from Livonia who were held as hostages and sent to Segeberg to be educated under the care of Bishop Albert's brother, Rothmar, who was abbot of the monastery.[56] Henry probably first came to Livonia in 1205 as a scholar in Bishop Albert's household. Albert ordained him as a priest in 1208 and assigned him to a newly formed parish. There, as Henry tells us us, he "lived with [the Letts] and, although exposed to many dangers, did not cease to point out to them the blessed future life."[57] He was still there as an old man in 1259.[58]

Henry began to write his chronicle no earlier than August of 1224. By the spring of 1226 he had completed the greater part of it.[59] He soon took it up again to add another concluding chapter that brought his narrative through the events of 1227 and the subjugation of Oesel (Saaremaa, in Estonian).[60] He may well have intended his chronicle as a report on the origins, progress, and achievements of the Livonian church for the papal legate, William of Modena, for whom Henry served as an interpreter in 1225–1227.[61]

Henry's chronicle records many of his personal experiences as a missionary in Livonia, fleshed out with stories that he heard from his contemporaries among the German colony there. "Nothing has been put in this account," he declared, "except what we have seen almost entirely with our own eyes. What we have not seen with our own eyes, we have learned

---

56. *Chronicle* IX.6; Johansen, "Die Chronik als Biographie," 11.

57. *Chronicle* XI.7. His parish is thought to have been at Papendorf (Rubene), about nine miles southwest of Wolmar.

58. Johansen, "Die Chronik als Biographie," 15.

59. *Chronicle* XXIX.9 marks the point at which his original version concluded.

60. *Chronicle* XXX.

61. Henry presumably added the concluding chapter as a postscript after the legate undertook a previously unforeseen campaign against the Oeselians; see James A. Brundage, "The Thirteenth-Century Livonian Crusade: Henricus de Lettis and the First Legatine Mission of Bishop William of Modena," *Jahrbücher für Geschichte Osteuropas*, n.s. 20 (1972): 1–9.

from those who saw it and were there."[62] Declarations of this sort are not uncommon in medieval chronicles; indeed Leonid Arbusow described them as "a rhetorical commonplace."[63] Nevertheless, in Henry's chronicle, the writer's declaration seems a reasonably accurate description of his methodology. The episodes that he relates from his personal experience strongly suggest that much of his work is autobiographical.[64]

It is possible to infer a good deal about Henry's personality and interests from his chronicle. Clearly he was first and foremost a priest, well trained in Latin, steeped in the language of the Vulgate and the liturgy, who had along the way acquired some scattered tags from the Latin classics.[65] He certainly took more than a casual interest in military affairs. His detailed descriptions of warfare, military engines, and siege techniques derive from his experiences with the conquering armies that he accompanied on at least several campaigns.[66] That his knowledge of military affairs drew upon experience in the field is evident from one of the most vivid personal recollections in the chronicle. Henry relates that while he was baptizing a pagan in Wierland,

[a] great clamor arose and a rushing of our army through all the streets and everyone ran to arms, crying that a great host of pagans was coming against us. We immediately put down the holy chrism and the other holy articles, therefore, and hurried to the ministry of shields and swords.[67]

Once it became clear that the approaching forces were friendly, Henry tells us, he returned to his more pacific duties and completed the interrupted baptism.

62. *Chronicle* XXIX.9.
63. Arbusow, "Das entlehnte Sprachgut," 137; cf. his *Colores rhetorici*, 109–10.
64. Johansen rightly concluded that "Heinrichs Chronik im Grund nur einen abgewandelten Erlebnissbericht darstellt"(Henry's *Chronicle* constitutes merely an expanded autobiography); "Die Chronik als Biographie," 6.
65. Arbusow, "Das entlehnte Sprachgut," 102–7.
66. Thus, e.g., *Chronicle* X.12; XIV.5; XV.1; XVI.4; XVIII.5; XXIII.9; XXVIII.5–6.
67. *Chronicle* XXIII.7.

Henry's frequent allusions to musical instruments suggest that he was sensitive to sounds and had more than a casual interest in music. He tells us, for example, how, during another battle, he "mounted the ramparts and, while the others fought, sang prayers to God on a musical instrument."[68] Occasional wordplay[69] and an account of his amusement at the naiveté of some villagers[70] likewise suggest that Henry was not without a sense of humor. One might even suspect that a shade of mirth may lurk behind his account of the episode in which some Livonians cast their immolated goats and dogs into Bishop Albert's face.[71]

Although Henry did not identify himself ethnically with his Baltic parishioners, his chronicle expresses sympathy and affection for them. He clearly saw himself and the other Germans in Livonia as agents of a higher culture who had come to bring the blessings of the Christian religion and civilization to the Letts and Livonians among whom he labored. He also shows scant sympathy for his those among his compatriots who wished to oppress the native peoples with excessive demands, financial or otherwise. He insists, especially in the closing sections of his chronicle, that the burden of Christ should be sweet and light. Several times he reproved those who were excessively harsh toward the Livonian converts.[72] Henry rarely commiserates with the afflicted in so many words, but his compassion comes through clearly enough when, for example, he reports the lament of the prince of Gerzike over the burning of his city.[73] Henry's interest in the Baltic peoples is also evident from the Livonian, Lettish, and Estonian words and phrases that he scatters through his

---

68. *Chronicle* XII.6.
69. See, for example, his slightly heavy-handed play on the name of Riga and the verb "rigo" (irrigate) at *Chronicle* IV.5 and XIX.7, or "Lettus" and "laetus" at *Chronicle* XXIX.3.
70. *Chronicle* XXIV.5.
71. *Chronicle* XVI.4.
72. *Chronicle* XXV.2; XXIX.2–3, 5.
73. *Chronicle* XIII.4.

chronicle.[74] The attitude of this mere parish priest and chronicler—a humble man, as he calls himself—toward the Baltic subjects of Bishop Albert's new ecclesiastical principality contrasts strikingly with the haughtiness of the ambitious prelate who was Henry's superior.

[III]

Eight manuscript copies of Henry's chronicle survive in one form or another. The oldest known manuscript, the early-fourteenth-century Codex Zamoscianus, now in Warsaw, is unfortunately incomplete and lacks fully a third of Henry's text. The chronicle's editors have supplied the missing parts from a seventeenth-century transcript, the Codex Skodiesky, now in the State Library at Riga. In addition to these, a half-dozen more recent transcripts dating from the seventeenth and eighteenth centuries are known.[75]

Johann Daniel Gruber published the first printed version of Henry's chronicle in 1740 under the title *Origines Livoniae sacrae et civilis*.[76] Johann Gottfried Arndt brought out a German translation of this version with some textual corrections in 1747, and A. Hansen reproduced Gruber's text with Arndt's corrections with a new German translation in 1853.[77]

---

74. Among them, "draugs" (XVI.4); "maga," "magetac," and "magamas" (XV.3); "kilegunda" (XXVIII.2, 8; XXIX.7; and XXX.5); "nogata" (XIV.2 and XV.8); "watmal" (I.11); "maia" (XV.7; XXIII.7, 9); "malewa" (XIX.9; XX.2; XXIII.7); and "waipas" (XXVII.6). If Henry served as an interpreter for the Latin- and German-speaking clergy (*Chronicle* XVI.3 expressly identifies him as such), this close contact with the Baltic peoples and his knowledge of their languages may go far to explain his interest in and sympathy for them.

75. Albert Bauer's introduction to his edition, xliii–xlviii, provides further details of these manuscripts and their relationships to one another.

76. Henricus de Lettis, *Origines Livoniae sacrae et civilis seu chronicon Livonicum vetus*, ed. Johann Daniel Gruber (Frankfurt and Leipzig: n.p., 1740).

77. *Scriptores rerum Livonicarum: Sammlung der wichtigsten Chroniken und Geschichtsdenkmale von Liv-, Esth- und Curled*, 2 vols. (Riga: E. Frantzen, 1848–1853).

In 1874 a fresh edition by Wilhelm Arndt appeared in volume 23 of the *Scriptores* series of the *Monumenta Germaniae Historica.* Leonid Arbusow proposed a number of corrections to Arndt's edition in 1926 and 1927, and Albert Bauer incorporated most of these in his edition in the *Scriptores rerum germanicarum* series of the *Monumenta Germaniae Historica* in 1955.[78]

This is the first English translation of Henry's chronicle. I began work on it in 1950 and had substantially completed it by the end of 1951. The translation is based on Wilhelm Arndt's edition, with scattered emendations from the Bauer edition.

[IV]

In 1199, just as Bishop Albert was beginning his crusade in Livonia, Moses Maimonides in Cairo took time out from his busy medical practice to write to a Provençal scholar, Samuel ibn Tibbon, who was translating the *Guide for the Perplexed* from Arabic into Hebrew. In his letter, Maimonides offered some sage advice on the art of translating:

Whoever wishes to translate, and aims at rendering each word literally, and at the same time adheres slavishly to the order of words and sentences in the original, will meet with much difficulty; his rendering will be faulty and untrustworthy. This is not the right method. The translator should first try to grasp the sense of the passage thoroughly, and then state the author's intention with perfect clearness in the other language. This, however, cannot be done without changing the order of words, putting many words for one, or vice

78. See Bauer's introduction to Henricus de Lettis, *Chronicon Livoniae,* xlviii–liv.

versa, and adding or taking away words, so that the subject may be perfectly intelligible in the language into which he translates.[79]

I have kept Maimonides' counsel in mind while preparing this translation of Henry's chronicle. The translation was done with an eye to conveying the chronicler's meaning in English, rather than with the aim of transposing Henry's Latin words into English words. This has necessitated recasting many sentences, more than once expanding a single word into a phrase, and much less frequently compressing a Latin phrase into a single English word.

I have retained the chapter divisions devised by Hansen, since subsequent editors have continued to use them, as do virtually all modern authors when they cite Henry's text. The bracketed dates in the translation come from Arndt's edition, as do many identifications of persons and places in the footnotes.

Henry's fondness for biblical citations and allusions raises other problems for the translator.[80] I have followed the text divisions of the Vulgate throughout. I have taken translations of direct biblical citations either from the Douay-Challoner[81] or the Knox translation of the Vulgate,[82] depending on which

79. Maimonides, "Letter to His Translator," trans. Franz Kohler, *Commentary* 15 (1953): 394. Ronald A. Knox, in *Trials of a Translator* (New York: Sheed & Ward, 1949), offered similar advice in slightly greater detail, as did Hilaire Belloc in his lecture *On Translation* (Oxford: Clarendon Press, 1931) and Ezra Pound, in *Guide to Kulchur* (London: Faber & Faber, 1938), 326. For a more sophisticated treatment, see Umberto Eco, *Experiences in Translation*, trans. Alastair McEwan (Toronto: University of Toronto Press, 2001), 9–29.

80. Arbusow, in "Das entlehnte Sprachgut," noted several hundred biblical allusions, as well as more than a hundred further borrowings from liturgical texts. Some of the references that he listed seem strained, and this translations cites only those that seem clearly well founded.

81. *The Holy Bible: Douay Version*, rev. Richard Challoner (London: Catholic Truth Society, 1956; reprint 1960).

82. Ronald A. Knox, *The Holy Bible: A Translation from the Latin Vulgate in the Light of the Hebrew and Greek Originals* (New York: Sheed & Ward, 1956).

seemed most appropriate in the context. References to liturgical texts, save for the Martyrology, are to modern editions.[83]

[V]

Henry wrote his chronicle of Livonia at a period when the young emperor, Frederick II (1197–1250), was attempting, with considerable difficulty, to rule Germany from Sicily,[84] while the popes were far too distracted by other matters, notably including a power struggle with Frederick II, to give Baltic affairs more than passing attention.[85] Henry's chronicle shows how in these circumstances an aggressive Saxon bishop was able to establish an independent theocratic state in an underdeveloped Baltic area and how German control of the Baltic lands came to be based upon the devastation of the indigenous peoples and their culture. Henry's chronicle vividly documents not only the triumphs and achievements, but also the mistakes and misfortunes that attended this medieval effort to bestow the "blessings" of a more technologically advanced culture upon a "backward" people.

Both the chronicler and the men whose actions he describes were no doubt convinced in good conscience of the righteousness of their cause and of the ultimate benevolence of the Livonian invasion in which they participated. Nor were all the brutal events that Henry recorded perpetrated solely

83. Citations of the Martyrology refer to the two most widely used medieval texts: Ado of Vienne, *Martyrologium*, ed. Heribert Rosweid, in PL 123: 139–436; and Usuard, *Martyrologium*, ed. J. B. Solleri, in PL 123: 453–860.

84. David Abulafia, *Frederick II: A Medieval Emperor* (New York: Oxford University Press, 1988), 109–63; Michael Toch, "Welfs, Hohenstaufen, and Habsburgs," in *The New Cambridge Medieval History*, 5 vols. to date (Cambridge: Cambridge University Press, 1991–), 5:375–92.

85. Helmut Roscher, *Papst Innocenz III. und die Kreuzzüge*, vol. 21 of *Forschungen zur Kirchen- und Dogmengeschichte* (Göttingen: Vandenhoeck & Ruprecht, 1969), 198–200.

by the invaders. Local rulers and their forces played support-
ing roles in the fighting and were routinely employed to collect loot, round up prisoners, and search out the hiding places
of those who fled before the crusading armies. The invaders
sought with considerable success to take advantage of the ethnic divisions and rivalries among the indigenous peoples,
while local strongmen, for their part, seized the opportunities
that the invasions afforded to attack traditional enemies with
whom they had often struggled before the German armies
arrived.

The events whose beginnings Henry recorded proved to
have exceptionally long-term consequences. Although German settlers in the eastern Baltic were never very numerous,
they remained a dominant minority in the urban centers and
commercial life of the Baltic states, especially Latvia and Estonia, well into the twentieth century. In 1939, as part of his
pact with Josef Stalin, Adolf Hitler summoned the Baltic Germans to return "home" to the Third Reich. Since the alter-
native was to remain in place under imminent Soviet occupation, families whose ancestors had lived in the region for
centuries responded to the summons.

Still, unmistakable traces of their presence persist. Eight
hundred years after Henry wrote, the architecture, religions,
economies, and political culture of the Baltic Republics still
retain obvious and important traces of the events that he
chronicled. The admission of Latvia, Lithuania, and Estonia
into the European Union in December 2002 is only the most
recent testimony to the lasting imprint of those events.

THE BALTIC CRUSADE

THE HOLY ROMAN EMPIRE

Monasteries:
M = Marienfeld
S = Segeberg
R = Reinfeld
L = Loccum

NORTHERN CENTRAL EUROPE
AND THE BALTIC

Finland

Gulf of Finland

Karelia

Wierland

Baltic Sea

Dagö

Harrien   Jerwen

Estonia

Novgorod

Lake
Peipus

Oesel

Saccalia

Ungannia

Pskov

Gulf of
Riga

Isborg

Gauja River
Adsel

Visby

Gotland

Thoreiden
Holm
Uexküll Kokenhusen

Lettgallia

Gerzike

Selonia

Daugava
River

Polozk

Semgallia

Kurland   Aa River

Nalsen

Baltic Sea

Samogitia
(Lithuanian lowlands)

Aukstaitija
(Lithuanian
highlands)

Smolensk→

Nemunas River

Samland

Pregel
River

Jatwigia
(Sudavia)

Gardinas
(Grodno)

Minsk

Pomerellia

Prussia

Novogrodek

Vistula
River

Culm

"Black Russia"

Masovia

Bug River

Great Poland

Volhynia

Sandomir

LIVONIA ON THE EVE OF THE CONQUEST

Gulf of Finland

KARELIANS

Narva River

Lake Peipus

Tallinn

ESTONIANS

RUSSIANS

Oesel

Tartu

ESTONIANS

Pskov

Gulf of Riga

Gauja River

Treiden

Visby

Gotland

LIVS

LETTS

Baltic Sea

Kokenhusen

Aa River

SELONIANS

Gerzike

RUSSIANS

SEMGALLIANS

Daugava River

Polozk

KURS

LITHUANIANS

PRUSSIANS

THE BALTIC DURING THE EARLY CONQUEST, 1200-1205

Gulf of Finland

Karelia

Wierland

Harrien

Jerwen

Novgorod

Lake Peipus

Estonia

Oesel

Saccalia

Ungannia

Pskov

Gotland

Visby

Gauja River

Tolowa

Treiden

Baltic Sea

Dünamünde

Riga

Lettgallia

Holm

Kokenhusen

Uexkull

Gerzike

Aa River

Selonia

Daugava River

Semgallia

Polozk

0   200 km

0   120 miles

Kurland

Lithuania

Bibliography

Primary Sources

Ado of Vienne. *Martyrologium*. Ed. Heribert Rosweid. In PL 123: 139–436.

Arnold of Lübeck. *Chronica slavorum*. Ed. J. M. Lappenberg. In MGH, SS 21:115–250.

Bernard of Clairvaux. *Opera*. Ed. Jean Leclercq et al. 8 vols. Rome: Editiones Cistercienses, 1957–77.

Corpus iuris canonici. Ed. Emil Friedberg. 2 vols. Leipzig: B. Tauchnitz, 1879. Reprint, Graz: Akademische Druck- u. Verlagsanstalt, 1959.

Henricus de Lettis. *Chronicon Lyvoniae*. Ed. Wilhelm Arndt. Vol. 23 of *Scriptores, Monumenta Germaniae Historica*. Hannover: Hahn, 1874.

Henricus de Lettis. *Chronicon Livoniae*. Ed. Leonid Arbusow. Rev. Albert Bauer. MGH, SSRG. Hannover: Hahn, 1955.

Henricus de Lettis. *Origines Livoniae sacrae et civilis seu chronicon Livonicum vetus*. Ed. Johann Daniel Gruber. Frankfurt and Leipzig [n.p.], 1740.

Liv-, Esth-, und Kurländische Urkundenbuch nebst Regesten. Ed. Friedrich Georg von Bunge. 14 vols. Reval: Kluge und Ströhm, 1853–1859; Riga: N. Kymmel (imprint varies), 1867–1910.

Livländische Reimchronik. Ed. Leo Mayer. Hildesheim: Georg Olms, 1963.

The Livonian Rhymed Chronicle. Trans. Jerry C. Smith and William

L. Urban. 2d ed. Chicago: Lituanian Research and Studies Center, 2001.

Maimonides, "Letter to His Translator." Trans. Franz Kohler. *Commentary* 15 (1952): 393–95.

Monumenta Germaniae Historica. Scriptores. 32 vols. Leipzig, Hannover: Hahn, 1826–1934.

———. *Scriptores rerum Germanicarum in usum scholarum.* Hannover, Leipzig: 1839–; in progress.

Patrologiae cursus completus . . . series Latina. Ed. J. P. Migne. 221 vols. Paris: J. P. Migne, 1841–1864.

Regesta pontificum romanorum ab condita ecclesia ad annum post Christum natum MCXVIII. Ed. Philip Jaffé. Rev. S. Loewenfeld, F. Kaltenbrunner, P. Edwald. 2 vols. Leipzig: Veit, 1885–1888. Reprint, Graz: Akademische Druck- u. Verlagsanstalt, 1956.

Regesta pontificum romanorum inde ab anno post Christum natum MCXCVIII ad annum MCCCIV. Ed. August Potthast. 2 vols. Berlin: Rudolf de Decker, 1874–1879. Reprint, Graz: Akademische Druck- u. Verlagsanstalt, 1957.

Scriptores rerum Livonicarum: Sammlung der wichtigsten Chroniken und Geschichtsdenkmale von Liv-, Ehst- und Kurland. 2 vols. Riga: E. Frantzen, 1848–1853.

Senās Latvijas Vēstures Avoti. Ed. A. Švabe. 2 vols. Riga: Latvijas Vēstures Institūta Apgaādiens, 1937

Usuard. *Martyrologium.* Ed. J. B. Solleri. In PL 123: 453–860.

Secondary Works

Abulafia, David. *Frederick II: A Medieval Emperor.* New York: Oxford University Press, 1988.

Ammann, A. M. *Kirchenpolitische Wandlungen im Ostbalticum bis zum Tode Alexander Newskis.* Vol. 105 of *Orientalia Christiana Analecta.* Rome: Pont. Institutum Orientalium Studiorum, 1936.

Arbusow, Leonid. *Colores rhetorici.* Göttingen: Vandenhoeck & Ruprecht, 1948.

———. "Das entlehnte Sprachgut in Heinrichs 'Chronicon Livoniae.' " *Deutsches Archiv für Erforschung des Mittelalters* 8 (1951): 100–153.

———. *Grundriss der Geschichte Liv-, Est- und Kurlands.* Riga: Jonck und Poliewsky, 1908.

Belloc, Hilaire. *On Translation.* Oxford: Clarendon Press, 1931.

Benninghoven, Friedrich. *Der Orden der Schwertbrüder: Fratres Milicie Christi de Livonia*. Vol. 9 of *Ostmitteleuropa in Vergangenheit und Gegenwart*. Cologne: Böhlau, 1965.

Bilmanis, Alfred. *A History of Latvia*. Princeton, N.J.: Princeton University Press, 1951.

Brundage, James A. "Christian Marriage in Thirteenth-Century Livonia." *Journal of Baltic Studies* 4 (1973) 313–20; repr. with original pagination in *The Crusades, Holy War and Canon Law* (Aldershot: Variorum, 1991), No. XVIII.

———. *Medieval Canon Law*. London: Longman, 1995.

———. *Medieval Canon Law and the Crusader*. Madison: University of Wisconsin Press, 1969.

———. "The Thirteenth-Century Livonian Crusade: Henricus de Lettis and the First Legatine Mission of Bishop William of Modena." *Jahrbücher für Geschichte Osteuropas*, n.s. 20 (1972): 1–9.

Christiansen, Eric. *The Northern Crusades: The Baltic and the Catholic Frontier 1100–1525*. London: Macmillan, 1980.

Constable, Giles. "The Second Crusade as Seen by Contemporaries." *Traditio* 9 (1953): 213–79.

Crusade and Conversion on the Baltic Frontier 1150–1500. Ed. Alan V. Murray. Aldershot: Ashgate, 2001.

Eco, Umberto. *Experiences in Translation*. Trans. Alastair McEwan. Toronto: University of Toronto Press, 2001.

Gnegel-Waitschies, Gisela. *Bischof Albert von Riga: Ein Bremer Domherr als Kirchenfürst im Osten, 1199–1229*. Hamburg: August Friedrich Velmede, 1958.

Grotefend, H. *Taschenbuch der Zeitrechnung des deutschen Mittelalters und der Neuzeit*. 8th ed. Hannover: Hahn, 1941.

Hauck, Albert. *Kirchengeschichte Deutschlands*. 8th ed. 5 vols. Berlin: Akademie Verlag, 1954.

Hellmann, Manfred. *Das Lettenland im Mittelalter: Studien zur ostbaltischen Frühzeit und lettischen Stammesgeschichte, inbesonders Lettgallens*. Münster, Böhlau, 1954.

———. "Die Anfänge der christlicher Mission in den baltischen Länden." In *Studien über die Anfänge der Mission in Livland*, ed. Manfred Hellmann. Vorträge und Forschungen, Sonderband 37. Sigmaringen: Jan Thorbecke, 1989. 7–38.

Hucker, Bernd Ulrich. "Der Zisterzienserabt Berthold, Bischof von Livland, und der erste Livlandkreuzzug." In *Studien über die*

Anfänge, ed. Manfred Hellmann. Vorträge und Forschungen, Sonderband 37. Sigmaringen: Jan Thorbecke, 1989. 39–64.

Holtzmann, R. "Studien zu Heinrich von Lettland." *Neues Archiv der Gesellschaft für ältere Deutsche Geschichtskunde* 43 (1920): 161–232.

Jensen, Carsten Selch. "The Nature of the Early Missionary Activities and Crusades in Livonia, 1185–1201." In *Medieval Spirituality in Scandinavia and Europe*, ed. Lars Bisgaard et al., 121–37. Odense: Odense University Press, 2001.

Johansen, Paul. "Die Chronik als Biographie: Heinrich von Lettlands Lebensgang und Weltanschauung." *Jahrbücher für Geschichte Osteuropas* n.s. 1 (1953): 1–24.

Johnson, Edgar N. "The German Crusade on the Baltic." In *A History of the Crusades*, ed. Kenneth M. Setton et al. 6 vols. Madison: University of Wisconsin Press, 1969–1989. 3:545–85.

Kedar, Benjamin Z. *Crusade and Mission: European Approaches Toward the Muslims.* Princeton, N.J.: Princeton University Press, 1984.

Knox, Ronald A. *Trials of a Translator.* New York: Sheed & Ward, 1949.

Lotter, Friedrich. *Die Konzeption des Wendenkreuzzugs: Ideengeschichtliche, kirchenrechtliche und historisch-politische Voraussetzungen der Missionierung von Elb- und Ostseeslawen um die Mitte des 12. Jahrhunderts.* Vorträge und Forschungen, Sonderband 23. Sigmaringen: Jan Thorbecke, 1977.

Mayer, Hans Eberhard. *The Crusades.* 2d ed. Trans. John Gillingham. Oxford: Oxford University Press, 1988.

Medieval Spirituality in Scandinavia and Europe: A Collection of Essays in Honour of Tore Nyberg. Ed. Lars Bisgaard et al. Odense: Odense University Press, 2001.

Murray, Alan V. "The Structure, Genre, and Intended Audience of the *Livonian Rhymed Chronicle.*" In *Crusade and Conversion on the Baltic Frontier, 1150–1500*, ed. Alan V. Murray, 235–59. Aldershot: Ashgate, 2001.

The New Cambridge Medieval History. 5 vols. to date. Cambridge: Cambridge University Press, 1991–.

Oman, Charles W. C. *A History of the Art of War in the Middle Ages.* Ed. John H. Beeler. Ithaca, N.Y.: Cornell University Press, 1943.

Pound, Ezra. *Guide to Kulchur*. London: Faber & Faber, 1938.
Riley-Smith, Jonathan. *The Crusades: A Short History*. London: Athlone Press, 1987.
Roscher, Helmut. *Papst Innocenz III. und die Kreuzzüge*. Vol. 21 of *Forschungen zur Kirchen- und Dogmengeschichte*. Göttingen: Vandenhoeck & Ruprecht, 1969.
Spekke, Arnolds. *History of Latvia*. Trans. H. Kundzins et al. Stockholm: M. Goppers, 1951.
Studien über die Anfänge der Mission in Livland. Ed. Manfred Hellmann. Sigmaringen: Jan Thorbecke, 1989.
Toch, Michael. "Welfs, Hohenstaufen, and Habsburgs." In *The New Cambridge Medieval History*, vol. 5, ed. David Abulafia. 5:375–404.
Urban, William L. *The Baltic Crusade*. 2d ed. Chicago: Lithuanian Research and Studies Center, 1994.
———. *The Livonian Crusade*. Washington, D.C.: University Press of America, 1981.
Vernadsky, George. *Kievan Russia*. New Haven, Conn.: Yale University Press, 1948.

THE CHRONICLE OF
HENRY OF LIVONIA

RECORDS OF WESTERN CIVILIZATION

Introduction

[I]

Western Christendom in the late twelfth century was expanding rapidly toward the East. In the Mediterranean area, the Crusaders had already built up a complex of feudal states in Palestine and Syria. In the opening years of the thirteenth century, the Byzantine Empire was attacked, overcome, and partitioned by West European Crusaders. For over two hundred years, since the time of Otto the Great, Western Christian armies, missionaries, and colonists had been pouring relentlessly eastward into the Slavic lands of Central Europe.

During the second half of the twelfth and the first half of the thirteenth centuries, great changes came over Germany in particular. By 1250 the Elbe, which in 1150 had been on Germany's eastern border, was in the heart of the country. Constant warfare on the frontier and the large-scale resettlement of colonists from the Western lands were pushing the Slavs further back into the central and eastern portions of the European continent.

In this expansionist movement, a new theater of operations was opened when German (primarily Saxon) merchants began to sail regularly after 1158 to the ports and harbors of the eastern coast of the Baltic Sea, there to trade with the native Livonians, Letts, Esthonians, and Kurs. German commercial interest in this area was quickly followed by the appearance of German armies, missionaries, and colonists. At the beginning of the thirteenth century, a full-scale German conquest of the Baltic coastal plains began. The beginning of this conquest is known primarily from the chronicle of Henry of Livonia, or Henricus de Lettis. Henry's chronicle provides virtually all of the information that is now available about the early stages of Western Christendom's expansion into the Baltic area. The chronicle is, furthermore, a fascinating personal record of the experiences and impressions of an eyewitness of this vast movement. Though Henry's account of the German conquest of the Baltic can be supplemented by another, later account, the *Livländische Reimchronik*,[1] and by some meager documentary evidence,[2] without Henry's invaluable narrative our knowledge of this whole conquest would be scant indeed.

The advance of Western Christendom into the Baltic was sponsored primarily by the church. About 1180, Meinhard, a canon of the Augustinian monastery of Segeberg, after listening to the stories of sailors and merchants who had traveled up the Dvina River to trade with the Livonians and Letts, decided to travel there himself and to try to convert those pagan peoples to Christianity. Accordingly, although he was already an elderly man, "with venerable gray hair," as Henry describes him,[3] Meinhard set out in the following spring for Livonia. When he reached the German trading posts on the banks of the Dvina, Meinhard stood among the booths set up

1. Edited by Leo Meyer (Paderborn 1876). There is also a further, very compressed account, in Arnold of Lübeck's *Chronica Slavorum* V, 30, in *MGH, SS*, XXI, 210–13.
2. The most comprehensive and convenient collection of documents is Friedrich Georg von Bunge's *Liv-, Esth- und Curländisches Urkundenbuch nebst Regesten*, 15 vols. (Reval, Riga, and Moscow, 1853–1914).
3. See below, p. 25 (I, 2).

by the merchants there and preached to the natives who happened along. As time passed, Meinhard's work met with some success. Converts were made and, in 1184, the missioner built a church in the village of Uexküll and baptized a few Livonians.[4] During the following winter, after the Livonians had been attacked by the Lithuanians, Meinhard offered to strike a bargain with the local inhabitants: if they would submit to Christian baptism, Meinhard would see that a stone fortress was built at Uexküll to protect them from future Lithuanian attacks. The Livonians, who knew a good bargain when they heard one, accepted the offer. Meinhard then had stonemasons brought in from Gothland and a stone fortress was built at his direction on the banks of the Dvina. When the building was finished and occupied, however, the Livonians went back on their part of the agreement and refused to be baptized.

Meinhard returned to Bremen, in 1186, to report to his ecclesiastical superiors what had been done. Remembering their see's former hopes for an ecclesiastical empire in the north, Archbishop Hartwig II and his cathedral chapter were quite willing to sanction Meinhard's work and to confirm his position by consecrating him bishop of Uexküll.[5] When he returned to his outpost in Livonia, however, Meinhard's posi-

4. The date is given as 1184 because it seems very likely that about two years elapsed between the building of the Uexküll church and Meinhard's consecration as bishop, which took place in 1186. See Albert Hauck, *Kirchengeschichte Deutschlands*, 5. Aufl., 5 vols. (Leipzig, 1925), IV, 654; Leonid Arbusow, *Grundriss der Geschichte Liv-, Est- und Kurlands* (Mitau, 1890), pp. 8–9.

5. See below, p. 27 (I, 8). See also Bunge, *Urkundenbuch*, I, 10–11; Manfred Hellmann, *Das Lettenland im Mittelalter* (Cologne, 1954), p. 115; Arbusow, *Grundriss*, p. 9; Arnolds Spekke, *History of Latvia* (Stockholm, 1951), p. 135; A. M. Ammann, S.J., *Kirchenpolitische Wandlungen im Ostbaltikum bis zum Tode Alexander Newskis*, in *Orientalia Christiana Analecta*, CV (Rome, 1936), 102–3; Peter Z. Olins, *The Teutonic Knights in Latvia* (Riga, 1928), pp. 21–22. Alfred Bilmanis in his *History of Latvia* (Princeton, 1951), states, for no apparent reason, that Meinhard founded his bishopric at Riga and transferred it later to Uexküll. Bilmanis also says that Meinhard "bribed the Livs with delicacies to obtain their permission to stay" (p. 56)—presumably the stone fort was the major "delicacy."

tion rapidly deteriorated. The Livonians of Holm attacked him and tried to drive him out of the country. Many of the Livonians who had already been baptized jumped *en masse* into the Dvina to try to wash off their baptism. At this point, Meinhard and the priests who had joined him in his missionary labors were virtually prisoners of the Livonians. An appeal to the papacy for help brought only a proclamation by Pope Celestine III that those of the faithful who assisted the struggling missionaries in Livonia were to enjoy an indulgence.[6]

When Meinhard died in 1196, Archbishop Hartwig II of Bremen appointed the Cistercian abbot of Loccum, Berthold, to the Livonian missionary diocese. Berthold at first made difficulties over the appointment, but finally he acceded to the archbishop's pleas. The new bishop decided first of all to try his luck at converting the Livonians peacefully. When the members of his flock plotted to murder him while he was consecrating a cemetery at Holm, however, Berthold changed his mind. Secretly he sailed to Saxony, there to recruit a crusading army which he brought back to Livonia. His return to Livonia was marked by the immediate outbreak of hostilities between Germans and Livonians. In a battle on July 24, 1198, Bishop Berthold was hit by a Livonian lance and was torn limb from limb by the enraged Livonians. The German army, in turn, began a campaign of terror to force the Livonians into submission. In short order the Livonians capitulated. A hundred and fifty of them were baptized in two days. They agreed to welcome missionaries into their forts and they promised to pay taxes for the support of the priests. Reassured, the army returned to Germany.

The departure of the German troops was immediately followed by another Livonian uprising. The sails of the German ships were not yet over the horizon when the Livonians once again jumped into the Dvina to wash off their baptism. They

6. See below, p. 30 (I, 12); Bunge, *Urkundenbuch*, I, 11-13.

also found a carving on a tree, which they took to be a figure of the hated Saxon god, and this they flung after the departing Germans. This done, the Livonians harried the remaining priests out of the country and put pressure upon the German merchants to make them, too, leave, but the latter, we are assured, "taking thought for their lives, gave gifts to the elders." [7] The whole German missionary venture in Livonia now seemed lost.

At this point, appeared the man who was to create a real, Western Christian, Saxon theocracy on the Baltic littoral in Livonia: Albert von Buxhövden, a nephew of Archbishop Hartwig II of Bremen and a canon of the Bremen cathedral chapter. In 1199, Archbishop Hartwig named Albert as third bishop of Uexküll. Albert was one of the great churchmen, diplomats, and empire-builders of the early thirteenth century. Able, ambitious, and greedy, Albert set out to create in Livonia an ecclesiastical empire for himself and his family. Unlike the saintly Bishop Meinhard, Bishop Albert came to Livonia rather as a prince than as a preacher.[8]

The career of Bishop Albert in Livonia takes up the major part of Henry's chronicle.[9] The bishop's plans for conquest were carefully laid from the first. Upon his arrival in his new diocese, the bishop was accompanied by an army of Saxon

7. See below, p. 34 (II, 10).
8. Hauck, *Kirchengeschichte*, IV, 657; Hellmann, *Das Lettenland*, p. 121. [On Bishop Albert, see now the able biography by Gisela Gnegel-Waitches, *Bischof Albert von Riga, ein Bremer Domherr als Kirchenfurst im Osten* (Hamburg, 1958), which came to hand too late to be drawn upon in this discussion.]
9. Even the chapter divisions of the chronicle are arranged with reference to the years of Bishop Albert's pontificate, which began probably on March 28, 1199. Henry counted Easter as the first day of the year. See Arndt's introduction to his edition of Henry's chronicle, in *MGH, SS*, XXIII, 240; R. Holtzmann, "Studien zu Heinrich von Lettland," *Neues Archiv*, XLIII (1920), 161–212, especially pp. 183–205. Holtzmann demonstrates convincingly that Bishop Albert's election must have occurred between March 27 and April 3 and that, since episcopal elections customarily took place on Sundays, Laetare Sunday, March 28, 1199, is the most probable date.

Crusaders and his legal position was secured by privileges granted to him by both the Empire and the Papacy.[10] The army which Albert brought to Livonia was a variable force of pilgrims, or Crusaders, who undertook to fight in Livonia for one or two years in return for the promise of a Crusader's indulgence. Year after year, as appears from Henry's chronicle, Bishop Albert journeyed back to Germany to raise another levy of pilgrims to replace those whose terms of service had expired. In addition to these levies of volunteers, Bishop Albert created, in 1202, a more stable force, a standing army of his own, in the Order of Sword-Bearers, otherwise known as the Brothers of the Militia of Christ or the Livonian Brothers of the Sword.[11] This military order, subordinate to the bishop, was to act as a permanent army of occupation in the newly-conquered lands. The occupation forces were further strengthened by the establishment of religious houses of the Cistercian and Augustinian orders. The monks and canons of these houses were charged both with missionary responsibilities and with administrative duties.

The secular administration of the conquered territory was placed in the hands of the bishop's magistrates, who were given charge of the conquered native villages. Care was taken, too, to safeguard the commercial interests of the German merchants who accompanied the bishop's armies. The merchants were provided with a city which was to be colonized by them and which was to be the center of the whole elaborate military, commercial, and ecclesiastical apparatus of the German conquest. This was Riga, founded in 1200, the year after Bishop Albert's arrival, on the site of an earlier Livonian port.[12] Here were built Albert's cathedral, the houses of his clergy, barracks for the pilgrims and the Brothers of the

10. See below, pp. 35–36 (III, 2–5); Bunge, *Urkundenbuch*, I, 11–13; Ammann, *Kirchenpolitische Wandlungen*, pp. 107–10; Hellmann, *Das Lettenland*, pp. 119–22.

11. See below, p. 40 (VI, 6); Bilmanis, *History of Latvia*, pp. 58–60.

12. See below, p. 37 (IV, 5); Spekke, *History of Latvia*, p. 135; Hellmann, *Das Lettenland*, p. 121; Bilmanis, *History of Latvia*, p. 58.

Sword, and warehouses for the merchants. Here, too, were cast the bells of the new cathedral, bells which were to call the citizens to arms and to celebrate the widening and tightening of the German grip on the land.

By 1208, the machinery of Bishop Albert's new principality was working smoothly and both the Livonians and the Letts had been compelled by force and fear to accept "the Christian name," as Henry so accurately put it. The bishop's missionary activities now began to turn in a new direction, toward Esthonia. The campaigns there are related in all their savage ferocity in the fourth book of Henry's chronicle.[13] The very repetitiveness of the chronicler's account of these Esthonian campaigns shows clearly that a stereotyped system had by this time been formulated for the Christianization and subjugation of the Baltic peoples.

First came the military expeditions against one after another of the fortified strongholds of the Esthonians. The Germans, with their superior military technology, overran them, village by village. The armor,[14] the siege machinery,[15] and even the musical instruments [16] of the Germans gave the conquerors a decisive advantage over their opponents. The Esthonians tried in vain to organize an effective resistance. They appealed to the Russian princes of Polozk, of Pskov, of Novgorod, and of Smolensk, all in vain. Neither the Russians nor the Esthonians were able to organize their forces effectively. Without more efficient organization and without considerable improvements in their armaments, there was no means of overcoming the persistent Saxon invaders, and the Russians, in any case, were too much taken up with their own domestic quarrels and with the Tatar invasions to be able to devote the necessary effort to combatting the Germans.

A struggle took place, too, between the representatives of Latin Christianity and the representatives of Russian Ortho-

13. See below, pp. 83–246 (XII, 6—XXX, 6).
14. See below, e.g., p. 49 (IX, 3); pp. 97–98 (XIV, 5).
15. See below, e.g., pp. 62–63 (X, 12).
16. See below, e.g., p. 85 (XII, 6); p. 98 (XIV, 5).

doxy for the religious allegiance of the Baltic peoples, but
again the Russians were overwhelmed by their better-or-
ganized opponents.[17] The Russian church had not hitherto
been very active in converting the Baltic areas subject to
Russian princes to Christianity. As Henry remarks, "It is, indeed, the custom of the Russian kings not to subject whatever
people they defeat to the Christian faith, but rather to force
them to pay tribute and money to themselves."[18] The Germans, however, insisted upon baptizing all of the peoples
whom they conquered in the Baltic area. Russian influence
in the Baltic area steadily diminished before the advance of
the conquering Saxons: the Russian princes of Gerzika and
Kokenhusen were defeated and their principalities were destroyed by the Saxon bishop and his men.[19] It was only after
Bishop Albert had been dead a dozen years that a Russian
army under Alexander Nevsky was able to turn back the
eastward drive of the Germans by defeating the German
knights in the famous battle of 1242 on the ice of Lake Peipus.

The Danes and Swedes, too, endeavored to stake their
claims in the Baltic territory where Bishop Albert was building his empire. Of the two, the Danes were much the more
serious menace, and a lively, frequently acrimonious, rivalry
between Saxon and Danish interests continued until the Danish
king was captured by the duke of Saxony.[20] The Danes, however, remained in control of northern Esthonia.[21]

When the military conquest of the various Baltic tribes was
achieved, the defeated people were baptized. Baptism was the
sign of surrender to German domination and the Germans
were anxious that all the people under their rule be baptized

17. On this struggle, see especially Ammann, *Kirchenpolitische Wandlungen*.
18. See below, p. 122 (XVI, 2).
19. See below, pp. 90–93 (XIII, 4); p. 76 (XI, 8); p. 88 (XIII, 1).
20. See below, p. 220 (XXVIII, 1).
21. Hellmann, *Das Lettenland*, pp. 142–43, 149–51; Bilmanis, *History of
Latvia*, pp. 62–65; Olins, *Teutonic Knights*, p. 33.

with the rites and ceremonies accepted in Saxony.[22] When the sacramental ceremony was completed, the conquered peoples also became subject to Christian law and, in particular, they were required to pay tithes to their new ecclesiastical overlords. Only after the initial period of conquest and baptism does it appear that some effort was made to acquaint the conquered with the doctrines and meaning of the Christianity which they had already been forced to accept. Slowly, in the wake of the conquering armies, came the priests who settled in the land as the rectors of parishes. One such priest was the chronicler Henry.

[II]

Henry of Livonia's origins are disputed. Many historians have held that Henry was a Livonian or Lettish priest, educated in Germany.[23] German writers, for the most part, have claimed, however, that he was German in origin.[24] On the whole, the probability that he was German seems very great.[25]

22. See below, e.g., pp. 193–95 (XXIV, 5–6).

23. See e.g., Bilmanis, *History of Latvia*, p. 55; Arndt, in *MGH, SS,* XXIII, 236–38; Spekke, *History of Latvia*, p. 129. The Latin title of Henry's chronicle, *Heinrici Chronicon Livoniae*, does not, of course, identify Henry as "of Livonia," since it must be literally translated as "The Chronicle of Livonia by Henry."

24. See, among others, Holtzmann, in *Neues Archiv*, XLIII, 161–64; Paul Johansen, "Die Chronik als Biographie: Heinrich von Lettlands Lebensgang und Weltanschauung," *Jahrbücher für Geschichte Osteuropas*, neue Folge I (1953), 1–24; Wilhelm Wattenbach, *Deutschlands Geschichtsquellen im Mittelalter*, 6. Aufl., 2 vols. (Berlin, 1894), II, 359; Olins, *Teutonic Knights*, p. 7, n.1.

25. The repeated and consistent use of the first person plural to refer to German armies and German deeds is perhaps the most convincing single argument in favor of this thesis. Johansen, in *Jahrb. für Gesch. Osteuropas*, n.F. I, p. 7, concludes: "Aber schon ein oberflächlicher Blick in die Chronik zeigt, dass Heinrich mit Leib und Seele Deutscher war: so begeistert vom allen Erfolgen, so hasserfüllt den Danen und Russen gegenüber, so bewust über das

All that is known of Henry's life and character must be
deduced from his chronicle, which is distinctly a personal
record of Henry's experiences as one of the parochial clergy
subject to Bishop Albert. From the chronicle we can readily
glean a great deal of information about its author.
Henry was born in the last quarter of the twelfth century,
perhaps about 1188, probably in Saxony.[26] He was educated
in Germany, perhaps at the monastery school at Segeberg,
where he received a thorough grounding in Latin. The style
of his chronicle shows that Henry was completely at home in
the Latin language and that he was steeped in the language of
the Vulgate Bible and of liturgical literature. Although Henry
does occasionally quote from, or allude to, classical Latin authors,[27] he refers to biblical and liturgical sources far more
often.[28] Henry's language is studded with references to the
Vulgate and some whole passages in his chronicle are veritable
mosaics, pieced together with phrases and figures taken from
the Vulgate and from the various liturgical books, especially
the Breviary.[29] Perhaps it was during his years at school, too,
that he made his first acquaintance with the languages of the
Baltic area where he was later to work as an interpreter. If he
was educated at Segeberg, it is quite likely that he came into
contact there with boy hostages from Livonia who had been

Schicksal des Römischen Reiches und vor allem so vol Kentniss über alle
kleinen Fürsten, Edelinge und Dynasten in Norddeutschland." See also
Holtzmann, in *Neues Archiv*, XLIII, 161–83.
    26. Johansen, in *Jahrb. für Gesch. Osteuropas*, n.F. I, p. 9. Johansen suggests
that Henry was born at Poppendorp, near Magdeburg, and that he was the
son of a *locator*, or real estate developer named Gerfridus, who worked in
Livonia; see also Holtzmann, in *Neues Archiv*, XLIII, 178–83.
    27. See below, e.g., p.26 (I, 2), p. 32 (II, 5)—Cicero; p. 55 (X, 3)—Horace;
p. 68 (X, 17), p. 245 (XXX, 5)—Ovid; and p. 47 (IX, 1), p. 55 (X, 3), p. 80
(XII, 2), p. 142 (XIX, 1), p. 237 (XXIX, 8)—Vergil. For some insight into
Henry's technical competence as a Latinist, note the many citations of the
chronicle in Leonid Arbusow, *Colores Rhetorici* (Göttingen, 1948).
    28. For a highly instructive account, to which I am much indebted, see
Leonid Arbusow, "Das entlehnte Sprachgut in Heinrichs 'Chronicon Livoniae,'" *Deutsches Archiv*, VIII (1951), 100–53, especially pp. 107–34.
    29. See, e.g., p. 25 (I, 1–2); pp. 150–51 (XIX, 6).

sent to Segeberg to be educated under the care of Bishop
Albert's brother, Rothmar, who was abbot of the monastery.[30]
Early in the thirteenth century, Henry came to Livonia,
perhaps in 1205, to join Bishop Albert's household.[31] Henry,
the bishop's scholar, was ordained, as he tells us in his chronicle, in 1208.[32] He was sent to Imera to assist the priest Alabrand in baptizing the Letts there, and, so far as we know, he
remained there, save for brief excursions, the rest of his life.
He built a church at a place named Papendorp, received it
from the bishop as a benefice, and settled among the Letts. He
was still there as an old man in 1259.[33]

Henry wrote his chronicle in 1225–26 and in its original
form the chronicle ended with the account of the events of
1226.[34] At some later date, probably in 1227–28, Henry added
a final chapter to the chronicle, to bring his narrative down
through 1227 and the subjugation of Oesel.[35] Perhaps he originally intended to continue his work to the death of Bishop
Albert in 1229, but failed for some unknown reason to do so.
It seems more likely, however, that Henry wrote his chronicle
as a report on the establishment of the Livonian church for
the papal legate, Bishop William of Modena, whom Henry assisted as interpreter in 1225–27.[36]

30. Johansen, in *Jahrb. für Gesch. Osteuropas*, n.F. I, p. 11.
31. If he was, as Johansen suggests, the son of the *locator* Gerfridus, he
may have visited Livonia with his father on an earlier occasion, perhaps
about 1200.—Holtzmann, in *Neues Archiv*, XLIII, 182–83; Johansen, in
Jahrb. für Gesch. Osteuropas, n.F. I, p. 10.
32. See p. 75 (XI, 7).
33. Johansen, in *Jahrb. für Gesch. Osteuropas*, n.F. I, p. 15.
34. Chapter XXIX, 9 (pp. 237–38), is evidently the original concluding
section of the narrative.
35. Johansen, in *Jahrb. für Gesch. Osteuropas*, n.F. I, p. 3.
36. *Ibid.;* Bilmanis, *History of Latvia*, p. 55. This explanation would account for the addition of Chapter XXX, which deals with the campaign
against the Oeselians under the legate's direction after William had left
Livonia proper. If Henry was William's interpreter, he may well have completed his chronicle before the legate's departure from Livonia and then
have added the concluding section as a postscript when the legate undertook the unexpected campaign against the Oeselians.

Henry's chronicle is a personal record of that writer's experiences in Livonia and of the episodes related to him by his colleagues among the German colony there. "Nothing has been put in this account," he declared, "except what we have seen almost entirely with our own eyes. What we have not seen with our own eyes, we have learned from those who saw it and who were there." [37] This type of declaration is, of course, not uncommon in medieval chronicles: Arbusow classifies it as "a rhetorical commonplace." [38] In Henry's chronicle, however, the writer's declaration seems to be a simple statement of the truth of the matter, and the episodes related in the chronicle fit in very neatly with the hypothesis that the work is largely autobiographical.[39]

Taking the chronicle as an expression of Henry's experiences and personality, then, we can discover a great deal about the chronicler himself from his narrative. Henry was, first and foremost, a priest, well trained in Latin, steeped in the Vulgate and the liturgy, though not particularly well read in other types of literature.[40] Further, it appears from his chronicle that Henry was interested in military matters. His detailed descriptions of warfare, of military engines, and of siege techniques in particular are the accounts of a man who undoubtedly accompanied the conquering army on many occasions and who was a keen and interested observer of military affairs.[41] His military knowledge was not entirely theoretical, either, as appears from one of the most vivid personal recollections in the chronicle. Henry relates that, as he was baptizing a heathen in Wierland, suddenly an enemy attack was

37. See below, pp. 237-38 (XXIX, 9).
38. Arbusow, in *Deutsches Archiv*, VIII, 137; cf. Arbusow, *Colores Rhetorici*, pp. 109-10.
39. Johansen, in *Jahrb. für Gesch. Osteuropas*, n.F. I, concludes (p. 6): ". . . dass Heinrichs Chronik im Grunde nur einen abgewandelten Erlebnissbericht darstellt."
40. Arbusow, in *Deutsches Archiv*, VIII, 102-7.
41. See below, e.g., pp. 62-64 (X, 12); pp. 96-99 (XIV, 5); pp. 105-8 (XV, 1); pp. 127-31 (XVI, 4); pp. 137-38 (XVIII, 5); pp. 222-26 (XXVIII, 5-6).

announced. "We immediately put down the holy chrism and
the other holy articles," he says, "and hurried to the ministry
of shields and swords." [42] When the attacking forces proved
to be friendly, however, Henry returned to his more pacific
duties and finished the interrupted baptism.

Henry's frequent allusions to musical instruments betray an
interest in music on his part and he tells us how, during another battle, he "mounted the ramparts and, while the
others fought, sang prayers to God on a musical instrument." [43] His occasional plays on words show, too, that Henry
was not without a sense of humor, though of a rather heavy-
handed variety. [44] He also tells us how he and another priest
were amused and laughed up their sleeves at the naïveté of
some villagers who had been baptized rather haphazardly by
the Danes in Esthonia. [45] One may even suspect, from the way
in which he relates the story, that Henry was not entirely un-
amused at the Livonians who cast their immolated goats and
dogs squarely into Bishop Albert's face. [46]

Lastly, Henry's chronicle shows his deep feeling of sympathy and affection for the Livonians and Letts among whom
he labored as a parish priest. He does not identify himself
with the native peoples, to be sure. He looks upon himself and
the other Germans in Livonia as the agents of a higher culture,
whose duty it is to convert the native peoples to the Christian
religion and to introduce them to the superior civilization of
the German West. Nonetheless, Henry had no sympathy for
those of his compatriots who wished to burden the Livonians,
Letts, Esthonians, and other peoples with excessive burdens,
financial or other. He emphasizes, particularly in the closing
sections of his chronicle, the fact that the burden of Christ

42. See below, p. 179 (XXIII, 7).
43. See below, p. 85 (XII, 6).
44. See below, e.g., the play on the name of the city *Riga* and the verb *rigo*
("irrigate"), p. 37 (IV, 5), n.28, and p. 152 (XIX, 7), n.174; and on *Lettus*
and *laetus*, p. 232 (XXIX, 3), n.303.
45. See below, p. 193 (XXIV, 5).
46. See below, p. 127 (XVI, 4).

should be sweet and light. Repeatedly he reproved those who
were excessively harsh toward the Livonian converts.[47]
Henry's sympathies, though not often overtly expressed, are
evident enough when he reports such an incident as the
lament of the prince of Gerzika over the burning of his city.[48]
Henry's interest in the Baltic peoples is further shown by his
use of Livonian, Lettish, and Esthonian words and phrases in
his chronicle.[49]

The attitude of this mere parish priest and chronicler—a
humble man, as he calls himself [50]—towards the Baltic subjects
of Bishop Albert's new ecclesiastical principality contrasts
strangely with the career of the ambitious prelate who was
Henry's superior.[51]

47. See below, e.g., p. 200 (XXV, 2); pp. 230–33, p. 234 (XXIX, 2–3, 5).
48. See below, p. 92 (XIII, 4).
49. See below, *draugs*, p. 128 (XVI, 4); *magetac*, p. 110 (XV, 3); *Maga
magamas*, p. 110 (XV, 3); *kilegunds*, p. 221 (XXVIII, 2) and p. 245 (XXX,
5); *nogata*, p. 95 (XIV, 2) and p. 119 (XV, 8); *watmal*, p. 29 (I, 11); *maia*,
p. 115 (XV, 7), p. 178, n.207 (XXIII, 7), and p.184, n.217 (XXIII, 9);
malewa, p. 154, n.176 (XIX, 9), p. 156, n.180 (XX, 2), and p. 179, n.212
(XXIII, 7); *waipas*, p. 219 (XXVII, 6). If Henry frequently served as an
interpreter for the Latin- and German-speaking clergy, this close contact
with the Baltic peoples may go far to explain his sympathy for them and
his interest in them; Henry is expressly identified as interpreter on page 126
(XVI, 3).
50. See below, p. 237 (XXIX, 9).
51. Henry's attitude also contrasts strikingly with that of some modern
German historians: Hauck, *Kirchengeschichte*, IV, 665, calls Bishop Albert
"the last great German missionary bishop." Rudolf Kötzschke, *Quellen zur
Geschichte der ostdeutschen Kolonisation* (Jena, 1924), in his *Vorwort*, calls
this expansion "one of the greatest performances of the German people in
the middle ages." Even more strangely, Rolf Gardiner in "German Eastward
Policy and the Baltic States," *Contemporary Review*, CXLV (1934), 324,
writes: "This astonishing movement . . . may be said truly to have sub-
stantiated the 'holy' title of the Empire." Johansen, in *Jahrb. für Gesch.
Osteuropas*, n.F. I, pp. 23–24, goes too far in the other direction, however,
when he identifies Henry's attitude with Livonian and Latvian patriotism.

[III]

The chronicle of Henry of Livonia has survived in several manuscripts. The oldest of these was the late thirteenth- or early fourteenth-century Codex Zamoyski, which was destroyed in Warsaw during World War II. Photographic copies of this manuscript, fortunately, survive at Marburg. The next oldest manuscript of the chronicle, the Codex Skodiesky, has long since been lost, but a seventeenth-century copy of it survives in the Riga city library. In addition to these two manuscripts, there are still in existence some seven other more recent and less reliable manuscript versions dating from the seventeenth and eighteenth centuries.[52]

The first printed version of the chronicle was published in 1740 by Johann Daniel Gruber under the title *Origines Livoniae Sacrae et Civilis*. The chronicle was edited and published twice during the nineteenth century: once, with a German translation, by A. Hansen for the first volume of the *Scriptores Rerum Livonicarum;*[53] a second time by Wilhelm Arndt for the *Monumenta Germaniae Historica*.[54] Arndt's edition is the standard modern edition and the one on which

52. See Wilhelm Arndt's introduction to his edition of the chronicle in *MGH, SS*, XXIII, 232-36; also, Johansen, in *Jahrb. für Gesch. Osteuropas*, n.F. I, pp. 1-2.
53. (Riga and Leipzig, 1853), pp. 50-311. This very imperfect edition reprints the text of Gruber's *Origines*. The notes of Hansen's edition are prolix, though sometimes useful.
54. *Heinrici Chronicon Lyvoniae*, in *MGH, SS*, XXIII (Hanover, 1874), 231-332. *MGH* editor Georg Heinrich Pertz reprinted this edition in the more easily available and more readily usable series of *Scriptores Rerum Germanicarum in Usum Scholarum* (Hanover, 1874). The folio edition in *MGH, SS*, XXIII, however, is still the preferred edition, both because it includes the notes of variant readings which are omitted in the smaller edition in the *Scriptores Rerum Germanicarum* and also because some typographical errors have slipped into the latter edition.

this translation is based.[55] In the twentieth century still another edition of the chronicle, with a Russian translation, has appeared.[56]

In addition to the German translation in the *Scriptores Rerum Livonicarum*, at least three other German versions of the chronicle have been published.[57] No English translation, however, has heretofore appeared.

[IV]

Moses Maimonides, in a letter to a Provençal scholar, Samuel ibn Tibbon, who was translating Maimonides' *Guide for the Perplexed* from Arabic into Hebrew, had some sage advice to offer on the technique of translating:

Whoever wishes to translate, and aims at rendering each word literally, and at the same time adheres slavishly to the order of words and sentences in the original, will meet with much difficulty; his rendering will be faulty and untrust-

55. Leonid Arbusow, the younger, had long proposed, before his death in 1951, to produce a definitive edition of the chronicle and his many useful studies of Henry's rhetoric gave promise that a brilliant version of the chronicle would someday appear under his name. Unfortunately, Arbusow's exile from Latvia during the last years of his life prevented the completion of this project. Arbusow's student, Dr. Albert Bauer, has taken over Arbusow's papers and it is hoped that Dr. Bauer may eventually be able to bring out a new and more perfect edition of the chronicle. [This edition has now appeared (Hanover, 1955), but came to hand too late to be used in this translation.]

56. S. Anninskiy, *Genrich Latvieskiy, Chronika Livonii* (Moscow, 1938). I have not seen this, but Johansen, in *Jahrb. für Gesch. Osteuropas*, n.F. I, p. 2, n.4, calls the edition a good one.

57. They are J. G. Arndt, *Der Liefländischen Chronik* (Halle, 1747), Hermann Hildebrand, *Die Chronik Heinrichs von Lettland* (Berlin, 1865), and Eduard Pabst, *Heinrichs von Lettland Livländische Chronik* (Reval, 1867). The last of these translations was based upon original manuscript studies, but as Wilhelm Arndt sadly notes (*MGH, SS*, XXIII, 231, n.4), the linguistic contortion of the author's style *creat taedium legentibus.*

worthy. This is not the right method. The translator should first try to grasp the sense of the passage thoroughly, and then state the author's intention with perfect clearness in the other language. This, however, cannot be done without changing the order of words, putting many words for one, or vice versa, and adding or taking away words, so that the subject may be perfectly intelligible in the language into which he translates.[58]

Maimonides' counsel has been followed as closely as possible in preparing this translation of Henry of Livonia's chronicle from Wilhelm Arndt's text in the *Monumenta Germaniae Historica*. The translation was done with an eye to conveying the chronicler's meaning in English rather than with the notion of presenting Henry's Latin style in English dress. This process has necessitated the frequent recasting of sentences, the expansion on many occasions of a single word into a phrase, and, much less frequently, the compression of a phrase into a single English word.

Following Arndt's text, this translation has retained the chapter divisions devised by A. Hansen, since they are convenient and have been employed by most modern authors in citing the text of the chronicle. The bracketed dates are also taken from Arndt's edition, as are many of the identifications of persons and places in the footnotes.

The great number of biblical citations and allusions has posed some problems.[59] The text divisions of the Vulgate have been used throughout and all biblical citations have been

58. *Commentary*, XV (1953), 394. Similar advice, with somewhat greater elaboration, is offered by Ronald A. Knox, *Trials of a Translator* (New York, 1949), and in Hilaire Belloc's lectures, *On Translation* (Oxford, 1931); see also the more abbreviated injunction in this same vein by Ezra Pound, *Guide to Kulchur* (London, 1938), p. 326.

59. Arbusow, in *Deutsches Archiv*, VIII, pp. 109–10, claims to have located some seven hundred biblical citations and allusions, as well as more than a hundred other borrowings from the Breviary, Missal, and other liturgical texts. Many of Arbusow's citations, however, seem rather strained and only a few of the citations and allusions referred to in the above article are cited in this translation.

checked against a standard edition of the Vulgate.[60] Whenever appropriate, direct biblical citations have been quoted either in the language of the Douay-Challoner version [61] or the Knox translation.[62] Citations from liturgical texts, save for the Martyrology,[63] have been taken from standard modern editions.[64]

[V]

Henry of Livonia, writing at a period when the German Empire as an effective government had largely ceased to exist and when the papacy was too far immersed in other matters to give Livonia any real consideration, shows in his chronicle how an aggressive Saxon bishop was able to establish a personal theocratic state in an undeveloped Baltic area and how German control of the Baltic lands came to be based upon the misery and devastation of the indigenous population. The ultimate importance of Henry's chronicle lies not merely in its significance for German and general European history, but

60. *Biblia Sacra Vulgatae Editionis*, nova editio (Paris, 1922).
61. *The Holy Bible . . . translated from the Latin Vulgate, . . . the Old Testament . . . by the English College at Douay. . . . the New Testament by the English College at Rheims . . . as revised by the Ven. Richard Challoner. . . .* (Boston, 1884).
62. *The Holy Bible: A Translation from the Latin Vulgate in the Light of the Hebrew and Greek Originals* [by Msgr. Ronald A. Knox] (New York, 1956).
63. Citations from the Martyrology are taken from two sources: (1) *Sancti Adonis Viennensis Archiepiscopi Martyrologium*, ed. Heribert Rosweid, S.J., in Migne, *P.L.*, CXXIII, 139–436, and (2) *Usuardi Monachi Sangermanensis Martyrologium*, ed. J. B. Solleri, S.J., in Migne, *P.L.*, CXXIII, 453–992, and CXXIV, 1–860.
64. The Breviary is cited from *Breviarium Romanum . . . Editio V Taurinensis*, 4 vols. (Turin, 1923). The Missal is cited from *The New Roman Missal in Latin and English*, ed. and tr. F. X. Lasance and F. A. Walsh, O.S.B. (New York, 1946). The Ritual is cited from *The Roman Ritual in Latin and English*, ed. and tr. by Philip T. Weller, 3 vols. (Milwaukee, 1946–52).

in the fact that it demonstrates clearly the mistakes and the misfortunes which attended this medieval effort to impose the "blessings" of a technologically more advanced and superior culture upon a "backward" people.

Both the chronicler and the other men whose actions he describes were convinced of the righteousness of their cause and of the ultimate beneficence of the Livonian invasion in which they participated. Many of the convictions betrayed in Henry's chronicle are the direct ancestors of that condescension which too often marks the twentieth-century Westerner's attitude towards those "lesser breeds without the law" who people the non-Western world. This medieval episode in the Baltic area which Henry of Livonia relates may stand, then, as a warning and object lesson to those who are concerned with extending the bounties of their own culture to those so unfortunate as to be without them.

THE CHRONICLE OF
HENRY OF LIVONIA

Book One

[Concerning Livonia: The First Bishop, Meinhard]

[I]

᠎᠎᠎ (1) Divine Providence, by the fire of His love,[1] and mindful of Raab and Babylonia,[2] that is, of the confusion of paganism, aroused in our modern times the idolatrous Livonians from the sleep of idolatry and of sin in the following way.

(2) In the monastery of Segeberg[3] there was a man of worthy life,[4] and with venerable gray hair,[5] Meinhard by name, a priest of the Order of Saint Augustine.[6] He came to

1. Cf. *Breviarium Romanum, Officium Matutini in Tempore Adventus, Benedictio ad Lect. vi.*

2. Cf. Ps. 86:4.

3. A military settlement and monastery, founded *ca.* 1131. The story of its foundation is told in Helmold, *The Chronicle of the Slavs* . . . , tr. with introduction and notes by Francis Joseph Tschan, (New York, 1935), Ch. 53.

4. Cf. Pope Gregory I, *Dialogorum Libri IV*, II, 1. in Migne, *P.L.*, LXVI, 126.

5. Cf. the Martyrology for March 18, in Migne, *P.L.*, CXXIII, 240.

6. I.e. an Augustinian canon regular.

Livonia with a band of merchants simply for the sake of Christ and only to preach. For German merchants, bound together through familiarity [7] with the Livonians, were accustomed to go to Livonia, frequently sailing up the Dvina River. (3) After receiving, therefore, the permission of King Vladimir of Polozk,[8] to whom the Livonians, while still pagan, paid tribute, and, at the same time, after receiving gifts from him, this priest boldly set out upon the divine work, preaching to the Livonians and building a church in the village of Uexküll. (4) And in the same village Ylo, the father of Kulewene, and Viezo, the father of Alo, were the first to be baptized, while the others followed in their turn.

(5) The next winter, the Lithuanians, after having laid waste Livonia, took many into captivity. The same preacher, together with the people of Uexküll, avoided the wrath of the Lithuanians and took to the forests. When the Lithuanians had withdrawn, Meinhard accused the Livonians of foolishness, because they had no fortifications; he promised them that forts would be built if they decided to become and to be considered sons of God. This pleased them and they promised and confirmed by an oath that they would receive baptism. (6) Therefore, stonemasons were brought from Gothland the next summer. The Livonians, meanwhile, confirmed the sincerity of their intentions a second time. Part of the people were baptized before the beginning of the fort of Uexküll, and, after the fort was completed, all promised, though deceitfully, to be baptized. The walls, therefore, arose from their foundations. Because Meinhard paid for the building of a fifth part of the fort, this part was his property. Meinhard had first bought the land upon which the church at Uexküll stood. When the fort had at last been finished, those who had been baptized relapsed; those who had not yet been reborn refused to accept the faith. Meinhard, himself, nevertheless, did not desist from the enterprise. At that time the Semgalls, pagans of the neighborhood, hearing of the building made of stones, and

7. Cf. Cicero, *De Officiis*, I, 17, 55.
8. Vladimir was a Russian prince, not a king, as Henry calls him.

not knowing that the stones were held together with cement, came with large ship's ropes, foolishly believing they could pull the fort into the Dvina. But they were wounded by the ballistarii [9] instead and went away after having suffered losses. (7) The neighboring people of Holm [10] cheated Meinhard by making a similar promise. After a fort had been built for them, they profited from their fraud.[11] But at first some were baptized, with whatever sort of intentions, and their names are: Viliendi, Uldenago, Wade, Waldeko, Gerverder, and Vietzo. (8) Between the construction of the two above-mentioned forts, Meinhard was consecrated bishop [1186] by the metropolitan of Bremen.[12] (9) After the second fort had been completed, in their iniquity they forgot their oath and perjured themselves, for there was not even one of them who accepted the faith. Truly the soul of the preacher was disturbed, inasmuch as, by gradually plundering his possessions and beating his household, they decided to drive him outside their borders. They thought that since they had been baptized with water, they could remove their baptism by washing themselves in the Dvina and thus send it back to Germany. (10) As a co-worker in the gospel the bishop had Brother Theodoric of the Cistercian order, subsequently a bishop in Esthonia. Because the crops in his fields were quite abundant and in their own fields dying because of a flooding rain, the Livonians of Treiden prepared to sacrifice him to their gods. The people were collected and the will of the gods regarding the sacrifice was sought after by lot. A lance was placed in position and the horse came up and, at the signal of God, put out the foot thought to be the foot of life. Brother Theodoric prayed

---

9. The ballista was a large, wheeled cross-bow, which was sometimes provided with a pouch and a double string and could thus be used for throwing stones. See H. S. Cowper, *The Art of Attack* (Ulverston, 1906), p. 271 f., and Sir Charles Oman, *A History of the Art of War* (New York, 1937), p. 545.

10. I.e. from the region of Kirchholm, on the Dvina River.

11. Cf. Pope Gregory I, *Homilia 9 in Evangelio,* cited in the Breviary, *Officium Commune Confessoris Pontificis, Lect. ix.*

12. Archbishop Hartwig II, 1184–1207.

aloud and gave blessings with his hand. The pagan priest asserted that the Christian God was sitting on the back of the horse and was moving the horse's foot forward; that for this reason the back of the horse had to be wiped off so that the God might slide off. When this was done, the horse again put forth the foot of life, as before, and Brother Theodoric's life was saved. When Brother Theodoric was sent into Esthonia, he likewise endured from the pagans a great many dangers to his life. Because of an eclipse of the sun which took place on the day of John the Baptist, they said that he was eating the sun. At that same time, a certain wounded Livonian from Treiden begged Brother Theodoric to cure him and promised to be baptized if he were cured. The brother pounded herbs together, therefore, and, not knowing the effects of the herbs, called upon the name of the Lord. The Livonian was thus healed in body and, by baptism, in soul.[13] He was the first to accept the faith of Christ in Treiden. A certain sick man called Brother Theodoric and asked to be baptized. He was kept from his holy purpose by the violent stubbornness of the women; but when his illness grew worse, the incredulity of the women was overcome and he was baptized and commended by prayers to God. When he died a certain convert saw his soul being carried into heaven by the angels and recognized him from a distance of seven miles.[14]

(11) Now that the aforementioned bishop had observed the stubbornness of the Livonians and had, accordingly, seen his labors falling to the ground, he abandoned his project, collected the monks and brothers, and, resolving to return, set out for the merchants' ships which were now preparing to go to Gothland at Easter. The tricky Livonians thus feared and suspected that a Christian army would come upon them. They therefore sought deceitfully with guile and tears and in many other ways to call back the bishop. They said to him —as was formerly said to Saint Martin, although the inten-

13. Cf. *Rituale Romanum, Ordo ad Faciendam Aquam Benedictam, Exorcismus Salis.*

14. Cf. the story in the Martyrology, Oct. 30, in Migne, *P.L.*, CXXIII, 432.

tion was not the same—: "Why do you desert us, father? And to whom are you leaving us desolate creatures? Does a shepherd by going away dangerously expose his sheep to the jaws of wolves?" [15] And these very Livonians again promised that they would fully receive the faith. The innocent bishop believed every word, and upon the advice of the merchants and upon the promise of an army, went back with the Livonians. For some of the Germans and certain of the Danes and Norwegians and each of the trading groups had promised that if necessary they would bring an army. After the departure of the merchants, certain of the people of Holm greeted the bishop on his return like Judas, and said: "Hail Rabbi! [16] At what price can salt or *watmal* [17] be bought in Gothland?" And with bitterness in his heart he wept and crossed over to Uexküll and was received in his home. He appointed a day on which the people were to assemble in order that he might admonish them concerning their promise. The day was not observed and they did not fulfill their promise. After taking council with his men he proposed to go into Esthonia in order to go on to Gothland with the merchants who were wintering in that place. The Livonians, in the meantime, prepared to kill him on the road, but he was forewarned by Anno of Treiden and advised to go back. Much perplexed and unable to get out of the country, he, therefore, went back to Uexküll.

(12) Then he secretly sent away his messenger, Brother Theodoric of Treiden, to take counsel with the lord pope.[18]

15. Cf. *Breviarium Romanum, Officium S. Martini Episcopi* (Nov. 11), *Resp. ad Lect. vi;* also, Sulpicius Severus, *Epistola III*, in Migne, *P.L.*, XX, 182.

16. Cf. Matt. 26:49.

17. *Watmal* was the Livonian name for a kind of crude cloth. The word is apparently a Scandinavian loan word: cf. the Icelandic *vaðmál*, meaning a plain woolen material. The word is derived from *vað*, meaning "cloth" and *mál*, meaning "a measure." In the old Scandinavian communities *vaðmál* was the standard medium of exchange. The word is used in modern Icelandic to refer to homespun goods, as distinguished from imported cloth. See R. Cleasby and G. Vigfusson, *Icelandic-English Dictionary*, 2d ed. (Oxford, 1957), *s.v. vaðmál.*

18. Pope Celestine II, 1191–98. There is also a decretal of Pope Clement III (1187–91) directed, according to Mansi's edition of the Lucca manuscript of the *Decretales Gregorii IX*, to the bishop of Livonia. This decretal

Brother Theodoric saw that he could not get out of the country, unless by a pious fraud he escaped the trap which the Livonians had set. Clad in a stole and carrying a book and holy water, he rode away on his horse, pretending that he was going to visit a sick man. When travelers questioned him, he insisted that this was the cause of his journey, and thus he escaped from the country and came at last to the supreme pontiff. When the supreme pontiff heard how many had been baptized, he thought that they should not be deserted and decreed that they ought to be forced to observe the faith which they had freely promised. He granted, indeed, the remission of all sins to all those who would take the cross and go to restore that newly founded church. (13) By this time the bishop, with the duke of Sweden, Germans, and the inhabitants of Gothland, had already attacked the Kurs. They were, however, thrown back by a storm and landed in Wierland, a province of Esthonia, and devastated its territory for three days. But while the people of Wierland were negotiating about receiving the faith, the duke, preferring to accept tribute from them, put to sail and to the annoyance of the Germans turned away.

(14) Bishop Meinhard of pious memory, after many labors and sorrows meanwhile took to his bed. Seeing that he was at the point of death, he called together all of the elders of Livonia and Treiden and asked them if after his death they would rather do without a bishop. They jointly declared that they preferred to rejoice in a bishop and father. After a short time the bishop died [1196].

---

grants two further favors to the Livonian missionaries: they are allowed to use any foodstuffs given them by the pagans and they are allowed to recruit for their work, *absque contradictione*, any cleric or religious who wished to join them and who could secure the permission of his superior. *Decretales Gregorii IX*, 5, 6, 10, *Quam sit laudabile (et infra:) Tuis frater*, in *Corpus Iuris Canonici*, ed. Aemilius Friedberg, 2 vols. (Leipzig, 1879–81), II, 774–75.

Book Two [Concerning the Consecration of Bishop Berthold]

[II]

[handwritten marginalia: ?]

[handwritten marginalia: Unfair - why should they cry otherwise?]

(1) The funeral was held according to custom, and the bishop was buried to the false wailing and tears of the Livonians. They then considered the matter of a successor and sent to the metropolitan of Bremen for a qualified person. A venerable member of the Cistercian order, Berthold, the abbot of Loccum, was indicated. At first, indeed, he made difficulties about going, but, overcome by the prayers of the metropolitan, he took on the burden of preaching. (2) Having been made a bishop [1197], he committed himself to the Lord alone and decided accordingly to test his fortune first without an army. He went to Livonia, came to Uexküll, took over the patrimony of the church, and gathered in his presence all of the more important Livonians, both Christian and pagan. He strove to please them with food, drink, and gifts, and said that he came at their invitation and that he had succeeded his

predecessor as sole heir.[19] They received him cordially at first, but at the consecration of the cemetery at Holm, some conspired to burn him in the church, others to kill him, and others to drown him. They charged that he came because he was poor. (3) After considering this beginning, he went secretly to the ships and back to Gothland and on to Saxony. He bewailed both to the lord pope and to the bishop, as well as to all the faithful of Christ, the ruin of the church of Livonia. The lord pope, therefore, granted remission of sins to all those who should take the cross and arm themselves against the perfidious Livonians. And he sent letters about these matters to Bishop Berthold as he had to his predecessor.

(4) The bishop, therefore, after collecting his men, went to Livonia with an army [1198], and made for the fort of Holm, which stands in the middle of the river. He sent a messenger across the water to ask if they had decided to accept the faith and to maintain it. They proclaimed that they wished neither to recognize the faith nor to maintain it. The bishop had left his ships behind and therefore could not harm them. Accordingly he returned with the army to Riga and took counsel with his men as to what he should do. (5) Meanwhile, all of the Livonians were called together against him and, preparing to fight, made a camp beyond the Riga mountain. Nevertheless, they sent a messenger to the bishop, asking why he had brought an army against them. The bishop replied that as dogs return to their vomit,[20] so they had returned too often from the faith to paganism. The Livonians then said: "We shall do away with this reason. If you send back your army, you may return with your people to your bishopric in peace, and you may compel those who have received the faith to keep it. You may lead others to accept it, but with words, not with blows." [21] As security, the bishop demanded their sons from them as hostages, but they utterly refused to give them.

---

19. . . . *dicens se . . . predecessori suo in solidum successisse.*
20. Cf. Prov. 26:11; II Pet. 2:22.
21. Cf. Cicero, *Tusculan Disputations*, III, xxvii, 64.

In the meantime, in order to collect a group of their men, the Livonians offered and received a short armistice, exchanging lances, according to the custom, to confirm the peace. During this peace, they killed several Germans who were seeking *Them who* fodder for their horses. The lord bishop, when he saw this, *break agreement* sent back their lance and called off the peace. The Livonians shouted and yelled in pagan fashion. (6) The Saxon battle lines were armed to fight against them and rushed headlong in an attack upon them [July 24]. The bishop, restraining his horse badly, was carried by its speed into the midst of the fugitives. Two of the Livonians seized him, a third, Ymaut by name, pierced him from the back with a lance, and the others tore him to pieces, limb from limb. (7) The Livonians, fearing that the army was following them, fled headlong, because they saw the military helmet of a dead German which his Livonian murderer had placed on his own head. The army, having lost its leader, was naturally wrought up, and with both horses and ships, fire and sword, laid waste the crops of the Livonians. When they had seen this, the Livo-*Scared?* nians renewed the peace in order to avoid greater damage, and called the clergy to them. About fifty were baptized at Holm on the first day, and about a hundred were converted at Uexküll on the following day. They received the priests into their forts and decided that a measure of grain should be given from each plow [22] for the expenses of each priest. Having seen these events, the army was placated and prepared to return home. (8) The Livonians, therefore, having now lost

---

22. "Plow" is used here to mean a measure of land. Ducange, *Glossarium Mediae et Infimae Latinitatis*, 10 vols. (Niort, 1883), I, 353, defines the term thus: *Aratrum, Idem quod corrucata terrae quantum terrae uno aratro arari potest.* ("A plow: the same as a carrucate of land; as much land as can be tilled with one plow.") In Helmold's *Chronicle of the Slavs*, tr. Tschan, the editor takes a different definition: "The Slavic plow consisted of so much land as could be worked by one pair of oxen or by one horse" (p. 78). See also James Westfall Thompson, *Feudal Germany* (Chicago, 1928), pp. 399, 485, n.3, and 352, n.2. Still another view is expressed by Spekke, *History of Latvia*, p. 171, who believes that the tax was levied on the agricultural implements themselves.

their shepherd, took the advice of the clergy and monks and sent messengers to Germany for a successor. And so, believing in this uncertain peace, the group of Saxons withdrew. The clergy and one ship of merchants remained. Now the wind filled the sails, and lo! the treacherous Livonians, emerging from their customary baths, poured the water of the Dvina River over themselves, saying: "We now remove the water of baptism and Christianity itself with the water of the river. Scrubbing off the faith [23] we have received, we send it after the withdrawing Saxons." Those who had gone away had cut the likeness of the head of a man on a branch of a certain tree. The Livonians supposed this to be the god of the Saxons and they believed that it was bringing flood and pestilence upon them. Accordingly, they cooked mead according to the rite, drank it together, and, having taken counsel, took the head from the tree, placed it on logs which they had tied together, and sent it as the god of the Saxons, together with their Christian faith, after those who were going back to Gothland by sea. (9) A month passed, the peace was broken, and they proceeded to capture the monks, to treat them badly, and to attack their property, taking it away secretly and violently. The horses having been taken away too, the fields remained uncultivated. Because of this, the church lost up to two hundred marks. The clergy, therefore, fled from Uexküll to Holm, not knowing to what place or fortune they should commit themselves. (10) During the following Lent [1199], the whole assembly of Livonians decided that any cleric remaining in the country after Easter [April 18] should suffer death. The clergy, leaving both because of the fear of death and because of the search for a shepherd, went to Saxony. The Livonians decreed too that the merchants who remained there were to be killed. But the merchants, taking thought for their lives, gave gifts to the elders.

23. *Fidem susceptam exfestucantes.* . . . The meaning is clear enough, although the wording is strange. *Exfestucantes* refers, in all probability, to beating with a rod (*festuca*), as is done when washing out dirty clothes.

Book Three

[Concerning Bishop Albert]

[III]

⚞⚞ (1) In the year of the Lord 1198,[24] the venerable Albert, a canon of Bremen, was consecrated bishop.

(2) In the summer following his consecration he went to Gothland and there signed about five hundred men with the cross to go to Livonia. (3) Afterwards, crossing through Denmark, he received gifts from King Canute, Duke Waldemar,[25] and Archbishop Absolon [1199].[26] (4) Going back to Germany, he signed many in Magdeburg at Christmas [Dec. 25]. There King Philip and his wife were crowned.[27] (5) In the presence of the king an opinion was asked for as to whether the goods of the pilgrims to Livonia were to be placed under the protection of the pope, as is the case of

24. 1199 by our calendar. See above, p. 7, n.9, for Henry's calendar.
25. Waldemar later became king of Denmark, reigning from 1202 to 1241.
26. Absolon was archbishop of Lund.
27. At this same meeting Bishop Albert was given Livonia as a fief by Philip.

those who journey to Jerusalem. It was answered, indeed, that they were included under the protection of the pope, who, in enjoining the Livonian pilgrimage for the plenary remission of sins, made it equal with that to Jerusalem.

[IV]

(1) In the second year of his episcopate [1200], Bishop Albert set out for Livonia with Count Conrad of Dortmund, Hartbert of Iburg, and many pilgrims, in a fleet of twenty-three ships. (2) After entering the Dvina River, he proceeded to the fort at Holm, commending himself together with all his men to God, and proceeding thence, he proposed to journey to Uexküll. The Livonians, however, made an attack as they sailed up the river. They wounded a few of them and killed the priest Nicholas and others. Although with difficulty, the bishop and his men arrived at Uexküll. The brothers, who had lived there from the time of the first bishop, and others received them with joy. The assembled Livonians there made peace with the Germans for three days, but deceitfully, that is, in order that they might meanwhile collect their army. (3) The peace having been made, the bishop went down to Holm and, being confident of peace, sent messengers to the ships in the Dvina for his throne, vestments, and other necessary articles. The messengers took with them from the ships what they wished; as if under the great security of peace, they went back over the route on which they had come down. After the bishop's messengers had gone up the Rummel on their return, the Livonians broke the peace and violently attacked them. One ship withdrew and escaped; they captured the other and killed almost all those on board. Then, proceeding to Holm, they besieged the bishop and his men. Since those who were besieged there had food neither for themselves nor for the horses, they were so put to it that they finally dug up the earth and found a great deal of grain and foodstuffs in various

pits. The Frisians, in the meantime, coming with only one ship, set fire to the crops of the Livonians and in this and in other ways damaged them as much as they could. The Livonians, having seen this and fearing a greater danger, renewed and confirmed the peace. With the bishop and other Germans they went to Riga, and there Asso and many other Livonians accepted the grace of baptism.

(4) Because of their treachery, the bishop did not trust in the peace of the Livonians, a peace which they had already broken many times. He therefore demanded hostages from Anno and Caupo and the elders of the land. Called by the Germans to a drinking party, they all gathered at the same time and were shut up in one house. Fearing lest they be brought across the sea into Germany, they presented about thirty of their better boys from the region of the Dvina and from Treiden to the bishop. He received them with joy and, committing the land to the Lord, returned to Germany.

(5) Before his departure, the Livonians showed to the bishop the site of the city which they call Riga. They call it Riga either from Lake Riga, or from irrigation, since it is irrigated both from below and from above.[28] It is irrigated from below for, as they say, it is well moistened in its waters and pastures; or, since the plenary remission of sins is administered in it to sinners, the irrigation from above, that is, the kingdom of heaven is thus administered through it. Or, in other words, Riga, refreshed by the water of the new faith, waters the tribes round about through the holy font of baptism.[29] (6)

28. Cf. Ps. 103:13.
29. Henry plays here upon the words *Riga* (the city) and *rigo* ("irrigate"): *Ante exitum suum Lyvones episcopo locum civitatis demonstrant, quam et Rigam appellant, vel a Riga lacu, vel quasi irriguam, cum habeat inferius irriguum ac irriguum superius. Irriguum inferius, eo quod sit aquis et pascuis irrigua, vel eo quod ministratur in ea peccatoribus plenaria peccaminum remissio, et per eam irriguum superius, quod est regnum celorum, per consequens ministratur, vel Riga nova fide rigata et quia per eam gentes in circuitu sacro baptismatis fonte rigantur.* Arbusow, *Colores Rhetorici,* pp. 43–44, deals with this type of elaborate pun in Medieval Latin and gives numerous other examples of this stylistic trick.

But the bishop, knowing the wickedness of the Livonians and seeing that he could not make progress among that people without pilgrims, sent Brother Theodoric of Treiden to Rome for letters authorizing an expedition. He revealed the business committed to him to the most holy Pope Innocent and through his kindness obtained the letters [30] which he requested. Upon Theodoric's insistence and request, the same venerable bishop of the Roman see strictly prohibited under anathema all merchants from using the port of Semgallia. (7) The merchants themselves rejoiced in what had been done and, by a common decree, placed the same port under their own interdict. If any of them for the sake of trade should for any reason presume to go there, he should be deprived both of goods and of life. When, two years after the construction of the city, certain ones wished to violate their promise, they were at first kindly called upon by the merchants not to go to Semgallia. But they, not attending to the apostolic mandate and ignoring the common decree of the merchants, sailed up the Dvina in their ships. The other merchants, seeing their recalcitrance, brought up other ships and attacked them. They finally took two men, the captain, namely, and the pilot of the ship, put them to a cruel death, and forced the others to return.

[V]

(1) In the third year of his consecration [1201], the bishop left the hostages in Germany and returned to Livonia with the pilgrims whom he was able to get. The city of Riga was built in the next summer in a spacious field, next to which

30. Presumably these are the letters which were incorporated in the *Decretales Gregorii IX*, 3, 1, 11, *Deus qui ecclesiam suam nova* (ed. Friedberg, II, 451–52); 4, 19, 9, *Deus qui ecclesiam suam* (*et infra:*) *Quia dispar* (ed. Friedberg, II, 724–25); and 5, 38, 8, *Deus qui ecclesiam suam* (*et infra:*) *Ceterum quum poenitentia* (ed. Friedberg, II, 886). Cf. Bunge, *Urkundenbuch*, III, 1, no. 13.

there was a potential harbor for ships. (2) At that time the bishop, binding to himself Daniel, a noble person, and Conrad from Meiendorf, enfeoffed them with two forts, Lennewarden and Uexküll.

(3) In the meantime, the Kurs, having heard of the coming of the bishop and the beginning of the city, not for fear of war, but rather at the call of Christ, sent messengers to the city to make peace. With the consent of the Christians, they confirmed the peace with the effusion of blood, as is the pagan custom. (4) The Lithuanians also, God so disposing, came to Riga that same year asking for peace. When peace had been made, they at once entered into a friendly alliance with the Christians. In the following winter they went down the Dvina with a great army and made for Semgallia. Before entering the country, however, they heard that the king of Polozk was entering Lithuania with an army. Leaving the Semgalls, they returned in haste and, finding as they went up country two fishermen of the bishop's by the Rummel, like ravening wolves [31] they raged against them and took away the clothes they were wearing. And thereupon the naked fishermen fled to Riga and exposed the injury they had suffered. The pilgrims then learned the truth of the matter, seized certain Lithuanians who were living in Riga at that time, and detained them in chains until the things stolen from the fishermen were returned.

[VI]

(1) In the fourth year of his appointment [1202], the city was committed to a few pilgrims who set themselves up as a wall for the house of the Lord,[32] and the bishop with the rest of the pilgrims set out for Germany.

31. Cf. Matt. 7:15.
32. Cf. Ezek. 13:5.

(2) After his departure, his brother Engelbert, a monk called from Neumünster,[33] came to Riga with the first citizens and, coöperating with Him who gave the Word to those who spread the gospel, began to spread the name of Christ among the people with Brother Theodoric of Treiden and Alabrand and the other brothers living in Livonia as monks. (3) After a short time, the brothers of the convent of the Blessed Virgin Mary in Riga, approving his life and order, elected him provost, because he came from the monastery of Segeberg and was of the same order as the first bishop of Livonia, Meinhard of blessed memory. With a desire to found a house of his own order, Meinhard had first established their convent in the parish of Uexküll. (4) Afterwards, Albert, the bishop of Uexküll, in the third year of his consecration moved the convent of regulars and the episcopal see from Uexküll to Riga and dedicated the episcopal cathedral with all of Livonia to Mary, the Blessed Mother of God. (5) He constructed a monastery for Cistercian monks at the mouth of the Dvina, which he called Dünamünde Cloister or Mount Saint Nicholas. He consecrated his co-worker in the gospel, Brother Theodoric of Treiden, abbot of the monastery. (6) At the same time Brother Theodoric,[34] foreseeing the treachery of the Livonians and fearing he would be unable to resist the multitude of pagans, and, moreover, to multiply the number of the faithful and to preserve the church among the pagans, founded certain Brothers of the Militia of Christ.[35] The lord Pope Innocent gave them the rule of the Templars and also, as insignia to be worn on their clothing, a sword and a cross. He commanded that they be under the obedience of their bishop.

(7) Thereupon, the Semgalls, not being at peace with the Livonians, burned down the church at Holm and all the vil-

33. A monastery in Holzatia.
34. This seems to be a mistake on the part of the chronicler, since other sources assign the founding of the order to the bishop, Albert, rather than to Theodoric, the abbot of Dünamünde.
35. I.e., the Livonian Brothers of the Sword.

lage likewise, and after besieging the fort for a long time and not being able to take it, they retreated. Wishing to strengthen the new plantation of the Christian faith and to confirm peace to it all around, God sent the Semgalls to Riga after this expedition to make peace. When peace had been confirmed according to the pagan custom, those who had formerly been enemies of the Germans and the Livonians, He made friends.

[VII]

～～ (1) In the fifth year of his pontificate [1203], the bishop brought back with him from Germany the noblemen Arnold of Meiendorf, Bernard of Seehausen, and his brother, Theodoric, together with many respectable men and soldiers. Not fearing to undergo prosperity and adversity for God, he committed himself to the raging sea. As he approached the Danish province of Lyster, he came upon pagan Esthonians of the island of Oesel with sixteen ships. They had recently burned a church, killed some men and captured others, laid waste the land, and carried away the bells and belongings of the church, just as both the pagan Esthonians and the Kurs had been accustomed to do heretofore in the kingdom of Denmark and Sweden. The pilgrims armed, wishing to avenge the losses of the Christians; but the pagans, knowing that they were going to Livonia, feared greatly and said deceitfully that they had made peace with the people of Riga. Since the Christians believed them, the pagans escaped their hands for the time being. But their trickery brought them no gain, for afterwards they fell into the same trap that had been prepared for them.[36] For the pilgrims, led by God, came to Wisby safe and unharmed [37] and were joyfully received by the citizens

36. Cf. Ps. 56:7.
37. Cf. *Rituale Romanum, Itinerarium Clericorum, Oratio.*

and foreigners living there. After a few days, the Esthonians approached with all their rapine. The pilgrims, seeing them sailing, blamed the citizens and merchants for permitting the enemies of the Christian name to cross their harbor in peace. The merchants and citizens pretended to agree but really wished to enjoy peace with them. (2) And so the pilgrims went to their bishop and requested permission to fight the Esthonians. The bishop, therefore, knowing their wish, endeavored to turn them aside from the project. For not only was it possible that they might be endangered by the enemy in battle, but also the church which had been established among the pagans and had long awaited their coming would not be able to make up their lack. They, however, for better or for worse, urgently and not distrusting the mercy of God, refused to turn their minds from the idea. Affirming that there was no difference between the Esthonian pagans and the Livonians, they asked that he accede to their petitions and deign to enjoin this battle on them for their sins. The bishop, seeing their obstinacy, thought it better that they should go into battle obediently, and since obedience is better than sacrifice,[38] in order to satisfy their wishes he enjoined them, as they asked, to go into battle with courage for the remission of their sins. Accordingly the pilgrims prepared to fight boldly for the name of Christ and girding their arms on tightly they speedily prepared the ships in which they were about to go. When the Esthonians heard this, on the other hand, withdrawing eight of their pirate ships a little from the others, they thought that they could surround the pilgrims as they came in between and so capture the ships prepared against them. And thus the Germans attacked them and mounted two of the Esthonian pirate ships. They killed sixty men and brought the ships, loaded with bells, sacerdotal vestments, and captive Christians, to the city of Wisby. A certain German, a man of great strength and courage, leaping upon a third pirate ship holding his drawn sword with both hands and striking here

38. Cf. I Kings 15:22.

and there, alone laid low twenty-two of the enemy. In this slaughter he labored beyond his strength. Therefore the sail was raised on high by the eight men who survived and, when wind filled the sails, this same man was taken captive and when the ships were brought together he was killed. That ship was burned by fire because of the scarcity of men. (3) These things having thus been gloriously accomplished, all the pilgrims gave thanks to Almighty God for the victory conferred upon them; and the bishop sent to the reverend Lord Andrew, archbishop of Lund, both the men and the things which the pagans had taken from the Danes.

(4) Then the pilgrims, not wishing to stay longer at Wisby, completed the journey they had begun and came at last to Riga. The citizens and others staying in Riga rejoiced greatly over their coming, went out to meet them, and received honorably with relics both the bishop and all his company. (5) After these events, Brother Theodoric with the pilgrims, who had soldiered under the cross for their God throughout this year in Livonia, returned to Germany and took with him a certain Livonian from Treiden, Caupo by name, who was a kind of king and elder of the Livonians, and, having traversed a large part of Germany, at length brought him to Rome and presented him to the apostolic father. (6) The latter received him most graciously, kissed him, asked many things about the status of the tribes dwelling about Livonia, and gave many thanks to God for the conversion of the Livonian people. After several days the venerable Pope Innocent presented his gift, namely a hundred gold pieces, to Caupo and, since he wished to go back to Germany, blessed him, bidding farewell with great and loving affection. By Brother Theodoric he sent to the bishop of Livonia a Bible written by the hand of the blessed Pope Gregory.

(7) That same summer the king of Polozk entered Livonia unexpectedly with an army and besieged the fort at Uexküll. Since the Livonians were unarmed they did not dare to oppose him and instead promised to give him money. The king ac-

cepted this and lifted the siege. Then certain Germans, having meanwhile been sent by the bishop with ballistas and arms, took over the fort at Holm. As the king came up and wished to attack this fort they wounded a great many horses and put to flight the Russians who, because of the arrows, did not dare to cross the Dvina. (8) The king of Gerzika,[39] also, proceeded to Riga with the Lithuanians, took the flocks of the citizens in the pastures, captured two priests, John of Vechta and Volchard of Harpstedt, who, with pilgrims, were cutting down trees next to the Old Mountain, and killed Theodoric Brudegame, who was pursuing him with citizens.

(9) At that time a certain monk named Siegfried was most devotedly carrying on the cure of souls committed to him as priest in the parish of Holm and, persisting in the service of God day and night, he imbued the Livonians with the example of his good manner of life. At length after long labors, God brought a happy end to his life and he died. A crowd of weeping converts bore and followed his little body to the church, as is customary among the faithful. As sons for a beloved father, they made a coffin for him out of good timber and found that one plank cut for the cover was a full foot too short. Disturbed, they sought for a long time and finally found a piece of wood to lengthen it. Fitting the piece to the above-mentioned plank, they tried to attach it with nails, but when they first placed it on the coffin they saw, as they gazed intensely, that the first plank, lengthened not by human but by divine skill had, according to their desires, been made to fit the coffin perfectly. The parishioners were jubilant over this event, threw away the uselessly cut wood, and, having buried their shepherd according to the custom of the faithful, blessed God who worked such miracles for his saints.

39. Like the "king" of Polozk, the "king" of Gerzika was a Russian prince.

[VIII]

⚶⚶ (1) In the sixth year [1204], the bishop, fearing that the city, which up to this time was small and weak, might, because of the scarcity of the faithful, be endangered by plots of the pagans, again went back to Germany to collect pilgrims. He was so zealous in administering the business of converting the pagans that had been laid upon him that he underwent the frequent and almost intolerable labor of going to and returning from Germany every year. After his departure some Lithuanians who abhorred the Christian name and who, with the still-pagan Livonians of Ascheraden and Lennewarden numbered together about three hundred men, descended on Riga and now tried a second time to lead away the flocks which they had seized from the fields. And since the few men who lived at that time in Riga feared ambush everywhere because of the woods all about, they dared not leave the city all at once. But about twenty courageous men from the city followed the enemy and searched for their flocks. After calling upon the aid of Almighty God, with the soldiers arriving from the city, they entered into battle with the pagans next to the Old Mountain. The battle grew so violent that they fought until they were separated from each other through fatigue. Moreover, certain Livonians descended the Dvina in a ship so that, in the absence of the people, they might attack the city from the other side. But under the protection of the Lord certain ones went out of the city with arrows to meet them and thus they were put to flight. Thus when these deeds had been done, the Livonians and the Lithuanians departed, having obtained only three of the horses of the citizens. All the Germans returned joyfully to the city, praising God for the conservation of men and the recovery of the flocks.

(2) After these events, since winter was coming on, certain

knights, namely Arnold of Meiendorf and Bernard of Seehausen and certain others who, after taking the cross a second
time, had remained there, wished to return to Germany. They
prepared the necessities for the journey, embarked in their
ship before the Nativity of the Blessed Virgin Mary [Sept.
8], and as they left the Dvina, God so arranged it that they
met three other ships of pilgrims outside of the harbor. (3)
Brother Theodoric and Caupo were coming back from Rome
in these ships and made the people of Riga, who had been very
sad, happy with their arrival. But to the extent that the joy of
the Christians was increased, so the multitude of the pagans
was made sorrowful and confused. (4) Thereupon the before-
mentioned knights labored long with their companions in the
struggle with the rough sea and at length came to a region of
Esthonia. The Esthonians, wishing to take their lives and
their possessions, attacked them with ten pirate ships and
twelve other ships. God preserved His people, however. They
suffered neither adversity nor sorrow from the enemy; rather,
one of the pirate ships was broken to pieces by the Christians,
some of the pagans were killed, and others miserably drowned
in the sea. They hooked another pirate ship with an iron hook
and tried to drag it toward themselves. The pagans, however,
wishing rather to be endangered in the sea than to be killed by
the Christians, jumped from the ship one by one. While they
fell into the danger of death, the other ships departed and
escaped. Although Almighty God does not cease to test his
elect ones, now placed in various tribulations, like gold in fire,
nevertheless He does not desert them entirely, but rather,
rescuing them from all evils, puts their enemies in greater fear.
They continued in many labors, spending especially many
days in hunger, thirst, and cold. Although they had very little
food, they received fifty shipwrecked Christians standing on
the shore and, mercifully helping them, shared and consumed
all their food. And when this alone remained, that they might
die of hunger, behold how the dawning visited them from on

high.[40] A large merchant ship arrived, gave and sold them
food, refreshed the starving ones, and they were filled. They
went on, however, and fell into very serious danger, for a
storm threw them among some very dangerous rocks out of
which they came with great fear and difficulty. They arrived
at the port of Wisby on the vigil of St. Andrew [Nov. 29],
took on food, and then sailed to the shores of Denmark. Being
unable to bring the ship to shore because of the great amount
of ice, they left it in the ice and, taking their possessions with
them, returned to Germany through Denmark.

[IX]

(1) In the seventh year [1205], about Lent, when these
tribes are more accustomed to engage in war, the Lithuanians
moved against Esthonia with a force of almost two thousand
men. They descended along the Dvina and passed by the city.
A certain one of them, a rich and very powerful man named
Svelgate, turned aside to the city with his companions. The
men of the city went out to meet them in peace, and a certain
citizen named Martin offered them a honeyed drink. When he
finished it, Svelgate followed the army which was going ahead,
and spoke as follows to his companions: "Did you not see the
Germans offering us mead with a trembling hand? They had
known of our arrival from rumor [41] and the fear which then
struck them still causes them to shake. At the moment, however, let us defer the overthrow of this city, but if we conquer
the places to which we are going, let us destroy this town and
capture and kill its men. For the dust of this city will scarcely
satisfy the fist of our people." (2) After a few days, Viesthard,
a noble of the Semgalls, hearing about the Lithuanian expedi-

40. Luke 1:78.
41. . . . *fama volante*. . . . Cf. Vergil, *Aeneid*, III, 121.

tion, came hurriedly to Riga and spoke in admonition to the
Germans for having permitted the enemy to cross their boundaries peacefully. For now that they had learned the location
of the place, they might possibly in the future destroy the city
with its inhabitants. Although they did not wish, because of
the weakness of their forces, to fight before the bishop's return, Viesthard, being a warlike man, excited them to battle
and promised to bring a great many Semgalls to their aid.
He asked, however, to be given at least a few men experienced
in war who knew how to organize an army and drill it for battle. The Germans recognized his steadfast spirit and said they
would willingly accede to his request if, however, he would
present them with one hostage whom they would choose from
each of the forts of the Semgalls. He rejoiced greatly at such
a reply, joyfully returned to his people, and collected a sufficient army, bringing with him the specified hostages. When
the army arrived, the hostages were delivered into the hands
of the Germans and, their loyalty thus demonstrated, the
Semgalls obtained both help and friendship. For the retinue
of the bishop, with the Brothers of the Militia of Christ, and
Conrad, a knight of Uexküll, together with a few others who
could be spared, went out to the army and in a high place
they and the Semgalls awaited the return of the Lithuanians.
(3) In the meantime, suitable scouts were sent to Treiden,
who were able to explore carefully the route of the enemy and
to report it. The leader of the Semgalls collected food from
each house in Riga and carried it to the army which had come
from afar. At length the Lithuanians returned with numerous
captives and indescribable booty in flocks and horses, entered
Livonia, and proceeded gradually from village to village. At
last they turned aside to the fort of Caupo and, trusting the
peace of the Livonians, spent the night among them. The
scouts of the Germans and Semgalls inquired discreetly about
their return and announced this to their own army. The next
day, some other scouts followed the former and reported that
the Lithuanians wished to return through the Rodenpois short

cut to Uexküll. When they heard these reports, the whole army rejoiced and all prepared in rivalry for the fight. The Lithuanians came with all their loot and captives, who numbered more than a thousand, divided their army into two parts, placed the captives in the middle, and, because of the excessive depth of the snow, marched single file over one path. But as soon as the first of these discovered the footprints of those who had gone before, they stopped, suspecting an ambush. Thus the last in line overtook the first and all were collected in one formation with the captives. When the Semgalls saw their great multitude, many of them trembled and, not daring to fight, wished to seek safer places. Thereupon certain of the Germans approached the knight Conrad and begged insistently that they go first into battle with the enemies of Christ. They asserted that it was better to go to death gloriously for Christ than, to the confusion of their tribe, to take flight dishonorably. Conrad, with his horse and himself well-armored, like a knight, attacked the Lithuanians with the few Germans who were on hand. But God sent such fear into the Lithuanians and they were so dazzled by the brightness of the German arms that they turned away on all sides. The leader of the Semgalls, perceiving that the Lithuanians were so terrified through the mercy of God, exhorted his men bravely to go into battle with them. Thus the army was assembled and the Lithuanians were dispersed on all sides of the road like sheep. About twelve hundred of them were cut down by the sword.

(4) A certain member of the bishop's household, Theodoric Scilling, came upon Svelgate, who had said that he would overthrow the city of God, saw him sitting in a cart, and pierced his side with a lance. Certain of the Semgalls saw him quivering, cut off his head, and put it on one of their wagons which they had loaded only with the heads of Lithuanians, and went into Semgallia. They killed a great many of the Esthonian captives with the sword, since they too were enemies, working at all times against the cultivators of the Chris-

tian name. Thus the Christians, joined with the pagan Semgalls, obtained a full victory over both countries, namely Lithuania and Esthonia.

After the slaughter of the Lithuanians and Esthonians, the Germans and the Semgalls turned to the spoils of each tribe. They took untold loot, both in horses and flocks, likewise in clothing and arms, and then all returned to their homes safe and unharmed [42] and, having been saved through the grace of God, they blessed God. (5) A certain priest named John who at that time was held captive in Lithuania reported that fifty women had hanged themselves because of the deaths of their husbands, without doubt because they believed that they would rejoin them immediately in the other life.

(6) Having signed many men throughout Germany with the sign of the cross, at length the bishop returned to the ships, taking with him his brother Rothmar from the monastery of Segeberg, by virtue of the authority given to him by the most pious apostolic father Innocent to take as a companion in his labor whatever brother he wished from each monastery. Led by Him Who commands the winds and the sea,[43] he arrived at Riga. Here the lord bishop, long desired by his people, was honorably received with all the army of pilgrims. There were in this same battle line the leader in war, Count Henry of Stumpenhusen, Cono of Isenburg, a nobleman, and a great many other knights and pilgrims from Westphalia as well as from Saxony. (7) The bishop wished to extend the vines of the Lord's vineyard among the heathen by the counsel and aid of such men, and after entering the Dvina, placing a monastery of Cistercian monks at Dünamünde,[44] and appointing his brother Theodoric as abbot, he sent Conrad of Meiendorf to the fort at Uexküll, which he had already bestowed on him as a benefice. He was to announce to the Livonians that the

42. See n.37, above.
43. Cf. Matt. 8:27; Luke 8:25.
44. The monastery had been built in 1202 (see above, p. 40, VI, 5), but this was, apparently, the first time monks had been brought to live there.

bishop and certain pilgrims were coming, so that, knowing this, they might as sons receive him kindly as a father and arrange with him about the maintainance of peace among themselves and the furtherance of the faith. (8) The Livonians, therefore, who, having accepted the grace of baptism from Meinhard, the first bishop of Livonia, had scorned the faith of Christ and often said they had removed it by bathing in the Dvina, heard of the approach of the bishop and prepared to flee with others who were still pagan. In the morning they called Conrad to them and strove to kill him secretly. But because the arrow which has been foreseen does not hit the mark,[45] he, knowing their trickery, put on his armor and went outside with his companions. As they conversed a great deal with him, he answered everything suitably. In the meantime those who preceded the bishop arrived. Thereupon the Livonians, more astounded than ever, fled and sought the aid of their little boats. They went up towards the fort of Lennewarden with their wives and children, thus demonstrating quite clearly by this that they cared little for the baptism which they had formerly received. The pilgrims therefore saw the converted Livonians turn away in this manner and, like dogs, go back to their vomit,[46] because they had forgotten the faith which they had formerly received. Burning with the zeal of God, therefore, they followed the fugitives. But as soon as they saw them join the other pagans of Lennewarden and leave the villages to go with them to the hiding places of the woods, the pilgrims burned up their city. (9) Then, as the pilgrims went up alongside the Dvina, the Livonians of the fort of Ascheraden heard of these events and fled to the safer places of the woods. Now that their fort, by the grace of God, had been burned, they made peace with the Germans, gave hostages, and promised that they would come to Riga shortly

---

45. *Sed quia sagitta previsa minus ferit.* . . . Cf. Pope Gregory I, *Homilia 35 in Evangelio,* cited in *Breviarium Romanum, Officium Commune Plurimorum Martyrum, Lect. vii.*

46. Cf. Prov. 26:11; II Pet. 2:22.

and be baptized there. This they afterwards did. (10) **King Vetseke of Kokenhusen**, hearing that Latin pilgrims had come in such great strength and that they were only three miles away from him, asked through an envoy for a safe conduct from the bishop. He thus came down to him on a ship and, after greeting the bishop by shaking hands, he made there a firm peace with the Germans. Yet this peace lasted but a short time. When he had made peace, he bade farewell to all and returned joyfully to his people.

(11) And when these things had been done, the Livonians of the two cities of Lennewarden and Uexküll most gravely attacked the pilgrims on their way back in very dense woods near the Memeculle road. Escaping from their attack without great danger, they came to Uexküll and perceived that this well-fortified city, formerly built by Bishop Meinhard, was empty. It seemed to them that the Livonians were unworthy of such a large fort, for, although they had been baptized, they were nevertheless still rebels and unbelievers. For this reason, they sent Conrad in to take possession of his benefice and left with him certain strong pilgrims ready for war. Since, moreover, they wished to provide grain for him, in preparation for the fight, they cut down the crops of the Livonians which were now ripe, both with scythes and with swords. Unable to endure the frequent ambushes of the pagans, they all went out armed to cut the crops and filled the town to the top. The lord bishop, overjoyed at such a deed, commended those remaining there to God and descended to Riga with the rest of the army of the pilgrims.

(12) A short time thereafter the pilgrims, leaving the fort of Uexküll to collect grain, were attacked by Livonians hiding in the woods. Seventeen of them were killed, some of whom suffering a cruel martyrdom were immolated to the pagan gods. Neither by this nor by similar deeds could the enemy keep the Christian voices from preaching the Word of God; indeed through the increase of the faith they saw that in preaching and fighting they were daily growing stronger.

Thus the hearts of all the Livonians dwelling near the Dvina were perturbed. (13) Because of their dismay, they gave hostages and were reconciled to the lord bishop and the other Germans. Those among them who were still pagans promised that they would be baptized. Thus, therefore, this untamed people, overly given to pagan rites, through the summons of Christ was steadily led to the yoke of the Lord and, leaving behind pagan darkness, through faith looked upon the true light, which is Christ.[47] Accordingly, not undeservedly, those who seemed justly to have lost villages and fields and other possessions were permitted to regain them. They were, however, entirely excluded from the fortifications built next to the town of Uexküll. The people, both of Uexküll and of Lennewarden, returned to their homes.[48]

(14) That same winter a very elaborate play of the prophets was performed in the middle of Riga in order that the pagans might learn the rudiments of the Christian faith by an ocular demonstration. The subject of this play was most diligently explained to both converts and pagans through an interpreter. When, however, the army of Gideon fought the Philistines, the pagans began to take flight, fearing lest they be killed, but they were quietly called back. Thus, therefore, the church grew hushed and peaceful in a short time. This play was like a prelude and prophecy of the future; for in the same play there were wars, namely those of David, Gideon, and Herod, and there was the doctrine of the Old and New Testaments. Certainly, through the many wars that followed, the pagans were to be converted and, through the doctrine of the Old and New Testaments, they were to be told how they might attain to the true Peacemaker and eternal life.

47. Cf. the Mass for Good Friday, *Oratio pro Judeis.*
48. . . . *ad propria revertuntur.* Cf. *Rituale Romanum, Itinerarium Clericorum, Antiphon.*

[X]

~~~ (1) At the beginning of the eighth year [1206], the lord bishop, wishing to acquire the friendship and intimacy of King Vladimir of Polozk, which the latter had shown to his predecessor, Bishop Meinhard, sent a war horse with armor to him, through Abbot Theodoric, who was robbed on the road by a band of Lithuanian bandits. The abbot and his men lost all the things they had with them, but at length came to the king safe and unharmed [49] in body. Going into the city, they found there certain Livonians who had been secretly sent by the elders of Livonia to incline the heart of the king to expel the Germans from Livonia. They set forth in a bland and lying speech whatever they could deceitfully imagine or say against the bishop and his men, for they asserted that the bishop with his followers was excessively harsh to them and that the yoke of the faith was intolerable. The king, believing their story like a simpleton, ordered everyone living in his kingdom to prepare as hurriedly as possible for an expedition to descend on Riga speedily and efficiently, that is, with the current of the Dvina in a ship or on a raft of many logs, with provisions placed along the route. Thus it was that the German ambassadors, ignorant of the Livonians' proposals and of the intention of the king, were ordered to appear before the king, where, in the presence of the Livonians, they were questioned why they came. When they explained that they had come for peace and friendship, the Livonians protested that on the contrary they neither wished for nor preserved peace. Their speech was full of wrath and bitterness and they excited the heart and mind of the king more to wage war than to make peace. (2) The king, however, fearing lest his dark counsels be brought to light, had the Germans removed

49. See n.37, above.

from his presence and ordered them to stay in the guesthouse. The abbot, however, reflecting on the matter, corrupted one of the king's councilors with gifts and money, and the long-secret plan was made known without delay. When he had learned this through the wonderful providence of God, things went better for the abbot. For he discovered by a gift of God that there was a certain poor man from the fort of Holm there. He hired him for a half mark of silver and gave him a letter to tell the lord bishop of Riga and all the faithful of the church what he had seen and heard. Whence it happened that many of the pilgrims who had been preparing to cross the sea returned and again took up the cross. The bishop also, who had been preparing to leave with the others, said good-by to those sailing away and returned to Riga.

(3) The king, therefore, hearing what the abbot had done, sent for him and asked if he had sent a messenger to Riga; but he, not fearing to face the king, acknowledged that by a certain one he had sent a letter. The ambassadors, however, who had been sent with him from Riga, feared the severity of the king and begged and tried to persuade the abbot to deny what he had said. But he, knowing that a word once uttered can never be recalled,[50] refused for any reason to deny what he had said to the king. The king knew he could accomplish nothing in this way, since his plot had been betrayed. Since he could not use warlike violence, he concocted a trick, for he spoke sweet words in the manner of a dove and did harm like a snake in the grass.[51] He sent back the abbot and with him Russian ambassadors who were deceitfully instructed with peaceful words to hear the arguments on both sides and decide what was right between the Livonians and the bishop, and to consider this settled. Dismissed by the king, they made great haste to the Russian fort of Kokenhusen. There they sent a certain deacon Stephan, not, to be sure, the protomartyr, with the abbot to Riga; they summoned the bishop to meet

50. Cf. Horace, *Epistulae*, I, xviii, 71.
51. Cf. Vergil, *Eclogues*, III, 93.

with the ambassadors and fixed the third day before the
kalends of July [52] [May 30] as the date for the meeting, at a
place alongside the River Oger. The rest spread throughout
the land summoning the Livonians and Letts, who are properly called Lethigalls, with their arms. The Livonians came
prepared not so much to obey the king as to work for the
downfall of the faithful of Christ. The still-pagan Letts or
Lethigalls, who approved the life of the Christians and desired
their safety, did not come to the treacherous meeting. They
could not even be influenced by Russian gifts [53] to bring evil
on the Germans. (4) The lord bishop, when called to the
same meeting by the king's ambassador, the before-mentioned
Stephan, after consulting his men, gave this reply: "It is known
to be the common custom of all lands," he said, "that the
messengers who are sent by their lords approach or seek out
him to whom they are sent. No prince, however humble or
friendly he may be, goes outside his walls to meet legates. It
is, therefore, fitting that legates of such rank and representing
such principals, find us in our city where we and our men
may more honorably receive and deal with them. Let them
come, therefore, fearing nothing, to be dealt with honorably."
At the approach of the appointed day, the armed Livonians
came to the conference on the banks of the Oger River. The
elders of the fort of Holm, authors of the villainous scheme,
also sailed up the river to them and, landing at the fort of
Uexküll, summoned its occupants to go with them. (5) After
considering the cunning of the Livonians, the Germans refused to come up. The Livonians, however, continued on
their way and with their compatriots discussed the ejection of
the Christians. In the meantime, two converts from Uexküll,
Kyrian and Layan, begged Conrad, who commanded the fort,
very hard to permit them to be present at the meeting of the
Livonians. They urged that, after observing their obstinacy,

52. "July" is thought to be an error for "June."
53. . . . *muneribus eciam . . . flecti nequeunt*. . . . Cf. the Martyrology,
Oct. 31 (Migne, *P.L.*, CXXIV, 637).

they could report what schemes were being drawn up against the faithful of Christ. Because of their numerous friends and kinsmen they did not fear to approach the fearful battle line of the enemy. Conrad earnestly strove to dissuade them from this foolishness, warning them of the manifold malice of the Livonians, but when overcome by their earnest entreaty, he allowed them to go their way. When they entered the meeting they were immediately taken by the elders, who attempted to force them to put off the Christian faith and to renounce the Germans. Constant in the love of God, they confessed that they had embraced the faith they had received with all devotion and affirmed that no kind of torture could separate them from the love and society of Christians. Because of this, naturally, the hatred even of their kinsmen grew so great against them that henceforth this hatred was greater than the love which they had previously felt. Thus it was that by a conspiracy of all the Livonians their feet were bound by ropes and they were cut through the middle. They afflicted them with most cruel punishments, tore out their viscera and cut off their arms and legs. There is no doubt that they received eternal life with the holy martyrs for such a martyrdom. (6) Their bodies rest in the church of Uexküll and are beside the tombs of the bishops Meinhard and Berthold, of whom the first was a confessor and the second a martyr who, as is related above, was killed by the same Livonians. When this had been done, the Livonians agreed to come together as a group from all parts of their land and to occupy the fort of Holm, because it was closer to the city. From it they were to overcome the people of Riga, who were not very numerous at the moment, and destroy Riga. When the conspiracy and confederation had been completed, therefore, they proved unmindful of the oaths they had taken. Forgetful of their baptism, casting off the faith, not keeping the peace, beginning war, the whole multitude descended to Holm and, calling to themselves certain Lithuanians and inhabitants of Treiden and certain inhabitants of the Dvina region, they all came together as one. (7) Besides, the people of Holm, who are quick to shed blood, took their priest, John, cut off his head, and cut the rest of his body into pieces. John, indeed, was born in Wierland and was captured from the pagans as a boy. He was freed from captivity by the venerable Bishop Meinhard, who, in order to imbue him with sacred letters, placed him in the monastery of Segeberg, where he made great progress. He set out for Livonia with Bishop Albert, took holy orders, and converted many in the parish of Holm from the cult of idols. After the course of his labor was completed, he together with two others, Gerhard and Herman, as confessors of the faith, as we have said before, attained eternal life through the martyr's palm. The lord bishop with his chapter devotedly buried his body and bones, which were collected afterwards by other priests, in the church of Blessed Mary at Riga.

(8) When these things had been done and the crowd of Livonians was going together to the fort of Holm, certain converts of Lembewalde and others, showing themselves faithful, leaving their wives and families in Holm, since they wished more advantage for the Christians than for their own crafty Livonians, made suggestions to the lord bishop as to how he might defend himself from the enemy. All the Livonians, however, were at the same time in the camp for a few days. Certain of them, however, went out towards Riga, stole horses from the fields, killed the men whom they met, and did all the damage they could. Some who finally grew tired went home, while others still remained. When he heard of the departure of some of them, the bishop called together the Brothers of the Militia and the citizens and pilgrims and asked what it was necessary to do against the machinations of the Livonians. It seemed expedient to all that, after calling the aid of Almighty God upon themselves and commending the new church to Him, they should go to war with those in Holm, for it was better for all to die for the faith of Christ than for them to be daily tortured, one by one. After they had turned the city over to the lord bishop, therefore, the braver Germans

with their Livonian Rigans armed, took ballistarii and archers
with them and went up the river by ship. They reached the
fort at Holm on the fifteenth day after Pentecost [June 4].
After seeing their approach, the enemy rushed boldly up to
prevent access to the shore. Because of their own fewness the
Christians were at first dismayed, for they numbered scarcely
a hundred and fifty, while there was a multitude of the enemy,
but they implored the aid and mercy of God with a song and,
having recovered their spirits, at last sprang out. The first to
spring was Arnold, a Brother of the Militia, who was followed
by the servants of the bishop and others from another ship.
They all approached the enemy at once. And fighting at first
in the water, they received the hostile lances and the stones
from the shore which fell cruelly upon them; at length, after
a very brave fight, they took the beach. The enemy were
wounded here and there, where they were unprotected, by
flying arrows; [54] the battle lines came together and the enemy
was overcome. Some were killed in flight; others, wishing to
swim across the stream, were drowned; others were received
into the fort; others tried to escape by swimming but did not
escape the sting of the worms. Ako, their prince and leader,
was, moreover, among them; he had been the author of all the
treachery and of all the evil; he had incited the king of
Polozk to war against the people of Riga; he had collected
the Lithuanians; he had called together the people of Treiden
and all Livonia against the Christian name. He, among others,
was killed and, together with the news of the victory, his
severed head was sent to the bishop. Having just celebrated
Mass, the bishop was with his priests. He was waiting in the
fear of God and with prayers to see if by chance anyone
should appear to report to him what had been done. For his
heart had faith in the Lord. [55] And suddenly there appeared
in the distance a little ship in which a Brother of the Militia

---

54. *Vulneratur passim hostium nuditas a sagitta volante* . . . seems to in-
dicate that the Livonians were only partially protected by armor.
55. Cf. Prov. 3:5.

was returning with some wounded men. He presented the head of Ako to the bishop as a sign of victory. The bishop rejoiced with all who had remained at home and gave thanks to God, Who, through a few, wrought the salvation of His church. (9) In the meantime the Christians reached the walls of the suburbs, set fire to the walls of the fort, and with the paterells threw fire and stones into the fort. The ballistarii wounded a great many on the fortifications, and after the killing of so many the enemy were no longer able to defend themselves. Therefore, the people of Treiden begged for peace, which was given to them. Almost all of them were wounded, and they were permitted to leave the fort. The people of Holm also, the authors of the evil, were compelled to surrender; their elders were taken to Riga and, as they deserved, cast into chains. Those, however, who were left in the fort were spared because of the sacrament of baptism which they had formerly received, and no evil was henceforth done to them. God always worked through a few and not through the bravery of many in all those things which hitherto had gloriously happened in Livonia. Hence for the many victories let God be blessed forever. At that same time there was a great famine and a shortage of food in the city. God therefore sent Daniel, a priest of the bishop, from Gothland with two merchant ships filled to the gunwales with grain and similar necessary things. The bishop sent the same Daniel with his steward Gevehard, ballistarii, and certain others to take over the aforesaid fort of Holm. This was to prevent the Livonians from opposing the Christians by calling together the Russians and pagans. The bishop later took the elders of Holm with him to Germany so that by seeing and hearing Christian customs there they, who had always been unfaithful, might learn to become faithful.

(10) After this the people of Riga, mindful of all the injuries which the still-pagan inhabitants of Treiden had brought upon them and of the often interrupted peace, called the Semgalls to help them take revenge on their enemies. The

Semgalls were delighted, for they were always hostile to the people of Treiden. About three thousand men came with Viesthard, their prince, to meet the people of Riga. They proceeded to the Aa, where they divided their army and turned over half of it to Caupo, the leader of the army. After he returned from Rome he became most faithful and, because of the persecution of the Livonians, he fled to the town and lived there with the Christians for almost a whole year. The other half of the army was sent into Dobrel's territory. Caupo journeyed with his army towards that fort of his where his still-pagan friends and relatives were. When they saw the army come suddenly and unexpectedly, a few of them, struck by fear, mounted the ramparts to defend the fort. Many of them jumped down from the rear part of the fort and sought flight in the woods and mountains. The Christians, therefore, manfully attacked the fort and courageously climbed at length to the top of the walls. They conquered the enemy, pushed them from the walls, and were received in the fort. They pursued the pagans everywhere through the fort and killed almost fifty of them, while the rest escaped by flight. After taking away everything and many spoils, they burned the fort. When the Livonians who were on the other side of the Aa, in the fort of Dobrel, saw the smoke and flames ascending from Caupo's burning fort, they feared that the same would happen to them and their fort. They all collected in the forts, mounted the ramparts, awaited the enemy, and most bravely resisted them as they came. Dobrel, their elder, comforted and encouraged them, saying, as the Philistines once did: "Take courage and fight, ye Philistines, lest you come to be servants to the Hebrews." [56] The pilgrims, indeed, after attacking the fort with the Semgalls for a whole day were not able to take it. Certain of them tried to scale the walls at another spot with a few others and left there five of their men, killed by the Livonians. Seeing that the fort was strong and impregnable, therefore, they turned away from it and, after de-

56. I Kings 4:9.

spoiling the land, returned to their fellows. Upon their return they halted at Riga with the whole army and divided all the spoils which they had brought. The bishop, too, gave thanks to God and with joy sent the Semgalls back to their country.

(11) After this the bishop renewed peace with the Livonians and proposed to go to Germany. When he came out to sea he endured for a whole night a very serious storm and the following day was pushed back into the Dvina. Therefore he rested for several days, rejoicing between the outgoings of the morning and of the evening.[57] He was not burned by the sun of prosperity by day nor saddened by the moon of adversity by night,[58] and thus kept from the work of God on land and sea. Rather he gave thanks to God, committed himself again to the same perils which he had just escaped, and with God giving a calm sea, went to Germany to collect pilgrims to defend the church.

(12) After this, certain of the Livonians, persisting in their treachery, made their wounds and losses known to the king of Polozk through ambassadors. Since there were few left in Riga, the rest having departed with the bishop, they asked him to come to their aid against the Germans. He acquiesced in their pleas and summons and called together an army, not only from all parts of his kingdom, but also from those of other kings who were his neighbors and friends. He then descended the Dvina by ship in great strength. When he touched at Uexküll, certain of them were seriously wounded by the ballistarii of the knight Conrad. From this they knew that there were Germans in the fort, and they descended the river, therefore, and came suddenly to the fort of Holm, which they besieged on all sides. The Livonians, indeed, were totally ignorant of the approach of the army. Some escaped by fleeing to the woods; others gathered in a group with the Germans in the fort. When the fort was closed, ballistarii mounted the

57. Ps. 64:9.
58. Ps. 120:6.

ramparts and wounded many. The Russians, however, were ignorant of the art of the ballista, being familiar, rather, with the bow. Yet they wounded many on the fortifications during the many days they fought and, bringing up a huge pile of wood, they tried to burn down the fort. Their labor was in vain, however, for many of them fell wounded by the ballistarii as they gathered wood. The king, therefore, sent messengers to the people of Treiden, to the Letts, and to the pagans round about, urging them to join in an expedition against the people of Riga. Accordingly the people of Treiden at once came happily to the king and this one task was enjoined upon the newcomers, namely to bring up wood and set fire to the fort. As they brought up the wood, many of them, being without armor, were killed by flying arrows. The Letts, indeed, neither came nor sent messengers. The Russians also made a little machine like that of the Germans, but not knowing the art of throwing rocks, they hurled them backwards and wounded many of their own men. Indeed, since there were few Germans, scarcely even twenty, and since they feared betrayal by the Livonians, many of whom were in the fort with them, they sat armed night and day high on the ramparts, guarding the fort both from friends within and from enemies without. The Livonians, however, took careful counsel daily with the king as to how they might hold them by a trick and surrender them into the hands of the Russians; and unless the days of the war had been shortened, it is likely that neither the people of Holm nor those of Riga would have been able to defend themselves, because of their fewness. For in Riga they feared both for themselves, because the city had not yet been securely built, and for those of their people who were being besieged in Holm. Certain Livonian scouts, indeed, came back to the king saying that all the fields and roads around Riga were full of little three-pronged iron bolts.[59] They showed some of them to the king,

59. The chronicler uses here the expression *claviculis*. From his description it is clear that he refers to what is known as a caltrop.

and said that these hooks had everywhere gravely pierced both their horses' feet and their own sides and posteriors. Fearing this, the terrified king did not descend to Riga with his army. The Lord thus freed those who believed in Him. For the people of Treiden told the king that they had seen ships on the sea. And since he had gained nothing after besieging the fort for eleven days but rather had lost through the deaths of his men, and since he feared the arrival of the Germans, he rose up with his whole army and, taking the dead and wounded with him, sailed back to his own country. Geverhard, the bishop's steward, afterwards died from a small wound; the rest, however, safe and unharmed,[60] blessed God, Who again this time had defended His church in the hands of a few from the enemy.

(13) At that same time, the Danish king, with a great army that he had been collecting now for three years, came to Oesel. With him came Archbishop Andrew of Lund who, for the remission of sins, had bestowed the sign of the cross upon a great multitude who were to take vengeance on the pagans and subject the nations to the Christian faith. After the king had built a fort, he could find no one who, in the face of the attacks of the pagans, dared to remain there. Accordingly, the king burned the fort, and with the whole army returned to his own land. The archbishop of Lund and Bishop Nicholas, with two ships loaded with food and their whole retinue, turned aside to Riga. As they came into the Dvina, they were most devotedly received by Englebert, the provost of Blessed Mary, and all of the monastery. And after they had heard of such tribulation of the church and its liberation by God, they congratulated them and rejoiced and blessed God because, with so few men and in the midst of pagans, He always maintained His church. After this, the archbishop, calling together all the clergy, gave instruction in theology, and, reading in the psalter, they spent the whole winter in divine contempla-

60. See n.37, above.

tion. And quite properly theological doctrine followed the wars, since at that same time, after all the above-mentioned wars, the whole of Livonia was converted and baptized. For after the departure of the king of the Russians with his army, the fear of God took hold throughout the Livonian land. Both the people of Treiden and those of the Dvina, accordingly, sent messengers to Riga to ask for peace. The people of Treiden, however, were reminded of all the evils they had often committed, breaking the peace while there was peace. For they had killed many and inflicted many evils on Caupo who, after leaving his people, had always fought with the Christians. They had burned all his goods, taken over his fields, broken up his bee trees, and, moreover, instigated many wars against the people of Riga. Hence peace was denied them, and deservedly; for, not knowing how to be sons of peace, they disturbed the peace at all times. But they, insisting the more, begged to be baptized and promised to receive priests and to obey them in all things. The people of Lennewarden, indeed, in order to reconcile the lord Daniel, who had now for some time held the same fort as a benefice, promised a half talent [61] of rye from each "plow" each year, a tax which they still pay today.

(14) The provost of Riga, therefore, in the name of the archbishop, after accepting boys of the better people of all Livonia as hostages, sent out priests to preach. The first of these was Alabrand, who set out for Treiden, preaching the Word of God and administering the sacrament of baptism. After laying out parishes, he built a church in Cubbesele.[62] The priest Alexander was sent to Metsepole. After having baptized all the province, he began to live there, to sow the seed of the gospel, and to build a church. The priest Daniel, who had been, in a way, tested during the siege of the fort of Holm, was sent to the people of Lennewarden. They received

61. About twenty-five pounds.
62. The church of Kremon, not far from the Kipsal estate.

him kindly and were baptized by him. After he had gone on to the village called Sydegunde,[63] he at once called the people together to listen to the Word of God. A certain Livonian, coming at night from his hiding places in the forests and reporting a vision, said to him: "I saw the god of the Livonians, who foretold the future to us. He was, indeed, an image growing out of a tree from the breast upwards, and he told me that a Lithuanian army would come tomorrow; and for fear of that army, we dare not assemble." The priest, knowing this to be indeed an illusion of the devil, because at this time of autumn there was no road by which the Lithuanians could come, continuing in his prayers, commended himself to God. When, in the morning, they heard or saw nothing that the Livonian's phantom had foretold, they all came together. The priest then execrated their idolatry and affirmed that a phantom of this kind was an illusion of the demons. He preached that there was one God, creator of all, one faith, and one baptism, and in these and similar ways invited them to the worship of the one God. After hearing these things, they renounced the devil and his works, promised to believe in God, and those who were predestined by God were baptized.[64] After baptizing the people of Remi also, he went on to Ascheraden. After they had heard the Word of God with joy and the sacrament of baptism had there been celebrated, he went back to Treiden and came to the fort of Dobrel, where he was kindly received. Having sowed the seed of the Word of God there, he converted and baptized them, left that province, and went on to the Wends. The Wends, indeed, were humble and poor at that time, because they had been driven out from the Windau, a river of Kurland. They then lived on the Old Mountain, next to which the city of Riga is now built. They were again put to flight by the Kurs and many of them were killed. The rest fled to the Letts and, living there with them, rejoiced at the arrival of the priest.

63. Possibly the modern village, Siggund.
64. Cf. *Rituale Romanum, Ordo Baptismi Adultorum.*

After converting and baptizing them, Daniel the priest went back to Riga, committing to the Lord the now planted vineyard and sown field. (15) Later, indeed, he was sent to the Idumeans where he baptized a great many, both Letts and Idumeans. Here he built a church above Brasle and, by staying with them, showed them how to acquire eternal life. The people of Treiden, indeed, after they had accepted the mysteries of holy baptism and, with it, the whole spiritual law, asked their priest, Alabrand, just as he administered spiritual law for them, likewise to administer civil cases according to the law of the Christians, which by us is called secular law. The people of Livonia were formerly most perfidious and everyone stole what his neighbor had, but now theft, violence, rapine, and similar things were forbidden as a result of their baptism. Those who had been despoiled before their baptism grieved over the loss of their goods. For, after baptism, they did not dare to take them back by violence and accordingly asked for a secular judge to settle cases of this kind. Hence the priest Alabrand was the first to receive the authority to hear both spiritual and civil cases. He, administering quite faithfully the office enjoined on him, both for the sake of God and because of his sins, exercised his authority in cases of rapine and theft, restored things unjustly seized, and so showed the Livonians the right way of living. This Christian law pleased the Livonians the first year because the office of magistrate [65] was administered by faithful men of this kind. Afterwards, however, this office was very much degraded throughout all Livonia, Lettgallia, and Esthonia at the hands of divers lay, secular judges, who used the office of magistrate more to fill their own purses than to defend the justice of God.

(16) That same winter [1207] there was an eclipse of the

---

65. *Advocatus* has been translated here and elsewhere as "magistrate"; the term is used in an extended sense to designate an officer who is the equivalent of the German *Vogt*.

sun through a great part of the day [Feb. 28]. (17) Bishop
Albert made the rounds through Germany, through the villages, streets, and churches, seeking pilgrims. Having completely traversed Saxony and Westphalia, he came at length
to the court of King Philip and, since he could expect aid
from no king, he turned to the Empire and received Livonia
from the Empire.[66] Therefore King Philip of pious memory
promised to aid him with a hundred marks each year. If only
one could be rich through promises! [67]

[XI]

 (1) In the ninth year [1207] after all Livonia had been
baptized, the church rested, rejoiced in the quiet of peace,
and awaited the arrival of its bishop. The archbishop of Lund
and his chancellor with all their men, preparing to return
home, landed in Gothland on Palm Sunday [Apr. 15] and
celebrated the holy feast of Easter [Apr. 22] in their own
land. When the bishop of Riga came to Riga at Pentecost
[June 10], he was received with joy by all. With him came
Gottschalk, count of Pyrmont, a second count, and a great
many other pilgrims, noble and respectable men who, rejoicing in the peace of the church, so built up the wall of the
city that henceforth the attack of the pagans was not feared.

(2) King Vetseke of Kokenhusen heard of the arrival of
the bishop and the pilgrims, rose up with his men, and went
to meet them. When he came to Riga, he was honorably received by all. After having spent several days in the bishop's
house, with great show of charity, he at length asked the aid
of the bishop against Lithuanian attacks and offered him a
half of his land and his fort. The bishop accepted this offer

---

66. This happened during the first three months of 1207, possibly at
Gelnhausen on February 2. See Holtzmann, in *Neues Archiv*, XLIII, 205–12.
67. Cf. Ovid, *Ars Amatoria*, I, 444.

and, honoring the king with many gifts and promising help
both in men and in arms, with joy sent him back to his own
land. After this, the bishop, rejoicing over the conversion and
baptism of all the Livonians, sent priests everywhere, that is,
to Treiden, to Metsepole, to Idumea, and the area next to the
Dvina. Churches were built and priests were placed in their
parishes.

(3) It happened also at the same time that the Lord increased from day to day the number and retinue of the
Brothers of the Militia. It seemed to them, however, that just
as their numbers and labors increased, so ought their possessions and goods to increase, in order that those who bore the
burden of the day, and the heats, in wars and other continual
labors, should likewise receive the reward of their labors: the
penny a day.[68] Daily, therefore, they vehemently begged the
bishop for a third part of all Livonia and also of the other
lands or tribes roundabout, not yet converted, tribes whom
the Lord, through them and others from Riga, might subject to Christianity in the future. Thus as they would be called
upon for greater expenditures, so would they have greater
revenues. The bishop, indeed, like a father, desired to favor
these men who day and night set themselves up as a wall for
the house of the Lord and to multiply their number. He
wished likewise to repay their labors and expenses and, accordingly, conceded to them a third part of Livonia. Since he
had received Livonia from the emperor with every right of
lordship and law, he relinquished his third part to them with
every right of lordship and law. Since he could not give what
he did not have, he quite reasonably denied them the lands not
yet acquired or converted. When they continued to press him
with their entreaties in and out of season, the matter finally
reached the ears of the supreme pontiff.[69] He committed the
lands not yet acquired to God and assigned them a third part

68. Cf. Matt. 20:2, 12.
69. Cf. the bulls on this matter in Innocent II, *Opera Omnia*, Migne, *P.L.*,
CXVI, 326–27. The documents are dated October 20, 1210.

of what had been already acquired, leaving the bishop a quarter of the tithes in their areas, in recognition of their obedience to him. The Brothers of the Militia, therefore, at the request of the bishop, divided Livonia into three parts and conceded to him, as to a father, the first choice. The bishop took first the region consisting of Caupo's lands, namely Treiden. The Brothers then chose for themselves as the second third, the region on the other side of the Aa and left Metsepole to the bishop as the third part. The Brothers subsequently received compensation in other regions of Livonia for all those provinces or other estates that had already for some time been given out as benefices.

(4) After Livonia had thus been divided, the bishop sent priests into his parts and left the Brothers to administer their own part. That year a certain pilgrim knight, Gottfried, was also sent to Treiden to administer the office of magistrate in secular law. He went through the parishes, settling the disputes and quarrels of men, collected money and a great many gifts, and, sending a little bit to the bishop, kept most of it for himself. Accordingly, certain other pilgrims who resented this broke open his chest and found nineteen silver marks which Gottfried had realized from property that he had stealthily collected, not counting much more which he had already dissipated. Because he had acted unjustly in perverting judgment and oppressing the poor, in justifying the iniquitous and levying toll on the converts, by the just judgment of God it so happened that, to the terror of other such men, he should incur such a humiliation, and he afterwards died a shameful death, as some report.

(5) After this the Lithuanians remembered all of their people who had been killed by the people of Riga and the Semgalls two years before. They sent, accordingly, through all Lithuania, collected a huge army, and, after crossing the Dvina all through the night on Christmas Eve [Dec. 24], came to Treiden, crossed the Aa at dawn [Dec. 25], dispersed through all the villages, and, finding the land forewarned by

no rumors, killed many and took many more into captivity. On this very Christmas Day there were two priests celebrating divine services for the Livonians in the church of Cubbesele, namely, the one John Stric and the other Theodoric, with his servant. When John had finished the first Mass and was celebrating another, the parishioners, hearing the army coming, fled from the church. Some committed themselves to the hiding places of the forests and escaped; some, as they were hurrying home, were captured on the road, and a great many were killed. When he had finished the sequence and was reading the gospel, the Lithuanians rode here and there around the church on their swift horses. God, however, looked out for His own and kept them from entering the church. They, however, hastened to the priest's house, seized horses and flocks, and put the clothes and food and everything else they found in their carts. Since they were greatly delayed in plundering the courtyard, the priest finished, in the meantime, the most holy mysteries of the body and blood of the Lord, and, not hesitating to offer himself as a sacrifice to God, commended himself to the Lord. Theodoric the priest, as a minister, and his servant, by watching the door, faithfully stood by him, encouraging him not to neglect the divine service for fear of the pagans. When, by the grace of God, the Mass had been finished, they took the coverings of the altar, put together with them all the furnishings, and placed them in a corner of the sanctuary. They then sat down together in the same corner and hid themselves. This had scarcely been done when, behold, one of the enemy came into the church, ran all around and almost into the sanctuary. When he saw that the altar was bare and that there was nothing that he could take away, he exclaimed "Bah!" and went back to his men. After plundering everything they found, the Lithuanians went back on their way. Scarcely had they left the courtyard, however, when, lo, another crowd of them, greater than the first, came and, finding the house plundered, hurried after the others. One of them entered the church without dismounting

from his horse and, finding nothing to plunder and not knowing about those lurking in the corner, likewise hastily withdrew. A third band of Lithuanians now came. One of them
passed through the church, seated in his cart, but did not see
the priests. They therefore gave thanks to God for keeping
them safe and unharmed [70] in the face of the enemy. After the
Lithuanians had departed, they left the church, about evening,
and fled to the woods. For three days they ate no bread and
on the fourth they came to Riga. The Lithuanians, indeed,
having laid waste the whole province, banded together at
night in a group in the village of Anno. At dawn they left the
land, taking with them women and children and great spoils.
On that very Christmas night the Livonians sent messengers
to inform the bishop that a Lithuanian army had entered
Livonia. Other messengers subsequently followed the first to
report on the men killed and captured, on the churches laid
waste, and on all the evils which the pagans had brought upon
the new church. When the bishop heard these things, he called
together the pilgrims, the Brothers of the Militia, the merchants, and all his own men, and told them all, for the remission of their sins, to make of themselves a wall for the house
of the Lord and to liberate the church from its enemies. They
all obeyed, prepared themselves to fight, and sent to all the
Livonians and Letts the following threat: "Whosoever does
not come out to follow the Christian army shall be punished
by a fine of three marks." Fear filled all and, hearkening to
this threat, they met the people of Riga on the banks of the
Dvina. They then went together up to Lennewarden, assembled within the town, and awaited in silence the return
of the Lithuanians. They then sent scouts to investigate their
route. The Lithuanians, with all their captives and loot, met
these scouts near Lennewarden and crossed the Dvina over the
ice at night. The leader of their army climbed the banks, and
approached the fort with his companions. He then called the
leader of the fort, demanded the whereabouts of the Christian

70. See n.37, above.

army, and said: "Go, tell the Christians who, two years ago, killed my army as if it were asleep, as it returned from Esthonia, that now they will find me and all my men awake." After they had heard this speech, the Christians hastened to the battle of the Lord and followed the enemy at dawn. They crossed the Dvina near Ascheraden about the third hour and found the enemy there. When the pagans saw that they were following them, they were terrified by the definite turn of events. They cried out at once with a great yell, called together their men, and turned to meet the Christians. The Christians, not fearing their yell and their numbers, and confiding in God, raised their banners and suddenly rushed upon them. Killing here and there, they made the war grow warm on both sides. The Lithuanians, who had just said that they were wide awake for the fight, as a people who were swifter and crueler than the other pagans, fought back long and bravely. They finally retreated, however, and showed themselves as swift in flight as they were agile in war. Leaving captives and spoils behind, accordingly, some fled to the forests and others over the road. The Christians pursued them for a whole day and killed many of them; the rest escaped through flight. After this, the Christians came back to the spoils and freed from their chains the women and children of the converts and all the captives. After the converts, both Letts and Livonians, had come together with the Germans, and after they had given thanks to God, as sheep lost and found again, or rather, as sheep snatched from the jaws of wolves, they divided the spoils and sent back all the liberated captives to their friends.

(6) After the Lord had freed His church from this attack of the pagans, the bishop feared lest, after his departure, they would do likewise and devastate all Livonia. He therefore considered destroying the fort of the Selones,[71] which was their refuge at all times when they entered or left Livonia. Accordingly he sent messengers throughout all Livonia and Let-

71. Selburg, east of Kokenhusen on the Dvina River.

tigallia to call to an expedition all those who were now Christians. When he had collected a great army, the bishop sent Abbot Theodoric and Engelbert, the provost, with his own men and the pilgrims, who had likewise been joined by the Brothers of the Militia of Christ, to attack the Selones. They marched toward Ascheraden, crossed the Dvina, and found the unburied bodies of the Lithuanians killed in the previous campaign. They trod over them on the road and, marching in ordered ranks, came to Selburg. From all sides they laid siege to the fort, wounded many on the ramparts with arrows, captured many in the villages, killed many, brought together logs, and made a great fire. They gave the Selones no rest day or night, and struck fear into their people. Hence the latter secretly called together the leaders of their army and begged for peace. The Christians then said: "If you wish true peace, renounce idolatry and receive the true Peacemaker, Who is Christ, into your camp; be baptized and, moreover, remove the enemies of Christ's name, the Lithuanians, from your fort." These terms of peace pleased the Selones and, after giving hostages, they promised to receive the sacrament of baptism. Moreover, after they had removed the Lithuanians, they vowed to obey the Christians in all things. After receiving their boys, therefore, the army was pacified. Accordingly the abbot and the provost, with the other priests, went up to them in the fort, instructed them in the beginnings of the faith, sprinkled the fort with holy water, and raised the banner of Blessed Mary over it. They then rejoiced over the conversion of the pagans, praised God for the advancement of the church, and, together with the Livonians and Letts, returned joyfully to their country.

(7) At the same time Alabrand the priest, with certain others, was sent to Ungannia to demand the goods that had been taken away from merchants before the construction of Riga. As the merchants were journeying from the Dvina toward Pskov in their carts, the Ungannians, upon the advice of the Livonians, had despoiled them on the road of many

goods, to the value of nine hundred marks and more. The Ungannians, indeed, neither gave back their goods nor gave any definite answer about returning them in the future. Thence Alabrand, concerning himself little in a matter of this kind, went back. Since all Livonia and a great many Letts had received now the Word of God, on the way back he preached the Word of God to the Letts living next to the Sedde, about their reception of baptism. They rejoiced over the coming of the priest, inasmuch as they had often been devastated by the Lithuanians and always oppressed by the Livonians and now hoped to be relieved and defended by the Germans. They thus received the Word of God with joy. First, however, they cast lots and asked the opinion of their gods as to whether, as the Letts of Tholowa had done, they should submit to the baptism of the Russians of Pskov or, on the other hand, to that of the Latins. For the Russians had come to baptize the Letts of Tholowa, who had always been their tributaries.[72] The lot fell to the Latins, however, and they were counted with the Rigans as members of the Livonian church. When Alabrand had baptized some villages, he returned to Riga and announced this to the bishop. The bishop, too, rejoiced and, since he desired always to provide for the church, sent back to that place with Alabrand his scholar, Henry,[73] now promoted to holy orders. When they had finished baptizing in those regions, Alabrand returned. Henry, however, when he had constructed a church and received it as a benefice, lived there with them and, although exposed to many dangers, did not cease to point out to them the blessed future life.

himself?

72. *Nam Rutheni eorum tempore venerant baptizantes Lethigallos suos de Tholowa sibi semper tributarios.*—*MGH, SS,* XXIII, 261. The use of *eorum* here is strange. Possibly *eodem* is meant. The chronicle as printed in the series *Scriptores Rerum Germanicarum in Usum Scholarum,* reprinted from *MGH, SS,* also uses *eorum* in this spot.—Vol. 7, *Heinrici Chronicon Lyvoniae,* p. 49.

73. This Henry, the bishop's scholar, is thought to be the "Henry of Livonia" who wrote this chronicle.

(8) At this time there arose a quarrel between the king of Kokenhusen and Daniel, the knight of Lennewarden. For the king had caused Daniel's men many inconveniences and, although warned, had not ceased his molestation. The armed men of this Daniel, therefore, rising up at night, went hastily with him to the fort of the king. They arrived at dawn and, finding those within the fort sleeping and the watch itself, moreover, less than properly watchful, they mounted the walls suddenly and reached the very center of the fort. After they had entered, however, they did not dare to kill the Russians because they, too, were Christians. Threatening them with swords, however, they put some to flight, captured others, and put them in chains. They seized the king, among others, cast him in chains, and, bringing all the wealth that was in the fort together in one place, they carefully watched it while they summoned their lord, Daniel, who was nearby. He, however, wishing to hear the counsel of the bishop on this matter, made everything known to the people of Riga. The bishop and all his men regretted this very much, for they did not approve what had been done. The bishop then ordered the fort to be restored to the king and all his wealth to be given back and, summoning the king, honored him with gifts of many horses and many suits of precious garments. Moreover, on the solemnity of Easter [Apr. 6, 1208], he treated him and all his men with most kindly affection, settled all the difficulties between him and Daniel, and joyfully sent him back to his fort. The bishop, moreover, mindful of the promise which he had given the king when he accepted half of his fort, sent back with him twenty strong men with arms, knights with their mounts, ballistarii, and masons to strengthen the fort and hold it against the Lithuanians. He likewise took care of all their expenses and all their needs. With these men, the king, to be sure, returned to Kokenhusen with a happy face, although he was meditating trickery in his heart. He left the bishop, who, as usual, was about to go to Germany to collect pilgrims for the following year, in Dünamünde. Those

who had completed their year of pilgrimage and were now preparing to return to Germany had been staying in Dünamünde for some time, inasmuch as God, repelling them by a contrary wind, did not permit them to leave. (9) This little king returned to Kokenhusen and, not doubting that the pilgrims had now left with the bishop and knowing very well that only a very few remained in Riga, he could no longer conceal in his heart his perfidious schemes. He took counsel with all his men and, at the awaited time and upon the opportune day, he set his schemes in motion. Almost all the Germans had gone out to their work and were quarrying rocks in the moat for the building of the fort. They had, in the meantime, laid their swords and arms outside the moat, for, looking upon the king as their lord or father, they did not fear him. Suddenly all the men and servants of the king ran up, picked up the swords and arms of the Germans, and killed many of them as they stood unarmed and naked at their work. Certain of them, by fleeing night and day, came to Riga to report there what had happened. The bodies of the seventeen men who were killed were thrown into the Dvina and sent back to the people of Riga; three escaped by flight. The people of Riga collected the bodies of those killed in the service of God from the water and, devotedly and with tears, buried them. After this the king sent the best German horses, ballistas, coats of mail, and similar things to the great King Vladimir,[74] with an urgent request that he call together an army and come as quickly as possible to take Riga, in which he said few men remained, the best having been killed by him and the others having gone away with the bishop. The excessively credulous king, after hearing these things, called together all his friends and the men of his kingdom to the expedition. The bishop, who was detained meanwhile in Dünamünde by a contrary wind, called all the pilgrims together when he learned of the killing of his men and of the betrayal of his church. Weeping, he made known to them

74. Vladimir was king, or more properly grand prince, of Pskov.

the damages to the church and invited them to become its
defenders and strong auxiliaries by resuming the sign of the
cross. He comforted them by reminding them of the previous
plenary remission of their neglected sins, and, because of the
greater labors they would now be undertaking on their long
pilgrimage, he promised a greater indulgence and eternal life.
After hearing these things, about three hundred of the better
ones did not fear, by again taking up the cross, to serve as a
wall for the house of the Lord and to go back to Riga. The
bishop, moreover, hired many more and sent them to Riga.
In addition all the Germans who were dispersed throughout
Livonia, together with the other Livonian leaders, assembled
for the defense of the Rigan church. The Russians, therefore,
hearing of the gathering of Germans and Livonians in Riga,
feared for themselves and their fort, because they had acted
amiss. They did not dare, accordingly, to await in their fort
the arrival of the Rigans. They thus collected their belongings,
divided the arms and horses of the Germans among themselves, set fire to the fort of Kokenhusen and fled, each one on
his own way. The Letts and Selones who were living there
sought the dark hiding places of the woods. The king, however, since he had acted evilly, departed for Russia, never to
return thenceforth to his kingdom.

[XII]

⟨⟨ (1) These things having been accomplished, therefore, the bishop, now in the tenth year of his consecration
[1208], committed his church in Livonia to the Lord and to
the pilgrims and all those living in Livonia who bore the
Christian name. He then went to Germany to arrange for
various matters of the church, that is, to collect both pilgrims
and goods to help the still-new and very indigent church. In
going about and preaching in many places he endured many

hardships. But those who remained in Riga gave each other mutual comfort and worked manfully at fortifying the city on all sides. Hearing of the burning of the fort of Kokenhusen and of the flight of the Russians, they sent some men to follow them. Among them were Meinhard and certain other men of the bishop, who followed the fugitives and found a great many of them, namely Letts and Selones, in the forests and swamps. These latter were tributaries of the king, were privy to his plans, and helpers in the betrayal and death of the Germans. They seized these and also some of the Russians, took away their loot and their goods, and recaptured from them certain German arms. All of those whom they found guilty of being partners in the treachery, they killed with a cruel death, as they deserved, and thus rooted out traitors from those regions.

(2) At this time the Rigans and the Christians who were in Livonia, desired peace, but it did not come; they were seeking good things, and behold, trouble! [75] For they hoped, after the flight of the Russians, that they had escaped Charybdis; yet the danger of Scylla was still imminent. For Viesthard, the leader of the Semgalls, was still mindful of the wars and hardships which the Lithuanians had inflicted upon the whole territory of Semgallia and in which they had often vanquished and despoiled him. He was, therefore, preparing an expedition against them and begged humbly for the aid of the Christians in Riga. This he claimed in return for the aid which, at another time, he had given the Rigans in overcoming other pagans. He declared, moreover, that the lots of his gods had fallen in a manner favorable to this war. In reply, the Rigan elders, not caring for the lots of his gods, rather denied him aid because of their own fewness and altogether forbade war at this time against the Lithuanians. But at length, overcome by his insistent requests and by the stubborn boldness of the foolish men who were about to go with him, they decided not to forbid them to go to war, but rather

75. Jer. 14:19.

to send them on obediently, lest they endanger soul as well as body. There were sent with Viesthard, therefore, fifty or a few more men, knights and ballistarii, and also several of the Brothers of the Militia of Christ. Taking with them Daniel, the priest of the Idumeans, they set out for the land of the Semgalls. As they came up on their horses, resplendent in their armor, they were most kindly received by the Semgalls. The Semgalls gathered together from all their land a great army and, advancing toward Lithuania, rested for the night. While resting, they sought the future from their gods. They cast lots, demanded their favor, and inquired especially if the news of their coming had flown ahead [76] and if the Lithuanians were about to come to fight against them. The lots told them both that the news had spread and that the Lithuanians were prepared for war. Thereupon the Semgalls, greatly astounded, invited the Germans to return, because they feared exceedingly the attack of the Lithuanians. The Germans replied: "Let us shun to do this thing, for to flee from them would be to bring reproach upon our people. Let us rather go to meet our adversaries and see if we may fight them." And the Semgalls could not dissuade them. There was a great multitude of Semgalls in whom the Germans still had faith, even though the region was flooded from heavy rains. Yet they proceeded boldly into Lithuania. After dividing their forces among the villages, they found them empty. All the men with their wives and children had escaped by flight. Therefore, fearing that an attack was threatening them, they gathered together as soon as possible and without delay prepared to return on the same day. When the Lithuanians learned of this, they flew around them on their speedy horses. As was their custom, they rode about here and there, sometimes fleeing, sometimes pursuing, threw their lances and staves, and wounded many. The Germans, however, grouping themselves together in a single wedge and protecting the army from

76. . . . . si videlicet fama adventus ipsorum pervolaverit. Cf. Vergil, Aeneid, III, 121.

the rear, permitted the Semgalls to go ahead. The Semgalls, however, suddenly fled, one after the other; some of them trampled each other in their flight, others sought the woods and swamps. Thus the whole weight of the battle was turned against the Germans. Some of the Germans defended themselves most bravely in a long battle, but since they were few, they were not able to resist such a multitude. Those very vigorous men, Gerwin and Rabodo, fought with many others in this prolonged battle. Some fell wounded and others were taken as captives by the enemy to Lithuania. Those who escaped by fleeing returned to Riga to report what had happened.

(3) When the city heard, therefore, of the flight of their men and of the daring of the Lithuanians, it was greatly pained, and suddenly the harp of the Rigans was turned to mourning and their song into the voice of those that weep.[77] Praying to heaven, all the elders and discreet men decided that thenceforth they ought not to confide in the multitude of the pagans nor ought they to fight with pagans against other pagans, but that they ought, hoping in the Lord, to proceed boldly against all the tribes with the now baptized Livonians and Letts. This they did. For in the same years the banner of the Blessed Virgin was carried by the Livonians, the Letts, and the Germans into Ungannia, and thereafter, with the help of God, Who alone is supreme over all kingdoms,[78] to all the Esths and the tribes round about.

(4) After this, however, the Lithuanians entered Semgallia with a great army and began to kill and lay waste all they found. The Semgalls, indeed, ambushing them on the road and felling trees, killed almost all of them on their way back. And the Semgalls honorably sent gifts to the Rigans from their spoils.

(5) At the same time God sent a great many religious men to the Dvina to console His church: Florence, an abbot of the

77. Cf. Job 30:31.
78. Cf. Isa. 37:16.

Cistercian order; Robert, a canon of the church of Cologne; Conrad of Bremen, together with some others. Some of these chose the life of a monk in Dünamünde, some joined the Brothers of the Militia, and others went over to the work of preaching. The still-small church rejoiced greatly over their coming and was thus much comforted after the sad wars. They gave thanks to God, Who never lets His people lack consolation in every tribulation, and to Whom be honor and glory forever. Amen.

Book Three, Concerning Livonia, Ends

Book Four, Concerning
Esthonia, Begins

(6) It came to pass,[79] now, after all Livonia and Letti-gallia had been baptized, that the elders of the Letts, Russin of Fort Sotekle, Waridote of Autine, Talibald of Beverin, and also Berthold, a Brother of the Militia from Wenden, sent messengers to the Esthonians in Ungannia to demand satisfaction for all the injuries which they had suffered from them. The Letts, indeed, were humble and despised before receiving the faith and had borne many injuries from the Livonians and Esthonians. Hence it was that they rejoiced greatly at the coming of the priests, because, after baptism, they would all enjoy together the same law and the same peace. The Esthonians, however, paid little attention to the words of the messengers and rendered no justice, but, on the contrary, sent their own messengers back with them to Lettigallia. Since the Brothers of the Militia were now living in Wenden, they sent their leader, Berthold, to the meeting of the Letts with the Esthonians. Henry [80] the priest came on behalf of the

79. *Et factum est.* . . . Cf. I Macc. 1:1; Luke 24:15.
80. This is, again, the author of this chronicle.

83

bishop, and there were also many Letts present. They began, accordingly, to consider again matters of peace and justice. The Esthonian ambassadors, however, both scornfully rejected the peace of the Letts and disdained to restore what they had unjustly taken. Moreover, they contradicted the Letts in everything, and, threatening each other with very sharp lances, they withdrew without any arrangement for peace. After merchants and some other Germans had meanwhile arrived from Gothland, Waridote rose up with the other Lettish elders and, coming to Riga, humbly asked for aid against the injuries which the Esthonians were inflicting upon them. The Rigans, recalling to mind their own injuries and the innumerable goods which the Ungannians had earlier taken from their merchants, acceeded to this request and promised an army. They did this especially since the Ungannians had often contemptuously and scornfully sent back the messengers whom they had sent for these same goods of their merchants, being unwilling to return the things they had unjustly taken. Having called upon the aid of Almighty God and of Mary, the Blessed Mother of God, the Rigans, together with the Brothers of the Militia, Theodoric, brother of the bishop, the merchants, and some other Germans arrived in Treiden. They called together a great and strong army from all Livonia and Lettigallia and, marching night and day, came to Ungannia. There they laid waste the villages, killed the pagan men, and thus avenged their injuries with fire and sword. At length they came together before Fort Odenpäh, that is to say, Fort Bear's Head, and burned the fort. After resting for three days, they returned on the fourth to their own country with the flocks, captives, and all the loot. The Letts also went back to their own country, reinforced their forts, and prepared most bravely for a fight. After they had gathered all their things in the forts, being ready for its coming, they awaited the Esthonian army. The Ungannians, therefore, called upon the Saccalians for aid and suddenly entered Lettish territory at the boundary of Tricatia. They burned alive a certain Lett named Wardeke, captured others, and brought many evils upon the Letts. They besieged Fort Beverin and attacked the Letts living in the fort for a whole day. The Letts leaving the fort and bravely meeting them in battle, killed five of them and, taking their horses, ran back into the fort to their priest.[81] Together with him, they all blessed the Lord, Who, they felt, was fighting for them. One of the braver men was Roboam, who had come down from the fort into the midst of the enemy, killed two of them, and returned to his people safe and unharmed through an adjoining part of the fort, praising God for the special honor which He had conferred on him at the cost of the pagans. The priest, indeed, paying little attention to the attack of the Esthonians, mounted the ramparts and, while the others fought, sang prayers to God on a musical instrument. When the barbarians heard the song and the sharp sound of the instrument, they stood still, for in their country they had nothing similar to it. They stopped fighting and inquired about the cause of such rejoicing. The Letts replied that they were rejoicing and praising the Lord because they saw that God was defending them for their recent acceptance of baptism. Then the Esthonians made a proposal concerning a renewal of the peace. But the Letts said: "You have not yet restored the goods stolen from the Germans and also the things often stolen from us. Neither can there be one heart and soul nor a firm treaty of peace between Christians and pagans unless you accept with us the same yoke of Christianity and of perpetual peace and serve the one God." The Esthonians were exceedingly angry and turned away from the fort. The Letts followed them from behind and wounded many of them. They sent messengers to Wenno, the master of the Militia of Christ, who was then present in Wenden, to request him to come with his men to follow the Esthonians. He called together all the Letts in the neighborhood and in the morning came to Beverin. Here he found that the pagan army had already long

81. This priest is thought to be Henry, the author of this chronicle.

scattered and he followed them for all that day. On the following night there was a great frost. Since almost all their horses were limping, the Christians could not make contact with the enemy, for the latter, after having killed the flocks and let go the captives, did not wait for battle and fled down the road, each returning to his own country. Then the Letts of Beverin, sad because of the deaths of their men, whom the Esthonians had slaughtered and cremated, sent word to all the Letts round about to be ready to march, in order that, when God gave the opportunity, they might take vengeance on their enemies. Thereupon Russin, who was the bravest of the Letts, and Waridote, with all the Letts who were within his territory, came together in a great multitude before the aforesaid fort of Beverin. They made plans against the Esthonians and, preparing to despoil their land, they put on such arms as they had and marched for one day. They then stopped, arranged their army, and marched on night and day, until they entered the province of Saccalia. Here they found in all the villages and places men, women, and children in their houses, and from morning to evening they killed those whom they found, both women and children, together with three hundred of the better men and leaders of that province, not counting innumerable others. Finally, on account of the exceedingly great slaughter of the people, the tired hands and arms of the killers failed them. On the following day, after all the villages had been colored with much pagan blood, they returned. Collecting many spoils from all the villages, they took back with them beasts of burden, many flocks, and a great many girls, whom alone the army was accustomed to spare in these lands. Returning slowly, they delayed many days on the way, being prepared for the eventuality that the remaining Esthonians, again taking up the war, might fall upon them from the rear. But the Esthonians, because of the great slaughter of their men, did not presume to follow the Letts; but for many days they collected and cremated the pitiful bodies, a task inflicted on them by the Letts, and held funerals, according to their custom, with much wailing and much drinking. The Letts, however, stopped by Lake Astigerwe [82] to divide all the spoils among themselves, and returned to Beverin rejoicing. There they found Berthold, a Brother of the Militia and also their own priest, together with soldiers and certain ballistarii of the bishop, upon whom they conferred gifts from all their booty. Since it was Gaudete Sunday [Dec. 18], all, without exception, joyfully blessed God, because, through new converts, the Lord had taken such vengeance, even on other nations. When Russin returned to Fort Beverin, he opened his mouth, saying: "The sons of my sons will tell their sons to the third and fourth generations how Russin wrought slaughter on the Saccalians." When he heard this, Hermann, the magistrate of the Livonians, was exceedingly indignant toward the Letts because they were constantly renewing the war against the Esthonians. He, therefore, called together all the elders of the Livonians and Letts and took counsel with them and also with the German residents, who were still scattered and few in the land. They all agreed that peace should be negotiated with the Esthonians, at least until the return of the lord bishop, who was in Germany, collecting pilgrims for the following year. This decision pleased the Esthonians, also, and they accepted the terms of peace. After the killing of their leaders, they had begun to have great fear of the Letts, and, since the dispute was not yet settled, they arranged terms of truce for a year.

[XIII]

(1) In the eleventh year of his consecration [1209], Albert returned from Germany, having in his company a copious multitude of pilgrims. Among them were Rudolph of Jerichow and Walter of Hammersleben and many other

82. The Burtneek'sche See. In Esthonian *jerw* (-gerwe) means a lake.

nobles, knights, and clerics, together with all their people, who committing themselves to the dangers of the sea, arrived in Livonia. After taking counsel with them, he called together all the Livonians and Letts, who had long been converted. He reminded them of the fearful loss which had been brought upon himself and his men during the past year by King Vetseke when he killed through trickery and great fraud the soldiers and members of his household whom, at the king's request, he had sent at great expense to help against the Lithuanians. Thereupon, with all the pilgrims and his army, he went off to Kokenhusen. Finding the mountain deserted and, because of the filthiness of the former inhabitants, full of snakes and worms, he ordered and asked that it be cleansed and renovated, and had it strongly fortified.[83] He built a very strong fort there and left knights, ballistarii, and his household to take care of it. At great expense to himself, he had it most diligently guarded, so that no subtlety of the Lithuanians or false trickery of the Russians could deceive them as before. He granted the aforesaid Rudolph of Jerichow one-half of the fort and the Brothers of the Militia a third. After everything had been well arranged, he left them there and returned to Riga. The Letts, meanwhile, had entered Lithuania with two armies and, after killing some and capturing others, returned to our men in Kokenhusen and, with the bishop and all his men, returned home.[84]

(2) There was at that time a certain Wickbert among the Brothers of the Militia, whose heart was rather more inclined to love of the world than to religious discipline, and he sowed many discords among the Brothers. He, abhorring the fellowship of holy living and disdaining the Militia of Christ, came to the priest of Idumea, said he wished to await there the arrival of the bishop, and wished to obey the bishop in all things. The Brothers of the Militia, Berthold of Wenden and

83. The fort of Kokenhusen had been burned by King Vetseke and his army when they withdrew to Russia. See p. 78 (XI, 9), above.
84. See n.48, above.

certain other Brothers and servants, followed this Brother as
if he were a fugitive, seized him in Idumea, led him back to
Wenden, and threw him in chains. When he heard of the
coming of the bishop, he asked that he might be released and
permitted to return to Riga, promising that he would obey
the bishop and the Brothers. The Brothers rejoiced and, hoping that after his trials and tribulations he, like the prodigal
son,[85] would repent, sent him back honorably to Riga and
restored him to the society. He, indeed, like a Judas among
the Brothers, or rather, like a wolf among the sheep, behaved
for a little while, but not knowing how to disguise the deceits
of his false conscience, awaited the opportune day when he
might carry out the evil in his heart. And it happened on a
solemn feast day, as the rest of the Brothers were going, with
the other men, to the monastery, that he, meanwhile, called
to him the master of the Brothers and their priest, John. In
the upper story of his house, while proposing to reveal to
them his secrets, he struck the head of the master a sudden
blow with the double-edged axe which he was accustomed to
carry with him, and, together with the master, slaughtered
and killed the priest. This was discovered by the other
Brothers, who pursued him as he fled from the house to the
chapel. He was taken and, in accordance with civil judgment,
killed with the cruel death that he deserved. After they had
buried with great lamentation their faithful and pious master,
Wenno, together with the priest, they then put Volquin in his
place, a man no less pious, kind, and full of all virtues. He
afterwards, whether the bishop were present or absent, was
leader and commander of the army of the Lord on all expeditions; he fought with joy the battles of the Lord, and set
out again and again against the heathen tribes in the neighborhood. All his Brothers helped him and the aid and victory of
the Lord was always with them.

(3) Englebert, the provost of the church of Blessed Mary,
died that same year. The bishop brought up from the mon-

85. Cf. Luke 15:11-32.

astery of Scheida a quiet, discreet, and altogether prudent man, named John, and substituted him for his brother, that same venerable provost, and set him to rule over the church of Blessed Mary. Since this John was of the rule and order of Saint Augustine and accordingly wore white, signifying purity, the bishop, to confirm this habit, changed the cassocks and black cowls of the canons of the same church to white. And since they were still afraid of pagans within and without the city, the canons lived in the first-built church, within the bounds of the first city. After the burning of this church and the city,[86] however, they began to build the church of Blessed Mary outside the walls next to the Dvina and to live there. The pilgrims of this same year were always ready to obey in the matter of heightening the walls and in other things of service to God. (4) Since autumn was now approaching, the bishop, always solicitous to promote and defend the Livonian church, took counsel with his more discreet men in order to consider how the new church could be freed from the plots of the Russians and Lithuanians. Mindful of all the evils which the king of Gerzika, together with the Lithuanians, had brought upon the city of Riga, the Livonians, and the Letts, they decided to go to war against the enemies of the Christian name. For King Vsevolod of Gerzika had always been an enemy of the Christian name and especially of the Latins. He had taken the daughter of one of the more powerful Lithuanians as his wife and was, accordingly, almost one of them, since he was their son-in-law. Joined thus to them in all the bonds of friendship and family ties, he often acted as the leader of their army and helped them cross the Dvina and supplied food whether they went to Russia, Livonia, or Esthonia. The Lithuanians were then such lords over all the peoples, both Christian and pagan, dwelling in those lands that scarcely anyone, and the Letts especially, dared live in the small villages. Not even by leaving their houses deserted

86. The burning took place in 1215, about March. See below, p. 139 (XVIII, 6).

to seek the dark hiding places of the forests could they escape them. For the Lithuanians, laying ambushes for them at all times in the forests, seized them, killing some and capturing others, and took the latter back to their own country, seizing all their possessions. The Russians also fled through the forests and villages from the face of the Lithuanians, however few, as rabbits flee before hunters, and the Livonians and Letts were food and provender for the Lithuanians and like sheep in the jaws of wolves, since they were without a shepherd. Sending a shepherd, therefore, namely Bishop Albert, God freed his Livonian sheep and the now-baptized Letts from the jaws of the wolves. Albert called together an army from all over Livonia and Lettigallia and, with the Rigans and pilgrims and all his people, went up the Dvina towards Kokenhusen. And since Gerzika was always a trap and a kind of great devil for all those living in this section of the Dvina, whether baptized or unbaptized, and since the king of Gerzika was always carrying on hostilities and wars against the Rigans and disdaining to enter into an agreement of peace with them, the bishop turned his army toward the city. The Russians, indeed, seeing the army coming from a distance, ran to the gate of the city and, when the armed bands of Germans attacked them and killed a few of them, they fled, not being able to defend themselves. The Germans followed them, entered the gate with them, and, out of respect for the Christian name, killed only a few of them. They took more captive and rather permitted them to escape by flight. When they had taken the city, they spared the lives of the women and children and captured many of them. While the king, with many others, fled by ship across the Dvina, the queen was captured and presented with her girls, women, and all her possessions to the bishop. The whole army remained in the town that day, collecting much booty from all its corners: clothes and silver and purple cloth and many flocks. They carried away with them the bells, icons, other ornaments, money, and large amounts of property which they took from the churches, and they blessed God, inasmuch as He had both given them a sudden victory over their enemies and, without the loss of any of their men, opened the city. The following day when everything had been extracted, they prepared for the return and set fire to the town. The king saw the burning from the other side of the Dvina, heaved a great sigh, bewailed with huge groans, and exclaimed: "O Gerzika beloved city! O inheritance of my fathers! O unexpected downfall of my people! O woe is me! Why was I born to see the burning of my city and the sorrow of my people!" [87]

After this the bishop and the whole army, having divided all the spoils among themselves, went back to their own land with the queen and all the captives. The king was ordered to come to Riga, that is, if he at last wanted peace and desired to recover the captives. He came and begged pardon for his excesses; he called the bishop "father," and, pleading in extenuation the extremely sharp whips, that is, the fire and the sword, with which he had been scourged by the Latins, humbly prayed them, as fellow Christians, to forget his past misdeeds, to give him peace, and to return the queen and the captives. Then the bishop with all his men, taking pity on the suppliant king, proposed to him the following terms of peace: "If," he said, "you will avoid henceforth association with pagans and, accordingly, not destroy our church through them and, at the same time, not lay waste, through the Lithuanians, the land of your Russian Christians; if, moreover, you will grant your kingdom in perpetuity to the church of Blessed Mary, in order to receive it back again from our hands, and rejoice with us joined in peace and harmony, then, when these things have been done, we will restore the queen with all the captives to you and always furnish you faithful aid." The king, accepting these terms of peace, promised henceforth always to be faithful to the church of Blessed Mary, to avoid pagan counsels, and to adhere to the Christians. Moreover, he conferred his kingdom upon the same church and,

87. Cf. I Macc. 2:7.

from the hand of the bishop, who solemnly handed over to
him three banners, received it back as a fief. He then chose
the bishop as a father and affirmed that hencefore he would
reveal to him all the evil counsels of the Russians and Liutha-
nians.[88] After the queen, together with the other captives, had
been given back to him, he returned joyfully to his own land,
called together those of his men who had escaped, and began
to rebuild his fort. Yet no less than before he mixed himself
up in the plans of the Lithuanians and, forgetting his promise
of fidelity, often incited the pagans against the Germans who
were in Kokenhusen.

(5) When the peace which had been made with the Ungannians had run out, Berthold, the commander of the Militia in
Wenden, summoned Russin with his Letts and also other Letts
from Autine and with his Wends went to Ungannia. There
they found in their villages the men who had not yet fled to
the fort, killed a great many in all the villages to which they
were able to come, and, having killed many, took others
captive and collected much loot. Taking the women and girls
with them, they left the villages, as it were, deserted, and,
after great slaughter and burning, returned to their people.[89]
When the Livonians of Treiden, who still continued to take
secret and characteristically disloyal counsel with the Esthonians, heard this, they were indignant because Berthold of
Wenden and the Letts had renewed war against the Esthonians. They suggested, therefore, to the bishop that he send
legates to Ungannia for peace. The bishop sent Alabrand the

---

88. Albert's charter appears in Bunge, *Urkundenbuch*, I, 20-21: "When he
had sworn homage to us and taken an oath of fealty, he was solemnly in-
vested, by means of three banners from our hand, with the aforementioned
city [i.e., Gerzika] and the land and properties pertaining thereto, as a
benefice. These things were done in the cemetery of Blessed Peter in Riga
in the year of the incarnation of the Lord 1209, during the pontificate of
Pope Innocent III, and during the reign of the most glorious Emperor Otto,
in the eleventh year of our pontificate." Arndt concludes, therefore (*MGH,
SS*, XXIII, 268), that this investiture must have taken place sometime after
October 4, 1209, the day on which Otto IV's coronation took place.

89. See n.46, above.

priest to Odempäh, both to renew peace and to ask for the
goods of the merchants.[90] The Esthonians throughout Ungannia, hearing that the legates of the bishop had arrived, gathered
for a meeting, and Alabrand spoke to them and taught them
about the faith of Christ. When he finished, the Esthonians
as a group ran forward to kill him with their lances and
swords. But some of their elders defended him and said: "If
we now kill the bishop's legate, who will believe us henceforth or send us a messenger?" And, not wishing to hear the
words of salvation, they sent Alabrand back to the bishop and
sent men with him to make peace. Peace was, therefore, made
with the Livonians and with the Letts of the bishop on one
side of the Aa. Berthold of Wenden, however, and Russin
and his Letts did not accept peace and accordingly prepared
for battle.

[XIV]

(1) During the bishop's twelfth year [1210], the
church was at rest only for a few days, for after the bishop
and his pilgrims had returned to Germany and had left his
men in Livonia with a few pilgrims, the Kurs, enemies of
Christ's name, suddenly appeared with eight pirate ships off
the shore of Sunde.[91] When they saw them, the pilgrims left
their cogs,[92] entered smaller boats, and hurried to the pagans.
With insufficient caution, each boat went ahead of the others
in haste to meet the foe first. Then the Kurs, by unloading the
fore parts of their pirate ships, raised them up to meet those
who were coming, arranged them two by two, and at the

90. For Alabrand's previous experience in these matters, see above p. 67
(X, 15), pp. 74-75 (XI, 7).
91. Sunde is the strait between Kurland and Oesel.
92. The cog was a large, broad sailing vessel used for transporting both
men and goods. It characteristically displaced about 250 tons and carried a
crew of 130, besides passengers.

same time left a space between each of the pairs. For this reason the pilgrims who came on first in the two skiffs, or small boats, were trapped in the space between the pirate ships and, because they were in small boats, were not able to get at the enemy who stood high above them. When some of them had been killed by the enemies' lances, some drowned, and some wounded, the others returned to the larger ships and escaped. The Kurs then collected the bodies of the dead, stripped them, and divided their garments and the other loot among themselves. The citizens of Gothland later devotedly collected the bodies and buried them. About thirty knights and others were killed there. The bishop mourned several days over his men, knowing, however, that persecution is useful to the suffering, since blessed are they who suffer persecution for justice' sake,[93] and because the furnace trieth the potter's vessels and the trial of affliction, just men.[94]

(2) At the same time, the great king of Novgorod,[95] and likewise the king of Polozk,[96] came with their Russians in a great army to Ungannia. They besieged the fort of Odempäh and fought there eight days. Since there was a lack of water and a shortage of food in the fort, the Ungannians sought peace from the Russians; and the Russians gave them peace. They baptized a few of them with their baptism, received four hundred *nogata* marks,[97] left them, and went back to their country, saying that they would send back their priests to them to finish the holy regeneration of baptism. This they afterwards neglected, for the Ungannians later received priests of Riga, were baptized by them, and were numbered among the Rigan Christians.

(3) Several years afterwards, the Frisians came with pil-

93. Cf. Matt. 5:10.
94. Cf. Ecclus. 27:6.
95. Mstislaw.
96. Vladimir, the brother of the king of Novgorod.
97. In the language of the Esths, pelts were called *nahad*, while in the Livonian language they were *nagöd* or *nogöd*. The coins derive their name from this merchandise.

grims to the aforementioned island of Gothland and found there Kurs with much plunder. After surrounding them, they suddenly attacked them and killed almost all of them. They took away with them to Riga four pirate ships with all their spoils. They also took away from them an infinite number of sheep, which had been taken from Christian lands, and brought these too to Riga. And great joy ensued over the revenge taken on the Kurs.

(4) The bishop, indeed, was saddened greatly by continual labors and the death of his men, but at length again took refuge in the Lord and, committing his journey and his business to Him, went back to Germany. There he complained to good and God-fearing men of his losses and sought, through highways and byways, through cities and forts, those who would set themselves up as a wall for the house of the Lord [98] and take on the sign of the cross in order to go by sea to Livonia for the consolation of the few who remained there. He found Yso, the bishop of Verden, Philip, the bishop of Ratzeburg, and also the bishop of Paderborn,[99] who prepared with their knights and many other men to make this journey the following year.

(5) After the departure of the bishop and the fight of the Kurs with the pilgrims, all the pagans round about, who had heard that some of the pilgrims had been killed by the Kurs, sent ambassadors to one another, first the Livonians to the Kurs, then the Kurs to the Esthonians, and also to the Lithuanians, Semgalls, and Russians. They sought from each other every counsel as to how they might destroy Riga, take all the Germans by trickery, and kill them. The Lithuanians, believing that few remained in Kokenhusen, came to the fort with a large army, found Rudolph of Jerichow with other men of the bishop in the fort, and attacked them most vigorously. The soldiers of the bishop and the Letts in the fort who went out against them killed many of them with their lances, and the ballistarii from the ramparts wounded some. Unable to

98. Cf. Ezek. 13:5.
99. By name, Bernard.

bear their attack, the Lithuanians withdrew. Then some Livonians from the Adia region, already baptized, filled with the
gall of their treachery, went to Kurland. After arousing the
whole country against the church of Riga and alleging, as
was quite true, that very few men remained in the city, they
collected a large, strong army. When the citizens heard this,
they sent scouts out to sea. The Kurs, indeed, gathered their
whole army and, while staying in the neighborhood for fourteen days, sought the aid of their gods and an opportune time
for battle by lot. The scouts, in the meantime, having seen
nothing, returned. Then the count of Schladen, the knight
Marquard, and other pilgrims who had remained for Easter,[100]
desiring to go back to Germany, went down to Dünamünde
in their two ships. Leaving a few in the ships, they spent the
night in the cloister [July 13]; the next morning at dawn, the
whole sea appeared as if covered with a dark cloud. When
they who were in the ships saw the multitude of pagans and
the great army descending upon them, some prepared to defend themselves, while others fled to the cloister. The pagans,
indeed, hoping to take the city suddenly and without warning, did not attack the pilgrims' ships, but instead rowed on
most rapidly to the city. But the fishermen from all parts of
the Dvina who saw them fled to Riga and reported that an
army followed. The citizens, the Brothers of the Militia, and
the ballistarii, few though they were, together with the clerics
and the women, all had recourse to arms, and having sounded
the bell which was rung only in time of war, they assembled
the people. They went out to meet the enemy on the banks
of the Dvina and wounded many of them with ballistas. The
Kurs, leaving their ships in the Dvina, organized their army
in the field. Each one of them carried before him a wooden
shield made out of two planks and, to support this shield, a
staff, like a pastoral staff.[101] The waters and the fields were
resplendent with the sun that reflected from their white

100. April 18, 1210.
101. I.e., a mantelet, or movable shelter used by besiegers for protection
when attacking the walls of a fortress.

shields. It was, indeed, a great and strong army that approached the city. The Livonians and ballistarii ran forward to meet them at the first fortifications which were in the field before the city gate and fought with them until the third hour of the day. The citizens, however, burned the village which was outside the walls. Some of our men, having with them little three-pronged nails,[102] threw them in the road over which the army was coming. Certain of the citizens went out manfully to fight and killed many of the enemy as they stood under their shields. Upon their return they fell over these nails, and some were killed while others escaped to us. After this the army returned to its ships and, having eaten, again prepared for battle. When they heard the sound of the great bell, they said that they were being eaten and consumed by this God of the Christians, and, approaching the city again, fought through the whole day. When they came out from under their shields in order to bring up wood for burning the fort, many of them were wounded by arrows and when any of their men fell, wounded by the stones of the machines or by the ballistarii, immediately his brother or some other companion killed him by cutting off his head. After they had encircled the city on all sides and set a great fire, the people of Holm came on their horses to the Old Mountain, threatened the enemy with their swords, and descended to the city on the other side. When the Kurs saw them, they withdrew from the city, collected their dead, and returned to the ships. After crossing the Dvina, they rested for three days while cremating their dead and mourning over them. The Treiden Livonians heard that Riga was being besieged by the Kurs and, since they wished for the destruction of the city, collected a numerous army to come to their aid. For there were certain perfidious Livonians, Semgalls, and other tribes awaiting the success of the Kurs so that they might all come together at the same time to destroy the city. But the people of Holm who, on the same day, had killed certain Kurs on the islands

102. Caltrops.

and taken away their boats, came to Riga. Marquard the knight, returning from Dünamünde through the midst of the enemy, entered the city and later joined the brotherhood of the Brothers of the Militia. On the following night, Caupo came into the city with all his friends and relatives and faithful Livonians. At dawn, Conrad of Uexküll came into the field next to the city with the Livonian leaders. As they made a great show with their horses and arms, all those in the city came out to them and great joy was manifested among them. They marched forward to meet the Kurs and, prepared either to die bravely or to win, called upon them to fight. Since the Kurs were more concerned about the burial of their men, they spoke of peace and went away three days later. The Livonians, however, who were guilty of this treason, without any harm to their men voluntarily made peace with God and the household of the bishop and promised to be faithful henceforth. The city which had thus been mercifully liberated from the pagans through the grace of God, gave thanks to Him and arranged that Saint Margaret's Day,[103] on which the liberation had taken place, was henceforth to be celebrated within the city. At the same time Berthold of Wenden came with the Letts from Ungannia, where they had burned many villages and killed many pagans and had thus inflicted heavy losses on them. He now came with a great force to help the Rigans, but, the Kurs having left, each one returned to his own country.

(6) After this the same Berthold collected an army. Siegfried and Alexander, soldiers of the bishop, went with him, together with many others, both Livonians and Letts. When they came into Ungannia, they found few men in the fort at Odempäh. Those in the fort, therefore, frightened because of their small numbers, peacefully received Berthold within the

103. Bonnell's *Russisch-Livländische Chronographie*, p. 74, cited in *MGH*, *SS*, XXIII, p. 271, n.26, shows that Saint Margaret's Day was celebrated on July 13 in Prussia and Livonia. See also H. Grotefend, *Taschenbuch der Zeitrechnung des deutschen Mittelalters und der Neuzeit*, 9. Aufl. (Hanover, 1948), p. 77.

fort. The soldiers of the bishop, with certain Livonians, not knowing that Berthold had been received within the fort, approached it from the other side. The whole army followed them, captured the summit of the hill, seized the stronghold of the fort, then became complete masters of it, killed men, captured women, and, while some escaped by flight, took away many spoils. They then rested there for a few days and, after having divided the loot and burned the fort, returned to Livonia.

(7) The Livonian church was thus now beset with many tribulations, inasmuch as it was in the midst of many nations and the adjacent Russians, who all took counsel together over ways to destroy it. Accordingly the Rigans decided to send messengers to the king of Pskov to see if perchance they could arrange some terms of peace with him. (8) Rudolph of Jerichow accordingly was sent with certain others to go to Russia. When they approached Wenden, behold the Esthonians came and besieged it with a great army. Rudolph with his men escaped into the fort. And the Esthonians fought for three days with Berthold and his Brothers and the people of Wenden at the old fort, in which at this time the Brothers were living with the Wends. Many of the Esthonians fell, wounded by the ballistarii, and likewise certain of the Wends were killed by the lances of the enemy. The Esthonians brought up a great deal of wood, which they set on fire in order to burn the fort. They dragged great trees with their roots out of the forest, made them into a sort of rampart, which they strengthened and reinforced with other logs, and, fighting from below and with fire and smoke from above, they greatly harassed those who were in the fort. And had not the time of the war been shortened,[104] they would have wrought even greater evils. For, although the Rigans, because of the negligence of certain ones, had not received news of the siege on either the first day or the second, but only on the third day, they did rise up on the fourth day and come to

104. Cf. Matt. 24:22.

Segewold. On the same day, the Esthonians heard that a great
congregation of Livonians had come together with Caupo and
his friends. They accordingly left Fort Wenden and, crossing
the Aa, spent the night near the lake which is on the Beverin
road. The Brothers from Wenden, however, and Caupo with
the Livonians and Letts, followed them at dawn and stopped
near the same lake to eat. When the scouts and guards of the
army, whom they had sent out, returned, they announced that
the Esthonians were fleeing most swiftly across the Sedde.
And at once, excessively credulous of their words, the Livonians and Letts, saying that they could never wait until the
Rigans came up, hurried to follow the Esthonians. But Caupo,
together with the Germans, said: "Let us await our Brothers,
and then we will be able to fight, and, having put on our
wings, to fly on high." But they, scorning this advice and
preferring rather the death of the Germans, followed the
Esthonians. Yet they arranged to set the Germans in the first
line of battle. Thus they, following from behind and awaiting
the outcome of the war, were well prepared either to follow
or to flee. And they marched to the Sedde, not knowing that
the army of the Esthonians was lurking in the forests near it,
and suddenly they saw the whole army coming out against
them. Then Arnold, a Brother of the Militia, took up a standard and said: "Let us come together, brother Germans, and
see if we know how to fight; let us not flee from them and
thus bring shame upon our people." And they attacked them,
fought with them, and killed some of them. Berthold, the son
of Caupo, fell, and also his son-in-law, Wane, a brave and
good man. Certain of the Brothers of the Militia and William
and Alder, soldiers of the bishop, were grievously wounded.
When the Livonians, however, who were following up the
rear, saw the multitude of the army coming on all sides from
the forests, they immediately turned to flight, and the Germans remained alone. When the Germans saw this and considered how few they were, for there were only about twenty
of them, they crowded together and returned over a direct

path to the Aa, fighting with the enemy as they withdrew. Rudolph of Jerichow fell to the ground, wounded by a lance, but Wigbold the Frisian lifted him to his horse. A Frisian himself, he trusted to the speed of his horse and, sometimes by fleeing, sometimes by returning to the enemy and by checking them in the narrow places, he freed many. The Esthonians, however, followed both the Germans, the Livonians, and the infantry of the Letts from right and left. They captured about a hundred of them, killed some, and, leading the others back towards the Sedde, tortured them in a cruel martyrdom. Of the fourteen of the latter, they roasted some alive, and, after stripping the others of their clothes and making crosses on their backs with their swords, they cut their throats, and thus, we hope, sent them into the heavenly company of the martyrs. Then the Esthonians, taunting the Christians, returned to their country and sent men through all the provinces to persuade them to swear and join together with one heart and mind against the Christian name. Caupo, the Livonians, and the Letts returned from the fight, bewailed their dead, and were joined by the whole church in grieving over the newly baptized who had been butchered by the pagans. The church, indeed, was like Arcturus, always pummeled but never broken; like the ark of Noah, raised up by great billows but not crushed; like the bark of Peter, shaken by waves but not submerged; like a woman whom the dragon followed but did not overtake.[105] For consolation followed after this tribulation, and after sadness God gave joy. (9) For Arnold, a Brother of the Militia, was sent with his companions to the king of Pskov, to see if he would accept peace and open a road for Rigan merchants into his country. The king received them with benign affection and, although deceitfully, rejoiced with them in the tranquillity of peace. In order that just and peaceful terms might be negotiated, he sent Ludolf, a prudent and rich man from Smolensk, back with them to Riga. When they came to Riga and made known

105. Cf. Apoc. 12:3-17.

the will of the king, it pleased the Rigans. So a perpetual peace was then made for the first time between them and the king. Yet it provided that either the Livonians themselves or the bishop for them should pay the annual tribute due the king. And all rejoiced, since they could now more securely wage war against the Esthonians and the other pagans. And this they did.

(10) For truly, at the approach of the solemnity of the birth of the Lord, when the harshness of winter was increasing, the elders of the Rigans summoned everyone from all Livonia, Lettia, and the whole area, and from all the forts of the Dvina and Aa to come and be prepared to take vengeance on the nations of the Esthonians. This word came to Pskov which was then at peace with us, and a great crowd of Russians came to help us. And the leaders of the land, Russin and Caupo, likewise Ninnus and Dobrel, came with the others and went ahead of the Rigans and pilgrims. The whole army followed them into Metsepole. After taking hostages from the Livonians whom they considered treacherous, they marched to the sea and, following day and night the direct route along the sea, they came to the first province, which is called Sontagana. When the guards of the roads saw the army, however, they fled to tell their people. But the speedier elements of the army, together with the scouts, entered the villages and found almost everyone at home in them. Then the army spread into all the roads and villages, killed many people in every spot, and followed the remainder into the adjoining provinces, captured from them their women and boys, and reassembled at the fort. On the following day and the third day, they went out and laid waste everything and burned what they found and took horses and innumerable flocks; for of the latter there were four thousand oxen and cows, not counting horses, other flocks, and captives, of whom there was no count. Many of the pagans, moreover, who escaped through flight to the forests and the ice of the sea, perished in the freezing cold. On the fourth day, having taken and

burned three forts, they began to leave the land with all their plunder. Deliberately turning back, they divided it equally among themselves and returned to Livonia with joy, blessing that Lord who gave them vengeance on their enemies. The Esthonians now no longer derided and taunted the Livonians and Letts over the martyrdom of their men. At the following new moon [Jan. 1211], the Livonians and Letts again assembled with the Rigans near Lake Astigerwe. They advanced to attack the army of Saccalensians and Ungannians that faced them there. But these turned their backs and fled. One of them, however, remained and, coming up to our men, announced that another great army from the maritime provinces was about to enter Livonia that same night by another road, which is next to the sea. When they heard this, the leaders of the Livonians, hastening to save their wives and children from the enemy, returned, each man to his own fortifications. On the following day, the Esthonians who had first escaped came hurriedly from Sontagana and the other near-lying provinces with a great army to Metsepole. While all the people stayed in the forts, they burned the empty villages and churches and, with their pagan sacrifices, committed many abominations around the churches and tombs of Christians. The Rigans assembled at Treiden to follow them; Berthold of Wenden, too, with Russin and all the Letts, came to Raupa. When they heard of this, the Esthonians, hastily leaving the land, did not await conflict with the Christians. At the third new moon [Feb. 1211], the Rigans prepared themselves to besiege Fort Fellin in Saccalia. They called together the Livonians and Letts from all the regions and forts and, by threatening to punish those who did not come and inculcating terror, they collected a strong army. Englebert, the brother-in-law of the bishop, who was serving as magistrate in Treiden that same year, some Brothers of the Militia, and pilgrims went with them. Taking with them the smaller machine, or paterell, ballistas, and other instruments necessary for besieging the fort, they went into Saccalia.

[XV]

〰〰 (1) In the year of the Lord's incarnation 1210, Bishop Albert's thirteenth year [1211], the Germans, Letts, and Livonians for the first time besieged the fort of Fellin in Saccalia. The Germans sent the Livonians and Letts to despoil all the adjoining regions and to secure food and grain. They went through all the villages, killed many of the pagans, and brought others as captives to the fort. Then Berthold of Wenden and Russin, together with other Letts and the elders, after taking all the captives, went up closer to the fort. "If you will renounce the worship of your false gods," said Berthold, "and will believe with us in the true God, we will return these captives alive to you. We will accept you in the charity of our brotherhood and will join you to us in the bonds of peace." The pagans would listen to nothing about God or the Christian name. They rather threatened war and donned the arms of the Germans which they had seized at the gate of the fort during the first engagement. On the heights of the fort they gloried in these arms, they prepared themselves for war, and with their shouting they jeered and mocked at the army. Russin and the Letts, however, having taken all the captives and slaughtered them, threw them into the moat and threatened to do the same to those who were in the fort. The archers, meanwhile, killed many men and drove them all back to the stronghold, while other men built a tower.[106] The

---

106. A *propugnaculum*, or movable wooden siege tower, which could be brought up next to the walls of a besieged fortress. From such a tower the attackers could then launch their arrows and other missiles at those within the fort. See Ducange, *Glossarium, s.v. Propugnaculum;* also Ferdinand Lot, *L'Art militaire et les armées au moyen age,* 2 vols. (Paris, 1946), II, 311. Henry also uses the term *propugnaculum* to designate a machine used in undermining walls and otherwise known as the "cat"—Sir Charles Oman, *History of the Art of War in the Middle Ages,* rev. ed. by John H. Beeler

Livonians and Letts carried wood and filled the moat up, from bottom to top, and pushed the tower over it. The Letts and the ballistarii went up on the tower, killed many men on the battlements with arrows and spears, wounded many, and for five days a very great battle raged. The Esthonians strove to burn down the first pile of wood by casting a great deal of fire from the fort onto the carts. The Livonians and Letts threw ice and snow and put it out. Arnold, a Brother of the Militia, labored there day and night. At last he was hit by a stone and crossed over into the brotherhood of the martyrs. He was an extremely religious man and was always praying. He found, as we hope, that for which he prayed. The Germans built a machine and, by hurling stones night and day, they broke down the fortified places and killed men and innumerable beasts of burden in the fort. Since the Esthonians had never seen such things, they had not strengthened their houses against the force of such missiles. The Livonians added dry wood to the pile of wood up to the plankwork. Eylard of Dolen climbed up on top. The Germans followed in arms, removed the planks, and, on the inside, found another wall which they could not get through. The men of the fort gathered up above and forced the Germans back by throwing stones and logs. The Germans came down, brought flames to the fort, and set it on fire. The Esthonians pulled apart the flaming planks and the burning timbers of the wall and dragged them away. On the next day, when the burning was over, they replaced everything, and the survivors nerved themselves once again for the defense. There were, however, many corpses of the slain in the fort, there was a shortage of water, and nearly everyone was wounded, so that now they gave out. On the sixth day the Germans said: "Do you still resist and refuse to acknowledge our Creator?" To this they replied: "We acknowledge your God to be greater than our

(Ithaca, N.Y., 1953), p. 68. In one passage of the chronicle, Henry seems also to make a distinction between the *propugnaculum* and a wooden tower, though the difference is far from clear in his text (XVI, 4).

Shows H's influence

Biblical but negative

gods. By overcoming us, He has inclined our hearts to worship Him. We beg, therefore, that you spare us and mercifully impose the yoke of Christianity upon us as you have upon the Livonians and Letts." The Germans, therefore, after calling the elders out of the fort, disclosed to them all the laws of Christianity and promised them peace and brotherly love. The Esthonians rejoiced greatly over peace simultaneously with the Livonians and Letts, and they promised to receive the sacrament of baptism on the same terms. When hostages had been given and peace had been ratified, therefore, they received the priests into the fort. The priests sprinkled all the houses, the fort, the men and women, and all the people with holy water. They performed a sort of initiation and catechized them before baptism but postponed administering the sacrament of baptism because of the great shedding of blood which had taken place. When these things had been done, therefore, the army returned to Livonia and they all glorified the Lord for converting the tribes.

After this, at the solemnity of Easter [April 3], the merchants, hearing all of the counsels of the Esthonians and of the other near-by pagans, about how they proposed to destroy Livonia and the city of Riga before the arrival of the bishop and the pilgrims postponed their journey to Gothland, put off their dealings and business, and remained there with all their ships until the arrival of the pilgrims. Emissaries, meanwhile, were sent into Esthonia to see what the pagans were doing. They returned and announced war. They brought the peace back with them [107] and disclosed the counsels of the infidel. Caupo, Berthold of Wenden and his men, and the bishop's men immediately rose up and went into the nearest Saccalian province. They burned all the villages to which they could penetrate, killed all the men, brought the women back as prisoners, and returned to Livonia. The Saccalians followed

107. *Qui reversi bella nunciant, pacem secum referunt.* . . . The emissaries brought back the peace in the sense that they announced the end of peaceful relations.

them and they, too, burned all of the villages around Astigerwe. They came up to the Sedde and, after killing some
Letts, took the women and children captives and carried the
spoils off with them. After these, Lembito and Meme, elders
of Saccalia, rose up, crossed the Sedde with another army,
came to a church, burned it, and laid waste everything which
belonged to the priest. They collected the herds and many
spoils throughout the parish, killed the men whom they
seized, and led off the women, children, and girls as captives.
There was great tribulation in all parts of Livonia. For the
Saccalians and Ungannians were attacking the Letts; the
Rotalians and the maritime provinces attacked the bishop's
Livonians in Metsepole and Loddiger with three armies, so
that one army followed another and when one returned another came. Day and night they gave the Livonians no rest,
but they followed them and killed them in the hiding places
of the forests, in the marshes, and in the fields. They captured
the women, drove off the horses and flocks, and carried off
many spoils. Few of the Livonians remained alive and God
humbled them in large part for their treachery at that time,
so that henceforth they might become more faithful. The
Oeselians entered the Aa in their pirate ships and came up to
Treiden. They completely devastated the parish at Cubbesele
and ravaged the whole province round about. They killed
some men and took others captive, while still others fled from
them, escaped to Riga, and sought help against the attack of
the pagans. The Rigans, however, were keeping careful watch
over the city and feared that they would be betrayed by some
treacherous people, so they awaited the arrival of the bishop
and the pilgrims.

(2) In the same year the bishop went to Rome with Volquin, the master of the Brothers of the Militia. The bishop
was most cordially received by the supreme pontiff, was
granted privileges concerning the division of Livonia and
Lettia,[108] received a renewed authorization to preach for the

108. These privileges are printed in Bunge, *Urkundenbuch*, I, 22–24.

remission of sins, and joyfully returned. After rescripts of the privileges had been sent through Prussia, all the people in Livonia rejoiced not a little, so that they met the messengers with tears, for after the many distresses of the wars, they were receiving the consolation even of the supreme pontiff.

It was the prelate's thirteenth year and the church did not rest from the wars. When the bishop returned from Germany there came with him three bishops: Philip of Ratzeburg, Ivo of Verden, and the bishop of Paderborn.[109] Helmold of Plesse,[110] Bernard of Lippe, and other noblemen together with a great many pilgrims came too. Their arrival was desired by everyone, so that they might free those who sat among perils. The Letts, accordingly, rejoiced over the arrival of the pilgrims and gathered at the Sedde. They went on with a few men and met a large pagan army. When they saw the multitude of the pagans, the Letts turned in flight. The Esthonians pursued them, killed some of them, and followed them to the Sedde. The Esthonians went on all night and came in the morning to Raupa. They burned the church and the church property and went around the whole province consigning villages and houses to the flames, killing men, dragging women and children out of the hiding places of the forests, and taking them captive. The Rigans heard this, went out with the pilgrims, and came to Treiden. The pagans, however, feared their arrival and, after three days, they swiftly returned to their own land with all their loot. Caupo with some Germans and others followed them in Saccalia, burned the forts of Owele and Purke as well as many villages, took much booty, killed many men, and led off the women and children as captives.

(3) The Oeselians, the Rotalians, and the people of Reval, meanwhile, gathered a large and strong army from all of the near-by maritime provinces. All of the elders of Oesel, Rotalia, and all of Esthonia were with them and they had with them

109. Bishop Bernard III.
110. From the castle of Plesse near Göttingen.

many thousands of cavalry and several thousand men who
came by ship. They marched into Livonia. The cavalry and
their infantry came to Metsepole and hurried to Treiden,
while others came across the sea in their pirate vessels and
went up the Aa. They all gathered together with their cavalry
one day at Caupo's large fort, where the Livonians were then
living because they feared the pagans. They besieged the fort
on every side, with the cavalry stationed in front of the fort
and the others at the rear by the river next to their pirate ships.
The ballistarii, who had been sent from Riga to guard the fort
together with the Livonians, went out to meet them in the
field. The ballistarii wounded many of them and killed many,
since the Esthonians were unarmed, for they are not accustomed to use armor as much as other nations do. After this
the Esthonians sent some of their stronger men through the
province to despoil the land. They burned villages and
churches, seized and killed some of the Livonians and took
others prisoners, took many spoils, drove the cattle and other
livestock to their base, and slaughtered the cattle and livestock, immolating them to their gods, whose favor they
sought. But the flesh which they cut off fell on the left side,
which indicated that their gods were displeased: this was a
sinister omen. The Esthonians, however, did not give up what
they had begun. They fought the men in the fort, they made
piles of wood, they dug at the hill on which the fort was
situated, they promised that they would *magetac*, that is that
they would stay there forever, until they had either destroyed
the fort or brought the Livonians around to their way of
thinking, so that the Livonians would march along with them
to destroy Riga. A Livonian from the fort said: *Maga magamas*, that is, "You will stay here for eternity." The Brothers
of the Militia in Segewold, therefore, seeing everything that
the pagans were doing, made it known to the Rigans and
sought the help of the pilgrims. Messengers from the Livonians besieged in the fort came next and tearfully made known
all the misfortunes which the Livonians and Letts had suf-

fered from the pagans. They begged the bishops to send their
men and liberate their church. The bishops immediately called
on their knights and commanded the pilgrims and all the people, for the remission of their sins, to relieve their Livonian
brethren and to take revenge, if God gave it, upon the Esthonian tribes. The Brothers of the Militia rose up with the pilgrims, and Helmold of Plesse with the knights. They donned
their weapons, put the trappings on their horses, and with
their infantry, the Livonians, and their whole company they
made their way to the Aa. They crossed the Aa, went on
through the night, and approached the pagans. They arranged
the army and instructed it for the war. The infantry they sent
ahead on the major road which leads to Wendendorf. The
knights, however, followed on the road which leads to the
right. The infantry marched cautiously and in orderly fashion.
When morning broke they came down from the mountain
and saw the fort and the pagan army, and the valley was between them. Immediately they beat joyfully upon their drum
and enlivened the spirits of their men with their musical instruments and their song. They called down God's mercy
upon them and swiftly hurried toward the pagans. After
crossing a little stream they halted for a moment to collect
themselves in a group. When the pagans saw them, they were
terrified by the unmistakable prospect. They ran, got their
shields; some of them rushed to the horses, others leaped over
the barricade, and they all assembled in one group. They
troubled the air with their shouts and came out in a great
multitude to meet the Christians, throwing a shower of spears
upon them. The Christians caught the spears with their shields,
and when the pagans had run out of spears, the Christians
drew their swords, marched closer, and commenced the fight.
The wounded fell and the pagans fought manfully. The
knights saw the strength of the pagans and suddenly charged
through the center of the enemy. The trappings of the horses
threw terror into the enemy. Many of them fell to the ground,
the others turned to flight, and the Christians pursued those

who fled. They caught them and killed them on the road and in the fields. The Livonians from the fort went out with the ballistarii and met the fleeing pagans. They scattered them on the road and enveloped them. Then they slaughtered them, up to the German lines. They pursued the Esthonians so that few of them escaped and the Germans even killed some of the Livonians as if they were Esthonians. Some of them, it is true, fled by another road which goes around the fort, towards the Aa. These came to another section of their army and escaped. More of them, however, were pursued by the knights as they descended the mountain and were killed. Everhard, a Brother of the Militia, was killed there and certain of our knights were wounded. The other section of the Esthonian army, meanwhile, saw the destruction of their men and gathered on the mountain which lies between the fort and the Aa. They prepared to defend themselves. The Livonians and the Christian infantry, however, ran toward the loot. They seized the horses, of whom there were many thousands there, and neglected the war against the remaining pagans. The knights and ballistarii, however, fought with the men who were located on the mountain and killed many of them. The Esthonians, therefore, sought peace and promised that they would receive the sacrament of baptism. The knights, believing their promise, made their words known to the bishops so that they might come to receive the Esthonians. The Esthonians, however, fled by night in their pirate ships and wished to go down to the sea, but the ballistarii on both sides of the Aa hindered their descent. Other pilgrims came with Bernard of Lippe to the Aa from Riga. They made a bridge over the river, built wooden structures upon the bridge, caught the pirate ships as they came with arrows and lances, and completely cut off the pagans' escape route. In the still quiet of the night, therefore, the Esthonians secretly disembarked from their pirate vessels, leaving all their things behind, and fled. Some of them perished in the forests and others yet died of hunger on the road; only a few of them escaped to their own land to announce the news at home. About two thousand horses were obtained there and another two thousand men were killed. The pilgrims and everyone who participated in the war returned to Riga, bringing with them about three hundred pagan pirate ships as well as smaller boats and horses. They divided the spoils equally among themselves, giving part to the churches, and, with the bishops and all the people, they greatly praised God, Who allowed such a glorious triumph over the pagans the first time that many bishops arrived. Then, indeed, the Livonian church knew truly that God was fighting for it, for in that same war Esthonia's head fell, that is the elders of Oesel and the elders of Rotalia and of the other provinces, all of whom were killed there. The Lord thus quieted their pride and humbled the arrogance of the strong.[111]

(4) The bishop of Livonia, therefore, having received from the supreme pontiff the authority in place of an archbishop to create and consecrate bishops in the overseas lands which God had subjected to Christianity through the Livonian church, took Abbot Theodoric of the Cistercian order in Dünamünde as his collaborator in his ceaseless labors. He consecrated Theodoric as a bishop, promising him a bishopric in Esthonia. He consecrated Bernard of Lippe, indeed, as abbot. This same Count Bernard, when he was formerly in his own land, had taken part in many wars, burnings, and assaults. He was punished by God and was afflicted with a debilitating disease of the feet so that, lame in both feet, he was carried in a litter for many days. He was chastened by this and received religion in the Cistercian order. After learning letters and religion for some years, he received authority from the lord pope to preach the Word of God and to come to Livonia. As he often told it, after accepting the cross to go to the land of the Blessed Virgin, his limbs were immediately made firm and his feet became sound. On his first arrival in Livonia he was consecrated as abbot at Dünemünde and afterwards was made bishop of the Semgalls.[112]

(5) The Livonians also rejoiced after the many misfortunes

111. Cf. Isa. 13:11.
112. In 1218; see p. 166 (XXII, 1) below.

of war,[113] both at the arrival of the bishops and at the victory over their enemies. They assembled from the Dvina, from Treiden, and from all the regions of Livonia and begged and petitioned the bishops that they be relieved of the Christian law and especially of the tithe. They promised perpetual fidelity both in the wars against the pagans and in all the affairs of Christianity. The bishops acceded to their requests and suggested to the bishop of Riga that he satisfy their wish, so that he would keep them ever faithful to him. The bishop desired with paternal interest to assist his people and he also considered the imminent threat of war with the peoples round about. He decreed, in accordance with their petition, that for the tithe they should pay annually a peck, measuring eighteen "fingers," [114] for each horse. He confirmed it by letters patent with the seals of the four bishops, but in such a way that, if the Livonians should ever forget their fidelity, should take part in the counsels of the infidel, and should besmirch the sacrament of their baptism with pagan rites, they should thenceforth be held strictly to the tithe payments and the other laws of Christianity.

(6) When these matters had thus been arranged, Bishop Albert left the three bishops in Livonia, having committed his own functions to the fourth bishop who was then consecrated, and returned to Germany to collect pilgrims and necessary things for the coming year, lest, if the pilgrims stopped coming, the Livonian church be more endangered.

(7) The Saccalians and Ungannians, meanwhile, were still safe and unharmed.[115] They summoned a large army, entered the provinces of the Letts, harassed them through the hiding places of the forests, and seized and killed many of Russin's friends and relatives. They despoiled Thalibald in Tricatia and the adjacent provinces and gathered next to the fort of

113. . . . *post bellorum multa incommoda.* . . . Cf. *Breviarium Romanum, Officio in Exaltatione S. Crucis* (Sept. 14), *Lect. iv.*

114. The "fingers" (*digiti*) were smaller subdivisions of a peck (*modius*) corresponding roughly to an English pint.

115. See n.37, above.

Beverin. They besieged the fort, fought with the Letts for a whole day, and brought up a quantity of fire. They said at last: "Have you forgotten the slaughter of your people at the Sedde, so that you still do not seek to make peace with us?" The men in the fort replied: "Do you not remember your elders and innumerable men who were slain at Treiden, so that you will believe with us in the one true God and will receive baptism and perpetual peace?" When they heard this, the attackers were enraged. They turned away from the fort and speedily returned with the loot to their own country. Dote and Paike, the elders of the Letts at Beverin, went to Riga and humbly sought aid against the Saccalians. The pilgrims rose up with the Brothers of the Militia, Theodoric the bishop's brother, Caupo with all the Livonians, and Berthold of Wenden with the Letts. They assembled a great army in Metsepole, marched to the sea, and went for a three-day journey beside the sea. They turned, after this, toward the province of the Saccalians and journeyed for three days through forests and swamps by a very bad road. Their horses gave out on the road and about a hundred of them fell down and died. At length, on the seventh day, they came to the villages. They dispersed throughout the land, killed the men whom they found, captured all the children and girls, and gathered the horses and flocks at the village of Lambit, where there was their *maia*,[116] that is, their assembly place. On the following day they sent the Livonians and Letts through the dark hiding places of the woods, where the Esthonians were lying hidden. They found a great many men and women, dragged them and all their goods out of the forests, killed the men, and took the rest back to the *maias*. The two Letts, Dote and Paike, went into the village and suddenly nine Esthonians rushed upon them and fought with them throughout the day. The Letts wounded and killed many of them until, at last, they too, fell. On the third day the stronger men from the army crossed the

116. In Esthonian the word *maja* (*mahja* in Lettish) means "house" or "place of hospitality."

Pala River and despoiled the whole province which is called Nurmegunde. They burned all the villages, killed the men, took away the women, horses, and livestock, and came to Jerwan. They returned at night and celebrated with great shouting and striking of shields. They burned the fort on the following day and returned by another road, dividing all the loot equally among themselves. With joy they returned to Livonia. A great pestilence broke out through all of Livonia. Men began to take sick and die and the greater part of the people died, beginning at Treiden, where the corpses of the pagans lay unburied, up to Metsepole and from there into Idumea, up to the Letts and Wenden. The elders who were called Dobrel and Ninnus died and many others as well. A great and mortal plague likewise prevailed in Saccalia and Ungannia and the other regions of Esthonia. Many men who, by fleeing, had escaped being struck by the sword could not escape the bitter death of the pestilence. The Letts from Beverin went again into Ungannia with a few men. They seized the Esthonians who were returning to the villages for food. The males they killed; the women they spared and took away with them. They also took away much loot. Returning home, other Letts met them on the road, going again into Ungannia. What the first had left, these took. What the first neglected, these took care of. Those who had escaped from the first were killed by these. Into the regions and villages which the first had not penetrated, these went and, taking many spoils and captives, they returned. As they were returning, they again met still other Letts on the road going into Ungannia. Whatever was left undone by the earlier men was fully completed by these. They killed all the men whom they caught: they spared neither the rich nor the aged; all were condemned to the sword. Russin, however, as the others were doing to avenge their friends, killed all whom he took, some by roasting, others by some other cruel death. When these men had returned to their forts, still other Letts from Beverin started out with a few men. They crossed through the woods into the province of Saccalia which is called Hallist. They found all the people in their houses and they fell upon them all, big and little. They slew many of them, took the women, horses, and flocks, and divided them among themselves along with all the loot. The Hallistians and other Saccalians were terrified thereby and sent emissaries to Riga. They gave their boys as hostages and received peace. They promised, likewise, that they would receive the sacrament of baptism.

Theodoric, the brother of the bishop, with his servants and Berthold of Wenden, also collected an army. Now that winter had returned, they went into Ungannia. They found the whole land laid waste by the Letts, and the fort of Dorpat was deserted, burnt by the Letts. They crossed the river which is called the Mother of Waters [117] and entered the villages. Finding few people, they went into the forests, where in the densest part of the woods the pagans had made a certain enclosure. They had felled the great trees on all sides so that when the army came they could save themselves and their possessions.

So when the Christian army approached, the pagans boldly went out to meet them and, after defending themselves for a very long time because of the roughness of the road, when they were finally unable to hold off the multitude, they turned tail and headed for the woods. But the Christians pursued those who fled and killed those whom they took. They captured the women and children, drove off the horses and flocks, and pillaged many goods, for people had fled there from that whole province and had all their goods with them. After the soldiers had divided all the spoils among themselves, they returned to Livonia with the captives.

After the solemnity of the Lord's Nativity [Dec. 25] had been celebrated, when the bitter cold had set in and the roads were deeply frozen, the bishops sent through all the Livonian forts and Lettish provinces, calling upon the Livonians and Letts to come on an expedition with the Germans. The bishops

117. The Embach River.

sent their knights with the pilgrims and the Brothers of the
Militia and ordered the army to assemble at the fort of
Beverin. Bishop Theodoric of the Esths went with them and,
after celebrating the Epiphany of the Lord [Jan. 6, 1212],
they marched into Ungannia. There were about four thousand German infantry and knights and the same number again
of Livonians and Letts. They went into the province of
Dorpat and, crossing the Mother of Waters, they came to the
stronghold which the Christians had destroyed earlier. While
the pilgrims rested there, the Livonians and Letts and the
swifter men from the army marched into Waiga. They despoiled the whole province and assembled at Fort Somelinde.
On the following day, they came to their people in Waiga
and, after resting for three days, they despoiled all the country
round about. The houses and villages they committed to the
flames. They captured many people, killed many, and took
much loot. On the fourth day they went to Jerwan. The army
spread out through all the provinces, villages, and houses.
They took and killed many of the pagans. They took the
women and children captive and carried off many flocks,
horses, and spoils. Making the village called Carethen [118] their
base, they laid waste everything round about with fire. The
village of Carethen was at that time large, well-peopled, and
very lovely, as were all the villages in Jerwan and in all of
Esthonia. Later all of these villages were frequently devastated
and burned by our men. After three days the army returned
with all its loot and burned the adjoining villages and provinces, namely Mocha and Nurmegunde, and at last they
reached the lake called Worcegerwe. [119] Going on the ice, they
returned joyfully to Livonia.

(8) The great King Mstislav of Novgorod, hearing about
the German army in Esthonia, likewise rose up and went with
fifteen thousand men into Waiga and from Waiga into
Jerwan. Not finding the Germans, he marched into Harrien

118. Gross-Karreda.
119. The modern Wirzjärw (in Esthonian, *Würtsjerw* or *Wortsjerw*).

and besieged the fort of Warbole.[120] He fought for a few days with them and the inhabitants of the fort promised him seven hundred *nogata*[121] marks if he would retire. The king returned to his own land.

(9) After the Germans had returned to Riga from their expedition, the bishop sent his priest, Salomon, to the Esths in Saccalia. He was to minister to them by preaching the Word and by celebrating the sacrament of baptism, which they had long since sworn they would receive. Salomon came to the fort of Fellin and was received by some of them. He was hailed with greetings from the mouth and not from the heart, as Judas hailed the Lord. He preached the message of salvation to them and baptized some of them.

But the Saccalians and Ungannians, hearing of the Russian army in Esthonia, gathered an army from all of their provinces. Salomon the priest, when he heard of their gathering, went out of the fort with his people and planned to return to Livonia. Lembit of Saccalia, however, took a crowd of Esths with him and followed the priest. He found Salomon at night and killed him and his interpreters, Theodoric and Philip, and some others. All of them succumbed for Christ's faith and, as we hope, passed over into the company of the martyrs. This Philip was of Lithuanian stock, was brought up at the bishop's court, and became so faithful that he was sent as an interpreter to teach the other people. As he was made a partaker of martyrdom, he thus merited the blessedness of eternal rest.

(10) After the slaying of these men, Lembit returned to his army. While the Russians were in Esthonia, the Esthonians went meanwhile to Russia, and entering the city of Pskov [Feb. 22], began to slay the people. But a din arose, so they suddenly fled from the Russians with a clamor and returned to Ungannia with the loot and some prisoners. The Russians, upon their return, found their city pillaged.

(11) Then the Livonians, Letts, and Esthonians, loathing

120. The modern Warbjala.
121. See above, p. 95 (XIV, 2) and n.97.

the misfortunes of war [122] because of the pestilence and famine which was upon them, sent messengers to one another and made peace, except with the Rigans. When the wars had ceased, the famine and deaths immediately stopped.

(12) After this, when the ice melted on the sea and in the Dvina, the bishop of Verden and the bishop of Paderborn returned to Germany with their pilgrims. Bishop Philip of Ratzeburg, who had been among the chief men at the court of the Emperor Otto, remained in Riga. Since the sentence of excommunication had been issued against Otto,[123] Bishop Philip remained as a pilgrim in Livonia for four years, in order to stay out of Otto's presence.[124]

(13) After the departure of the pilgrims [Feb.] the Russians of Pskov were enraged at their prince, Vladimir, because he had given his daughter as a wife to the brother [125] of the bishop of Riga. They expelled Vladimir and his family from the city. He fled to the king of Polozk, but received small consolation from him, so that he came down to Riga with his men and was honorably received by his son-in-law and the bishop's household.

[XVI]

∿∿ (1) In the year of the Lord's incarnation 1212, the bishop's fourteenth year, the Livonian church rejoiced over the bishop's return with the pilgrims. Everyone went out with King Vladimir to receive him with praise for God. The bishop gave the king a blessing and, in kindly love, gifts of all the

---

122. See n.113, above.

123. The sentence was given on November 18, 1210. See A. Potthast, *Regesta Pontificum Romanorum*, 2 vols. (Berlin, 1874–75), I, 356.

124. Bishop Philip had to remain away from the excommunicated emperor in order to avoid falling under excommunication himself. See *Decretum Gratiani*, C. 11, q. 3, c. 16–19 (ed. Friedberg, I, 647–48).

125. Theodoric.

things which he had brought back from Germany. With the zeal of piety, he had his needs in every respect adequately served.

The Esths from all of the maritime provinces had gathered a large army and were encamped at Coiwemunde. They had Isfrid, the messenger of the Rigans, with them. When they heard of the arrival of the bishop and the pilgrims, they sent him back to Riga, tortured with various cruelties.[126] They then fled and returned to their own land. The Livonians and Letts therefore sent messengers into Esthonia and urged the Esths to renew the peace which they had made among themselves. The Esthonians rejoiced and sent their men back with the messengers to Treiden. The bishop was summoned, together with the Brothers of the Militia and the elders of Riga. They met with the Esthonian emissaries, they sought what was just, and they inquired into the cause of so many wars. After much arguing, a three-year peace was made among them all. Yet the Saccalians up to the Pala River were left in the power of the bishop and the Germans, so that those who had given hostages and had promised to accept the Christian faith might fully rejoice in the right of baptism and in the acceptance of the Christian faith. When peace had been made with the Esthonians, therefore, human deaths ceased in Riga, as well as in Livonia and Esthonia. Yet the wars did not stop, for some perfidious Livonians, who were still sanguinary sons, tore at the breasts of Mother Church. They sought in every way to trap and cheat the Brothers of the Militia who were in Segewold, so that when the Brothers had been thrown out of the land they might the more easily expel the bishop's household and the other Germans.

(2) The king of Polozk, meanwhile, summoned the bishop to come before him at a designated place and time to answer to him about the Livonians at Gerzika who were formerly the tributaries of the king. The king also wished that by confer-

126. . . . . *diversis penis cruciatum*. . . . . Cf. the Martyrology, *s.d.* June 16 (Migne, *P.L.*, CXXIV, 159–160).

ring together they could arrange a secure route for the merchants on the Dvina and that by renewing the peace they could resist the Lithuanians more easily. The bishop went up to meet the king taking with him his own men and King Vladimir, together with the Brothers of the Militia and the elders of the Livonians and the Letts. The merchants went with them in their ships and they all armed themselves with their weapons as a precaution against the treachery of the Lithuanians on both sides of the Dvina. They came to the king and began to examine with him the things that justice demanded. The king asked, now blandly, now with pointed threats,[127] that the bishop cease baptizing the Livonians. The king maintained that the Livonians were his servants and that it was in his power to baptize them or to leave them unbaptized. It is, indeed, the custom of the Russian kings not to subject whatever people they defeat to the Christian faith, but rather to force them to pay tribute and money to themselves. The bishop, however, thought one should obey God rather than men, the heavenly King rather than an earthly king, as He commands in His gospel, saying: "Go, teach all nations, baptizing them in the name of the Father and of the Son and of the Holy Spirit." [128] He steadfastly affirmed, therefore, that he would not quit what he had begun, nor would he neglect the duty of preaching, which had been enjoined upon him by the supreme pontiff. On the other hand, he would not forbid the giving of tribute to the king, even as the Lord again says in His gospel: "Render to Caesar the things that are Caesar's and to God the things that are God's"; [129] for the bishop himself had once in turn paid the tax to the king for the Livonians. The Livonians, however, were unwilling to serve two masters,[130] namely both the Russians and the Ger-

127. . . . *modo minarum asperitatibus*. . . . Cf. Pope Gregory I, *Homilia 5 in Evangelio*, cited in *Breviarium Romanum, Officio S. Andrei Apostoli* (Nov. 30), *Lect. vii.*
128. Matt. 28:19.
129. Matt. 22:21.
130. Cf. Matt. 6:24.

mans. They suggested to the bishop all the time that he should liberate them completely from the Russian yoke. The king, however, was unwilling to agree to these just and logical arguments. He was, at last, enraged and threatened to commit all the forts of Livonia and Riga itself to the flames. He ordered his army out of the fortress and, pretending that he was going to war with the Germans, he ordered all of his people into the field with his archers and he began to approach the bishop's party. All of the bishop's men with King Vladimir, the Brothers of the Militia, and the merchants put on their weapons and boldly marched out to meet the king. As they came together, John, the provost of the church of Blessed Mary, and King Vladimir and some others crossed over between the battle lines and forcefully warned the king not to disturb the new church with his wars, lest he be set upon by the Germans, who were all strong in arms and who greatly desired to fight with the Russians. Their boldness frightened the king, who ordered his army to retire. He went over to the bishop, whom he saluted and revered as a spiritual father. The bishop, for his part, received the king as a son. They remained talking for a time and inquired diligently into all the questions pertaining to peace. At length the king, led, perhaps, by the inspiration of God, relinquished all of Livonia freely to the bishop, so that a permanent peace might be concluded between them, both against the Lithuanians and against the other pagans. A route for the merchants on the Dvina was to be kept free forever. When these matters had been arranged, the king went up the Dvina with the merchants and all his people and joyfully returned to Polozk, his city. The bishop and all his people went downstream with even greater joy and returned to Livonia.

(3) After their return a great contention arose between the Brothers of the Militia from Wenden and the Letts of Autine, the latter being in the bishop's area, over their fields and their bee trees. Some of the Letts were wounded by the Brothers and the quarrel came before the bishop. The lord

bishop rose up with the venerable Lord Philip, bishop of Ratzeburg, and called the Brothers of the Militia and the Livonians and Letts to a hearing so that, by checking the quarrel, he could restore them to their former harmony. They wrangled bitterly for two days and were unable to enter into any peaceful reconciliation among themselves. The Livonians and Letts thereupon left the Germans and took oaths among themselves. They confirmed their oaths, according to their pagan custom, by trampling on their swords. Caupo was the chief among them and his words were to this effect: that he would never fall away from the Christian faith, but that he would intercede with the bishop for the Livonians and Letts, so that the Christian law might be lightened for them. But all the others did not care for his intentions. They conspired against the Brothers of the Militia and planned to expel all of the Germans and the Christian nation from the land of the Livonians. When they saw this, the bishops and the Brothers of the Militia, with all the friends who had come with them, returned, each man to his own stronghold. The Livonians from Sattesele then gathered in their fortress and they sent to the people of Lenneworden, Holm, and Treiden and to all the Livonians and Letts, so that they might take counsel. They all agreed with them and began to strengthen all their forts, so that when they had gathered in their crops, they would suddenly retreat into the strongholds. The agreement was reported to Daniel of Lenneworden, who was procurator of the magistracy, and he sent men and seized all the Livonian elders of the province who were privy to the scheme and had them thrown in chains. Then he burned down their forts. The Rigans likewise learned the wicked thoughts of the people of Holm and they sent and destroyed the top part of their stone fortress, which their first bishop, Meinhard, had built.[131] They sent to Treiden and in the silence of the night they burned the fort there, lest, after gathering their men in the fort, the Livonians prepare more serious wars against the Rigans.

131. See above, pp. 26-27 (I, 5-7).

After the burning of their forts, the traitors' plan came to nothing. The Livonians of Sattesele, who had long been gathered in their fort, commenced a war against the Brothers of the Militia in Segewold and began to chase the members of the Brothers' household and to kill some of them. But the Brothers left their newly-built castle at Segewold and put them to flight when they came out to meet them. They pursued the Livonians and killed them. Other Livonians, more numerous and brave than the former, went out again to meet them, pursued them, killed some of them, and drove them back into their fort. In this fashion they struggled for several days. The bishop heard of their quarrel and sent messengers to discover the cause of their war. Livonian emissaries came to Riga and uttered many complaints about Rolf, the master of the Brothers of the Militia. They reported that he had taken fields, meadows, and money away from them. The bishop sent Alabrand the priest, who had baptized them, together with other men, but they went and labored in vain, for they were unable to settle the quarrel. The bishop himself came with Bishop Philip of Ratzeburg to Treiden. He called in the Livonians and the Brothers of the Militia and heard their cases. The Livonians sat on the other side of the river with their weapons and talked to the Germans. They accused the Brothers of the Militia on many scores. The bishop promised to restore everything that had been taken unjustly. As for the things that the Brothers had taken (as they justly deserved) on account of the Livonians' excesses, the bishop made no promise to restore them. The bishop, acting on the advice of prudent men, demanded the Livonians' boys as hostages, lest they abandon the Christian faith. The Livonians, however, would neither give up the hostages nor obey the bishop or the Brothers of the Militia. They planned, rather, to root out the Christian faith and all of the Germans from the land. The bishops, when they learned this, returned to Riga.

One following them,[132] however, begged tearfully that the bishop of Ratzeburg and the provost be sent again, on the chance that the Livonians might yet quiet down and accept the warnings of the doctrine of salvation. Philip of Ratzeburg, John the provost, Theodoric the bishop's brother, Caupo, and many others were sent to those Livonians. They all sat down with the Livonians in front of their fort and again discussed matters dealing with justice and peace. Some of the Livonians came behind their backs and falsely announced that the Brothers of the Militia with an army were despoiling the province. With much shouting and uproar, therefore, the Livonians seized the provost, Theodoric the bishop's brother, Gebhard the magistrate, and the knights and clerics and all their servants and dragged them into the fort. The Livonians beat them and put them in custody. They wished to seize the bishop, too, but his priest and interpreter, Henry of the Letts,[133] forbade them to do it and threatened them. When their noise and rage died down, the bishop asked that his provost and all the others be restored to him, and he further added threats about what would happen as a result of this kind of deceit. All the men were given back and the bishop warned the Livonians again and again that they were not to despise the sacrament of baptism, that they were not to profane the cult of Christianity, now their religion, and of God, and that they were not to return to paganism. He also demanded two or three of their boys as hostages. The Livonians replied blandly indeed, but did not take steps to give hostages. The bishop said: "O you of unbelieving hearts, hard faces, and smooth-talking tongues, acknowledge your creator!" He spoke so that they might perhaps quiet down, recognize the true God, and give up pagan practices. Making no headway, however, but as if vainly beating the air,[134] they returned to

132. The text is obscure and possibly defective here, for it seems likely that a proper name—possibly Alabrand or Henry, the author of this chronicle—has been omitted.

133. The author of this chronicle.

134. I Cor. 9:26.

Riga. The Livonians, nonetheless, began to war upon the Brothers of the Militia.

(4) Bishop Albert, however, wished to separate the tares from the wheat [135] and to root out the evils which had arisen in the land before they multiplied. He called together the pilgrims, the master of the Militia and his Brothers, and the Rigans and Livonians who still remained faithful. They all assembled and collected a great army. Taking all the necessary supplies with them, they marched to Treiden and besieged Dobrel's fort, in which there were the apostate Livonians, not only the Livonians belonging to the Brothers of the Militia, but also the bishop's Livonians from the other part of the Aa. The prince and elder of the latter was Vetseke.[136] The Livonians left the fort from the rear and, after wounding some men in the army, they took their horses and loot and returned to the fort, saying: "Take heart and fight, Livonians, lest you be slaves to the Germans." They fought and defended themselves for many days. The Germans destroyed the ramparts of the fort and killed many men and beasts with the many large rocks which they shot into the fort with their paterells. Some forced the Livonians from the defenses with arrows, wounding a great many of them. Others put up a tower,[137] which the wind knocked to the ground the next night. At this there was great noise and rejoicing in the fort and the Livonians sacrificed animals, paying honor to their gods according to their old customs. They immolated dogs and goats and, to mock Christianity, they tossed them from the fort, in the face of the bishop and the whole army. But all of the Livonians' work was wasted. The tower was put up more

---

135. Cf. Matt. 13:25.
136. The text is a trifle confused here. In *MGH, SS,* XXIII, 283, there is a misprint: . . . *quorum princeps ac Vsenior fuit esike.* In the text printed in *Scriptores Rerum Germanicarum in Usum Scholarum,* p. 101, the earlier error is compounded, so that the passage reads: . . . *quorum princeps ac Vesenior fuit sike.* The only plausible reading, of course, is: . . . *quorum princeps ac senior fuit Vesike.*
137. A *propugnaculum;* see above, p. 105 (XV, 1), and n.106.

strongly, another wooden tower was quickly strengthened, it was pushed across the moat, and the fort was sapped from below. From the highest point in the fort, meanwhile, Russin called Berthold, the master of Wenden, *draugs*, that is, his fellow.[138] Russin took off his helmet, leaned down from the wall, and uttered words about peace and their former friendship. Suddenly a bolt from a ballista struck his head. He fell and shortly thereafter he died. The Germans were digging day and night at the ramparts. They did not rest until they got near the top of the fort, until the rampart was cut in two, until it was expected that the whole fortification would tumble to the ground. The Livonians, seeing that the height of their strongest fort was being toppled, were bewildered in soul and confused in mind. They sent their elders, Asso and others, to the bishop. They asked for mercy and begged that they be not killed. The bishop, in order to persuade them to return to the sacraments of the faith, sent his banner into the fort. Some of them put it up; others then threw it down. Asso was bound for torture, war began again, and the final fight was worse than the earlier one. At length they gave up, raised Blessed Mary's standard on high, and bowed their necks to the bishop. They humbly besought him to spare them and promised that they would immediately accept the neglected faith of Christ, that they would henceforth observe the sacraments faithfully, and that they would never again call to mind pagan rites. The bishop had pity on them. He forbade the army to sneak into the fort or to kill the suppliants, or to deliver the souls of so many to hell fire. The army faithfully obeyed the bishop and in reverence to him stopped the battle and pardoned the unfaithful men, so that they could be made faithful. The bishop returned to his city with his men, taking with him the Livonian elders, enjoining the others to follow in order to renew the sacrament of baptism and to return to their former peaceful tranquillity. The messengers of the

138. *Draugs* in Lettish means "a friend."

Livonians followed the bishop to Riga, seeking pardon before the whole multitude.

The bishop said: "If you will renounce the worship of false gods and will return whole-heartedly to the worship of the one God, if you will make fitting satisfaction to God and to us for your atrocious crimes, then we will restore the peace which you interrupted and we will receive you in the love of fraternal charity."

But they said: "What satisfaction do you require of us, Father?"

The bishop took the advice of the other bishop—of Ratzeburg—and of the dean of Halberstadt,[139] who was present, and of the abbot and his provost and also of the master of the Brothers of the Militia and of his other prudent men.

He said to them in reply: "Because you rejected the sacraments of the faith, because you disturbed the Brothers of the Militia, your lords, with war, because you wished to drag all of Livonia back into idolatry, and especially because, out of contempt of the most high God and in order to mock us and all Christians, you threw the goats and other animals which you had immolated to the pagan gods in our face and in the face of the whole army, we therefore demand a moderate sum of silver from your entire province, namely one hundred *oseringi*, or fifty silver marks. You are furthermore obliged to restore to the Brothers of the Militia their horses and equipment and the other things which were taken from them."

The perfidious Livonians heard this and were still unwilling to give any satisfaction. They returned to their people, pondering and discussing among themselves and seeking some device by which they could hold on to the plunder of the war and could avoid rendering any of the aforesaid rights to the bishop. They sent other men, better than the first, and spoke straightforward words to the bishop, though they meditated on deceit in their hearts. Alabrand, their first priest, considered

139. Burchard, dean of the cathedral chapter of Halberstadt.

their perfidy and took them aside. He taught them and said: "Brood of vipers! How can you, who are always full of the venom of treachery, you who will make no satisfaction for your evil deeds—how can you escape the wrath of God? Do something, therefore, as a product of your penitence and, if you truly wish to be converted to God, God will surely be with you, that you, who have been inconstant and of two minds, may now be constant in your ways, so that you will see that God's help is with you. You do not yet have the full constancy of faith, you do not yet wish to honor God by giving your tithes. Now truly beseech the lord bishop to forget all of your excesses and to enjoin upon you a full remission of your sins, so that sincerely believing in God, you may fully receive all the laws of Christianity. Pay a tenth of your harvests to God and God's servants, as do all other nations who have been reborn in the font of holy baptism.[140] God will so increase the other nine parts for you that you will have a greater abundance of goods and of money than before. God will free you from the attacks of other nations and from all of your troubles as well."

The Livonians rejoiced to hear such salutary warnings. They returned to Treiden and announced to everyone the message of Alabrand the priest. Everyone was pleased because they were not at present compelled to pay any monetary fine, and they hoped that next year the Germans would be fighting the Esthonians. All of the elders who remained in good health came to Riga from the fort of Dobrel, as well as the bishop's Livonians from the other side of the Aa, Vetseke with his men, and others from Metsepole. They asked the bishop, as Alabrand had instructed them, to confirm them fully in Christ's faith and to lay upon them the annual payment of the tithe as satisfaction for their misdeeds. This speech displeased the bishop and the other prudent men, for they feared that the Livonians' promise was full of trickery and deceitful designs. The bishop, however, was at last overcome by their

140. Cf. *Rituale Romanum, Ordo Baptismi Adultorum, Orationes, passim.*

importunate begging. He assented especially because of the pleas of the pilgrims and of all the people. He agreed to their request and received them as sons. After giving them peace, he confirmed their promise that henceforth they would be faithful and would pay the annual tithes.

(5) So the Livonians from Dobrel's fort paid the tithes as they had promised and up to now the Lord has preserved them from every attack of the pagans or the Russians. The bishop's Livonians, out of his mercy and great kindness, have hitherto paid a measure instead of the tithe. The Idumeans and the Letts, who did not come to war and who have not violated the sacraments of the faith, annually pay instead of the tithe up to the present day the first measure established by the four bishops. But those of them who came to war, or who sent emissaries, or who were coming but returned while they were still on the way, or who even saddled their horses for that purpose, made satisfaction by giving money to their magistrates.

(6) The Letts from Autine came to Riga bringing a complaint to the bishops against the Brothers of the Militia from Wenden about injuries to their persons and also about their trees [141] which the Brothers had taken. They chose arbitrators and a decision was given. The Letts, after taking an oath, were to receive possession of their bee trees. The Brothers of the Militia, upon their oath, were to obtain the fields, and they were to satisfy the Letts with a sufficient sum of money for the injuries.

(7) King Vladimir went with these Letts to Autine. He stayed with them discharging the office of magistrate until an exchange was made whereby the Brothers of the Militia gave up the fort of Kokenhusen completely to the bishop. The Brothers, in turn, received possession of Autine in compensation for their one-third of Kokenhusen. King Vladimir was named to the magistracy held by his son-in-law, Theodoric, since Theodoric had gone to Germany.

141. Bee trees, i.e., natural beehives, are meant here.

(8) At this time the Lithuanians came to Kokenhusen seeking peace and a road to the Esthonians. Peace was given, as was a road to the still unconverted Esthonians. The Lithuanians came immediately with an army and peacefully crossed the land of the Letts. They entered Saccalia and took many men whom they killed and despoiled of all their possessions. They seized and took the women, children, and livestock away with them, returning by another route to their own land with much booty. The Germans were angry with them, since they had despoiled Saccalia, which was now subject to the bishop. They said in reply (as was true) that the Esthonians still held up their heads and would obey neither the Germans nor the other nations.

[XVII]

(1) In the fifteenth year of his consecration [1213], the bishop of the Livonian church returned to Germany. He appointed in his place the aforementioned venerable Bishop Philip of the church of Ratzeburg. Bishop Philip was most devout in religious matters and in his whole way of life. His eyes and hands were always fixed upon heaven and he scarcely ever relaxed his unconquered spirit from prayer.[142] He greatly illuminated the new church among the heathen with words and examples, by loving the knights, by teaching the clergy, and by encouraging the Livonians and Germans with the great charity of his piety. The church in those days was relieved a little bit from the tribulations of wars. People were, nevertheless, daily frightened within and without by the deceitful trickery of the evil-thinking Livonians and Esthonians, who were ever seeking to do harm to the Germans and to the citizens of Riga.

142. Cf. *Breviarium Romanum, Officio S. Martini Episcopi* (Nov. 11), *Resp. ad Lect. ii, iv.*

(2) The Lithuanians, too, cared nothing for the peace they had made with the Germans. They came up to the Dvina, called out some men from the fort of Kokenhusen, and threw a lance into the Dvina to abrogate their peace and friendship with the Germans. They gathered a large army and crossed the Dvina into the land of the Letts. They despoiled the little villages and killed many people and, coming even to Tricatia, they seized Thalibald, the elder of that province, and his son, Waribule. They crossed the Aa and at the Sedde they found the men in their villages. They seized and killed some of them and then they suddenly retreated with all their loot. Rameke, seeing that they had taken captive his father and brother, rose up with all the Letts. Berthold of Wenden and the Brothers of the Militia were likewise with them and followed after them. As he approached the Lithuanians, Rameke feared that his father would be killed if he attacked them from behind and he led his troops around by another route. The Lithuanians, knowing this, swiftly fled and escaped from them. When, after crossing the Dvina, they approached the boundaries of their own territory, Thalibald escaped from them and, after eating no bread for ten days, he returned joyfully to his homeland.

(3) At that time Daugeruthe, the father of King Vsevolod's [143] wife, went with many gifts to the great king of Novgorod and made a peace treaty with him. On his return, Daugeruthe was captured by the Brothers of the Militia, taken to Wenden, and cast into chains. He was held there for many days until some of his friends from Lithuania could come to him. After that he stabbed himself with a sword.

(4) Meanwhile, Vladimir, the magistrate of the Idumeans and the Letts, reaped many things that he had not sowed,[144] holding court and trying their cases. Since his judgments did not please the bishop of Ratzeburg or anybody else, Vladimir at last gratified the wishes of many people and went to Russia.

143. The Russian king (or grand prince) of Gerzika.
144. Cf. Luke 19:21.

(5) The knights of Kokenhusen and the Letts frequently despoiled the Selones and the Lithuanians at that time. They laid waste their villages and territories, killed some of them, took others captive, frequently ambushed them on the road, and brought many evils upon them. The Lithuanians thereupon collected an army and crossed the Dvina into the province of Lennewarden. They caught the Livonians in their villages, killed some of them, drove the women, children, and flocks away with themselves, and carried off much booty. They also took captive the elder of this province, Uldewene. But Volquin, the master of the Militia of Christ, whose Brothers had come up the Dvina with the merchants, came upon the scene. The master and a few men pursued the Lithuanians, attacked them from the rear, and fought with them. The prince and elder of the Lithuanians fell and was killed, and many men fell with him. The rest who were in the first ranks fled and escaped, taking Uldewene with them. The head of the Lithuanian who was killed was afterwards given for Uldewene's ransom, so that at least when they had received the head they could celebrate the funeral rites for him, according to the pagan custom, with drinking bouts.

(6) In the following winter Vladimir returned to Livonia with his wife and children and his whole household. The Letts and Idumeans received him, though not with much joy. The priests Alabrand and Henry sent him grain and presents and he settled at Metimne, where he gave judgments and collected what he needed from the province. The Lithuanians again crossed the Dvina with their warriors and their prince and leader Stecse was with them. The Germans rejoiced at Stecse's coming. They all assembled, Berthold of Wenden together with his Brothers, and summoned King Vladimir and the other Germans and Letts. They met the Lithuanians, ambushing them on the road, and overran them. They killed the Lithuanian leader, the aforesaid Stecse, and many others. The rest fled to announce the news at home and the church was quiet for a few days.

[XVIII]

(1) In the bishop's sixteenth year [1214], he returned to Livonia with many pilgrims and found the church rejoicing quietly in a little peace and the venerable bishop of Ratzeburg ruling in his place. After disposing of everything that had to be taken care of, Bishop Albert journeyed once again to Germany so that in the following year he could more easily attend the Roman council [145] which had already been announced for two years. He left Bishop Philip in his house and at his expense in Riga. King Vladimir's wife and his whole household were there and everyone helped them in kindly love. (2) Vladimir himself was in Idumea and the land of the Letts, where he collected money and goods by giving judgments in civil affairs. Alabrand, the priest of the Idumeans, came and spoke to him: "It was right, O king," he said, "that you, who have attained the post of judge of men, should give just and true judgments, neither oppressing the poor nor taking their belongings. Nor should you, even more, disturb our converts and make them swerve from the faith of Christ." The king was outraged and threatened Alabrand, saying: "I shall have to take away the riches and wealth of your house, Alabrand." He later did lead the great army of the Russian kings to Alabrand's house and devastated everything, as will be told below.[146] A short time later Vladimir went to Russia with all his household.

(3) Bishop Philip of Ratzeburg after this crossed over to Treiden with the pilgrims and Gerhard the magistrate. He built for the bishop a castle called Vredeland, that is, "pacifying the land," hoping that the district would be made peace-

---

145. The Fourth Lateran Council, which met in Rome in 1215. For Bishop Albert's part in the council, see below, p. 152 (XIX, 7).

146. See below, pp. 169–70 (XXII, 4).

ful by this fort and that it would be a refuge for the priests and all his men. The sons of Thalibald, Rameke and his brothers from Tholowa, came to him there to put themselves in the bishop's power. They promised to change over from the Christian faith as they had received it from the Russians to the Latin use, and they also promised to pay one measure of grain annually for each two horses, because they were protected by the bishop in peacetime as well as in war, were of one heart and spirit with the Germans, and rejoiced in the Germans' defense against the Esthonians and the Lithuanians. The bishop received them joyfully and sent his priest, who was near the Sedde, back with them to administer the sacraments of the faith to them and to initiate them into Christian discipline.

(4) Meanwhile the knights of Kokenhusen, Meinhard, John, Jordan, and others, complained about King Vsevolod of Gerzika, since he had not come to the presence of his father, the bishop, now for many years after he had received his kingdom from the bishop.[147] Rather, he was always giving aid and counsel to the Lithuanians. They summoned him many times and invited him to make satisfaction. He disdained them, he did not come, and he sent no reply. The knights, after first asking permission from the bishop, gathered together their servants and the Letts and went up alongside the Dvina with all their servants. As they approached the fort of Gerzika, they took a Russian whom they bound and carried with them by night to the fort. He mounted the ramparts first and spoke to the watchman, as he had been ordered, and the others followed him, one by one. The watchman thought that they were citizens who had been away and who were returning. Each of them went up until at last all held the strong point of the fortification. They gathered together and guarded the fort on all sides and allowed none of the Russians to leave the fort until they could see the light of day. When it was light they descended into the fort and seized everything that was

147. See above, pp. 92–93 (XIII, 4).

there. They took many men and allowed others to escape by fleeing. Taking much loot and leaving the fort, they returned to their own people and divided among themselves the booty they had carried off.

(5) This was the third year and the peace with the Esthonians came to an end. The bishop summoned all the priests and, holding a chapter to take counsel with them, likewise summoning the knights and the Livonian elders, he deliberated over making an expedition into Esthonia, since the Esthonians had not come and did not take steps to renew the peace, but rather were always seeking to destroy the Livonian church. The bishop sent to all the forts of the Letts and Livonians and gathered a large and strong army from every region of the Dvina and the Aa. There were in Riga many pilgrims and merchants, all of whom gladly went out with the master of the Militia and his Brothers. The army was ordered to assemble at Coiwemunde. The bishop came there with his men. Some of the Livonians wished to turn the army against Kurland, but the time had not yet come when God wished to take mercy upon those people.[148]

When the bishop had given his blessings he returned to Riga. The army marched to the Sallatse and came into the province called Sontagana. The Germans remembered their words and the peace which they had formerly given to the people of these provinces.[149] They crossed the province peacefully and did the people no harm, neither routing men from their houses nor pursuing them when they fled. They went on their way with all gentleness until they came to the other provinces which had never arranged to make peace with the Rigans, since they thought that their regions were so remote that the Rigans could not come there with an army. About three thousand of our men were Germans and there was an equal number of Letts and Livonians. They went over the ice of the sea, bypassing Sallatse, until they came to the place they

148. Cf. Ps. 101:14.
149. See above, pp. 106-7 (XV, 1).

wanted, namely Rotalia. When they came there the army spread out into all the roads and villages. They found all the men, women, and children, and everyone, large and small, in the villages, for they had not been forewarned of the army's approach by any rumors. In their wrath the soldiers struck them and killed all the men. Both the Livonians and Letts, who are more cruel than the other nations, like the servant in the gospel,[150] did not know how to show mercy. They killed countless people and slaughtered some of the women and children. They wished to spare no one in the fields or in the villages. They stained the streets and every spot with the blood of the pagans. They pursued them into all the provinces on the seashore round about, which are called Rotelewic and Rotalia. The Letts and some others also pursued some of them who fled on to the ice of the sea. They immediately killed those whom they took and carried off their belongings and everything. The sons of Thalibald seized three Livonian silver talents, as well as clothing, horses, and much loot and they brought it all back to Beverin. The whole army likewise followed the fleeing Esthonians everywhere on the first, second, and third days. They killed the Esthonians here and there until both they and their horses were worn out. Then finally, on the fourth day, they all assembled in one place with all their loot. They drove along the horses and many flocks and brought the women, children, and much booty with them. They returned to Livonia with great joy, blessing the Lord for the vengeance they had wrought upon the heathen. The Esthonians were confounded and did much weeping and wailing. Esthonia, too, wept for her sons and could not be comforted, for they were lost, both here and in the future life,[151] and especially she sorrowed because of the multitude of those who had been slaughtered, of whom there was no count.

150. Cf. Matt. 18:23 ff.
151. Cf. Matt. 2:18.

(6) After this, during Lent,[152] there was a great fire in the city of Riga in the dead of the night.[153] The first section of the city took fire, the part, that is, that was built first and was first enclosed by the wall, from Blessed Mary's church (which burned down with the great bells) up to the bishop's house and the nearby houses up to the church of the Brothers of the Militia. The people were especially sad at the loss of the sweet-sounding war bell [154] and at the damage done in the city. Another bell, larger than the first one, was cast.

(7) When they had rested from their exhaustion after the expedition and both they and their horses had renewed their strength, they decreed another expedition during Lent. The Rigans went with the Brothers of the Militia and they summoned the Livonians and Letts to come with them. They went into Saccalia, leaving the fort of Fellin behind. They despoiled the whole land round about until they assembled, on the spur of the moment, at the fort of Lembit, which is called Leole. The Esthonians who were in the fort boldly marched out against the advance parties. The invaders were somewhat dismayed, but gathered in a single group and awaited the arrival of their men. On the following day and the third day the army attacked the fort. They piled a heap of wood on the palisade and set it afire. They burned the palisade, which was made of earth and wood, and as the fire gradually went up it approached the higher ramparts. Those who were in the fort, seeing the palisade consumed by the fire and fearing that by this means the fort would be taken, promised money if the army would leave the fort. The Germans, however, stated that they wanted nothing from the Esthonians, save that they be baptized, and, being reconciled to the true

---

152. 1215. Lent began in that year on March 4 and ended on Easter Sunday, April 19.

153. . . . *intempeste noctis silencio.* . . . Cf. III Kings 3:20.

154. This is presumably the bell referred to earlier, p. 97 (XIV, 5), which was rung as a tocsin in time of war. The other bells which were destroyed probably included some of the bells taken from Gerzika, p. 91 (XIII, 4).

Peacemaker, become their brothers, in this world and in the world to come. The Esthonians loathed that prospect and feared to deliver themselves into the Germans' hands. The Livonians and Letts and the whole army built up the fire and threatened them with death and cremation. The Esthonians, now that the palisade was consumed, feared that they would be killed and humbly begged for quarter. They left the fort and promised to be baptized. The priests John Stric and Otto, the priest of the Brothers of the Militia, were there. The most treacherous man, Lembit, was baptized, as were all the others, men, women, and children, who were in the fort. They promised that they would always keep the Christian law faithfully. This promise, however, they later violated with their treacherous devices. The army, meanwhile, entered the fort and seized all the goods. They brought out the horses and cattle and all the flocks and took much loot, which they divided among themselves. They returned joyfully to Livonia, bringing with them the elders of the fort, Lembit with the others. After giving their sons as hostages, the elders were allowed to return to their own land. Everyone blessed the Lord, Who had miraculously delivered the fort into their hands without the use of ballistas or machines, and Christ's name went even into other provinces.

(8) A certain priest of the Cistercian order, Frederick of Selle, whom the bishop, by the authority of the lord pope, had brought for the work of the gospel, was in the fort of Vredeland. On Palm Sunday [April 12] he celebrated the mystery of the Lord's passion with many tears and he ministered to those who were present a word of exhortation [155] about the Lord's cross, with sweet warnings. After celebrating the solemnity of the Lord's resurrection [April 19], he wished to go down to Riga by ship with his scholar and some others. Encountering him at the mouth of the river, the

---

155. . . . *exhortationis verbum.* . . . Cf. Pope Gregory I, *Hom. 17 in Evangelio,* cited in *Breviarium Romanum, Officium Commune Evangelistarum, Lect. viii.*

Oeselians rushed upon him and captured him and his boy and some of the Livonians. They took him away in their pirate ships, and going up on the bank of the Adia River they there tortured him with various torments.[156] For while intent upon heaven, he and his scholar poured forth praise and thanksgiving in their prayers to the Lord, the Oeselians jeered and struck both on the head and the back with their clubs, saying: *Laula! Laula! Pappi*,[157] even as it is written, "The wicked have worked upon my back. But the Lord, Who is just, will cut their necks," [158] as will be told below. Afterwards the Oeselians sharpening hard, dry wood, inserted it between the nails and the flesh and tormented every member with the points. They set the wood afire and tortured them cruelly. At last they killed them by hacking with their axes between their shoulders. Beyond any doubt they sent their souls to heaven to the company of the martyrs, while casting aside their bodies as it is written: "The flesh of Thy saints for the beasts of the earth. They have poured out their blood as water, roundabout Jerusalem, and there was none to bury the dead." [159] The Livonians they took with them to Oesel as captives; these, after their return, reported the foregoing to us.

(9) Meinhard of Kokenhusen and his fellow soldiers again collected an army to fight King Vsevolod of Gerzika. Vsevolod heard of this and sent messengers to the Lithuanians, who came and awaited the army on the other side of the Dvina. Those who were with Meinhard did not know about them, but came and seized Gerzika and took a great deal of loot and horses and livestock. The Lithuanians appeared on the opposite bank of the Dvina and asked them to send over ships, so that they could come and renew the peace. The simple men put too much faith in their fraudulent words and sent the ships to them. The Lithuanians crossed over at once and, as

156. . . . *diversis* . . . *tormentis cruciaverunt*. Cf. the Martyrology, Jan. 1 (Migne, *P.L.*, CXXIII, 601–2).
157. That is, "Sing, sing, priest."
158. Ps. 128:3–4.
159. Ps. 78:2, 3.

some brought others across, more and more of them followed. At last the whole army threw itself into the Dvina and began swimming towards the Germans. The knights saw the large size of the Lithuanian army and feared to stay and fight with them. Some of the Germans descended the Dvina in a ship and returned safely to Kokenhusen. The others, with the Letts, were attacked by the Lithuanians from the rear as they were returning by the road. The Letts saw the paucity of their numbers and turned to flight. The knights, Meinhard, John, and Jordan, fought but were unable to resist such an army and at last fell, killed by them. The bishop and the Rigans heard this and mourned for them, saying: "How are the valiant fallen in battle and the weapons of war perished." [160]

[XIX]

~~~ (1) In Bishop Albert's seventeenth year [1215], war was renewed in all parts of Livonia. After the expedition to Rotalia and the subjugation of Lembit of Saccalia, all of Esthonia began to rage against [161] Livonia. The Esthonians planned to come with three armies simultaneously and to destroy Livonia. The Oeselians were to besiege Riga and to shut off the port on the Dvina. The Rotalians were to attack the Livonians of Treiden. The Saccalians and Ungannians were, meanwhile, to devastate the territories of the Letts, so that the Livonians and Letts would be hindered by their own wars and would not be able to come to the aid of the Rigans.

(2) The Oeselians came with a great naval force to Dünamünde, bringing pirate ships and brigantines with them. These they filled with rocks and sank in the depths of the

160. II Kings 1:25-27.
161. . . . *tota Esthonia sevire cepit.* . . . Cf. Esther 14:11; also Vergil, *Aeneid,* X, 569, and *Georgics,* I, 511.

sea at the entrance of the river. They built wooden structures which they similarly filled with rocks and they cast these into the mouth of the Dvina to close the route and the harbor to anyone who was coming. Some of them in their brigantines went up to the city and, rowing here and there, they finally took the coast and the plain. The Brothers of the Militia with the other men of the city stood at the gate. Some of the servants and Livonians, seeing the enemy on the plains, suddenly rushed upon them and, slaying some, pursued them to the ships. When they were fleeing, one of their pirate ships was struck and sank with everyone aboard. The others escaped and returned to their men at Dünamünde.

The Rigans rose up with all the men they could muster and went down, some by ship and others by land, after the Oeselians. When the Oeselians saw them, they turned away and went to another region of the Dvina, not waiting to fight with them. The Rigans peered out into the distance and suddenly they saw two cogs coming. In them were Count Burchard of Aldenborch and Rothmar and Theodoric, the brothers of the bishop. When they approached the Dvina, the men in the ships saw the enemy around them on one side of the sea shore and the Rigans on the other shore, but they did not know which were the Christians. The Rigans, however, gave them a sign by showing their banner. As soon as they recognized them and at the same time realized the size of the enemy force, they turned their ships toward the enemy and sped toward them. Some of the Rigans were out on the Dvina in their own ships, following the enemy, while the others awaited the outcome on the shore. The enemy saw that they were surrounded by Christian armies on every side and sped quickly to their ships, in which they scattered over the sea through the midst of the Christians and vanished from their eyes. The Rigans followed them and took some ships from them and the rest escaped. The Rigans received the pilgrims with joy and blessed the Lord, Who had comforted His people in this present tribulation. The waters of the river wishing

to have their strong course free and likewise the sea, in the
violence of its storms, afterwards broke up the objects which
the Oeselians had put out in the depths. The Germans also
destroyed what remained by dragging it out and so they restored a free route to all who wished to enter the Dvina.

(3) While the Oeselians were still on the Dvina, the
Rotalians gathered an army from their maritime provinces
and entered Livonia. They despoiled and burned villages in
Metsepole, but they could find none of the Livonians, for the
latter had all fled with their women and children to the forts.
The Livonians gathered an assembly of their men to meet the
enemy. The Rotalians heard of their intention and, at the
same time, of the flight of their friends the Oeselians from the
Dvina. They, too, fled and returned to their own land.

Meanwhile, the Saccalians and the Ungannians had also
come into the land of the Letts with a great army. They besieged the fort of Autine, and the Brothers of the Militia, wishing to fight with them, left Wenden. When the Saccalians
and Ungannians got word of this, they, too, fled. They came
to Tricatia toward evening and found that Thalibald had
come back from the hiding places of the forest for a bath.
They seized him and cruelly burned him, still alive, before a
fire, threatening to kill him unless he would show them all of
his money. He showed them fifty *oseringi*, but, nevertheless,
they burned him. He said: ."If I were to show you all my
money and all my sons' money, you would burn me nonetheless," and he would show them no more. They put him
again into the fire, therefore, and roasted him like a fish, until
he gave up the spirit and died. Since he was a Christian and
one of the number of faithful Letts, we hope that his soul is
gladly rejoicing for such a martyrdom in eternal happiness in
the company of the holy martyrs. The Esthonians returned to
their own land and the Lord reduced their plan to nothing.
Then Rameke and Drivinalde, the sons of Thalibald, seeing
that their father was dead, were greatly angered at the Esthonians. They and their friends and relatives collected an army of

Letts, and the Brothers of the Militia from Wenden and other Germans went with them. They entered Ungannia, despoiled all the villages, and delivered them to the flames. They burned alive all the men they could capture in revenge for Thalibald. They burned down all the forts, so that they would have no refuge in them. They sought out the Ungannians in the dark hiding places of the forests and the Ungannians could hide from them nowhere. They took them out of the forests and killed them and took the women and children away as captives. They drove off the horses and flocks, took many spoils, and returned to their own land. As they returned, other Letts again met them on the road and they marched into Ungannia. What the former had neglected, the latter performed. For these men went to the villages and provinces to which the others had not come and whoever had escaped from the earlier men could not escape from these. They seized many people, killed all the men, and dragged away the women and children as captives. They took away with them the flocks and much loot. As they returned, again they met other Letts on the road, prepared for an expedition into Ungannia; they, too, wished to take booty. They also sought to kill men in revenge for their parents and relatives who had earlier been killed by the Esthonians. They proceeded into Ungannia, which they despoiled no less than the former army had and they took no fewer captives than the earlier ones had. They seized the people who were coming out of the forests to their fields or villages for food. Some they burned, while they cut the throats of others. They inflicted various tortures upon them,[162] until the Esthonians showed them all their money and until they led them to all the hiding places of the woods and delivered the women and children into their hands. But even so the hatred of the Letts was not slaked. After carrying off the money and all the possessions, the women and children, at last they took life, too, the only thing left. They crossed all

---

162. . . . *diversis tormentis afficiunt.* . . . Cf. the Martyrology, *s.d.* Jan. 1 (Migne, *P.L.,* CXXIII, 601–2.

of the provinces up to the Mother of Waters at Dorpat and spared no one. They killed all of the males, took the women and children captive, and took revenge upon their enemies. Then they joyfully returned to their homes with all their loot. Likewise Berthold of Wenden with his men, Theodoric the bishop's brother with his knights and servants, and the sons of Thalibald with their Letts gathered together. They went with an army into Ungannia and seized many of the Esthonians, who had earlier escaped from the Letts, and killed them. They burned the villages which remained and whatever had been done incompletely by the first groups was carefully completed by them. They went around through all the provinces and, crossing the Mother of Waters, they went up to Waiga. They ravaged and burned the villages no less in the land across the river. They killed the men, took the women and children, and after doing all the harm they could,[163] they returned to Livonia. They arranged for still other men to return immediately to Ungannia and to do similar harm to the Ungannians and when they came back they sent still others in turn. The Letts did not stop nor did they allow the Esthonians in Ungannia to rest. They did not have any rest themselves, until during that same summer, devastating the land with nine armies, they made it so deserted and desolate that now neither men nor food were found there. Their aim was to fight long enough so that either those who were left would come to seek peace and baptism or they would be completely wiped out from the earth.[164] It came to pass that by now the sons, in order to avenge their father, had killed over a hundred men, either by burning them alive or by various other tortures. These were in addition to the innumerable others

---

163. . . . *peractis omnibus malis, que potuerunt.* . . . Cf. I Macc. 7:23.

164. Cf. the dictum of St. Bernard of Clairvaux when preaching the Crusade against the Slavs in 1147: "They shall be either converted or wiped out."—*The Letters of St. Bernard,* trans. Bruno Scott James (London 1953), p. 467.

whom each of the Letts, Germans, and Livonians had slaughtered.

(4) The people who still remained in Ungannia, seeing that they could in no way escape from the fury of the Germans and Letts, sent messengers to Riga to ask for peace terms. They were told that they must restore goods once stolen from the merchants. But they said that those who had stolen the goods had been killed by the Letts and they maintained that there was no way in which they could make restitution. When all these matters were settled, they asked to be baptized, so that they could get a true peace and perpetual brotherly friendship with the Germans and Letts. The Germans rejoiced and confirmed the peace with them and promised to send priests to baptize Ungannia. The Saccalians, hearing of all the harm that had been done to the Ungannians, feared that something similar might befall them. They sent and asked that priests be sent to them so that when baptism had been administered in their province they might become friends of the Christians. Priests were sent: Peter Kakuwalde [165] from Finland and Otto, the priest of the Brothers of the Militia. They went into Saccalia and administered baptism up to the Pala River and in Ungannia up to the Mother of Waters. When this was done they returned to Livonia, for they were not yet able to live in those parts because of the hostility of the other Esthonians.

(5) The bishop of Ratzeburg and Bishop Theodoric of Esthonia hurried to the Roman council. They embarked by sea with the pilgrims who were going to Germany and sailed to Gothland with nine cogs. On the following night there was a contrary wind and thunder and they suffered a great storm through the whole day. At last they were forced into the new port on Oesel. When the Oeselians learned that they came from Riga, they threatened them with war. They sent throughout Oesel and gathered a large naval force. Others of

165. *Kaikkiwalta* in Finnish means "Almighty."

them came on horseback and built structures of wood on the seashore. These they filled with rocks, seeking to block off the harbor, whose entrance was narrow, so that when the port was closed off, they might capture the Germans and kill them. The Germans, who were unaware that the army was on the shore nearby, went off to shore in their skiffs, or small boats, and reaped the crops with their swords. They did the same on another shore each day. The Oeselians set an ambush and at last they caught eight of the Germans, some of whom they killed, and took the others captive, and they seized one skiff. They were too greatly encouraged by this, for they sent to all the provinces of Esthonia to say that they had captured the bishop of Riga and his whole army. All of the Esthonians came with a large army. At the first light of dawn the sea opposite us looked black with their pirate ships and they fought against us throughout the day. Some of them brought out the wooden structures and their old brigantines, which they filled with rocks and sent to the bottom, and so they closed off the entrance of the port to us. We were greatly frightened at this and thought that we could not escape their clutches. Some of them launched three big fires, kindled from dry wood and animal fat, and set upon structures made of huge trees. The first fire, which burned more fiercely than the others, was impelled over the sea toward us and a strong south wind gave it a big push and thrust it upon us. The Esthonians circled around the fire in their pirate ships and kept it going. They steered it straight toward the midst of our ships. Our ships were all gathered together, so that we could defend ourselves more easily from the enemy, so we feared all the more that we could not escape the fire. When the flames of this fire, which was taller than all of the ships, reached out toward us, we called the bishop from his cabin, where he was praying day and night. He came and saw that there was no counsel or help for us save in God. He raised his eyes and both hands to heaven and prayed to be saved from the present fire. We all watched, and suddenly the wind changed from south to east. The east wind turned the weathervane on the sails around and took the fire away from us. It gently forced the fire around the ships and behind us out to sea. And we all blessed the Lord, for He had visibly freed us from this present fire. The Esths launched the second and third fires and we worked for a long time fighting them and pouring water on them and at last the wind also removed them from us.

Other Esthonians, meanwhile, were rowing around us and they wounded many of our men with their lances and arrows. Still others returned, took the same route around us, and threw their stones and staves at us. Our people were afraid, both because of the fact that the harbor was closed and because of the mishaps of war.[166] Our skipper, Albert Sluc, said: "If you will be patient and obedient, the Lord will free us from these present dangers.[167] For," said he, "our ships are light and are not heavily loaded and scant depth is enough for us. We can get out by another channel if you strong armed men will get into the skiffs and take the anchors and throw them overboard. You will then return to us again through the midst of the enemy and the rest will follow, pulling the ships along by the ropes attached to the anchors, until we come to the deep sea." We all obeyed and pulled until, after passing the difficulties, we came into the great open sea. The knights and servants who had taken the anchors out in the skiffs had suffered a very severe attack and they were gravely wounded by lances, arrows, and stone missiles. At last they took with them an iron hook, or grappling iron, which they might throw into one of the pirate ships and so catch it. Throwing it into one of the ships, they thought they could drag it alongside, but the Esthonians rowed violently away and headed toward the other pirate ships. Since the

---

166. See n.113.

167. . . . *liberabit nos Dominus a periculis presentibus.* Cf. *Missale Romanum, Missa in Ascensione Domini, Secreta.*

bishop at this very moment was praying to the Blessed Virgin:
"Show Thyself a mother, show Thyself a mother," [168] She did
indeed show Herself a mother. For, as that pirate ship, which
was large and full of men, fled, it ran with great violence into
another one. It split down the middle with a great noise and
filled with water. The men fell into the sea and drowned and
all of the others were confounded. Seeing that we had now
reached the deep ocean, the Esthonians gathered on the seashore. There were many thousands of them, both cavalry and
infantry, who had come from all parts of Esthonia, and there
were about two hundred pirate ships. They raged violently
at one another with a good deal of noise and blows too, since
they had gained nothing from two weeks of work and had
lost many of their men who had drowned in the sea, and more
who had been killed by our ballistarii. They raised their sails
and dispersed on the sea and each of them went away by his
own route. Our men followed after them in the skiffs and took
from them a large pirate ship, which they brought along to
Gothland. The Blessed Virgin freed us that day, as She has
freed the Livonians from all their troubles up to the present
day.

(6) After the Lord had liberated us from the Oeselians, we
stayed in that port for three full weeks, during daily storms
at sea, sudden squalls, and contrary winds. There was a great
famine and food shortage. The bishop gave away everything he had in charity and we were making vows and praying
daily that the Lord would set us free from that place. And
on the vigil of Mary Magdalene [July 21], when we, who
were barely half alive, were chanting the responses, it came
to pass that the south wind began to blow, all the contrary
winds stopped, and the Lord gave us a favorable wind. We
raised our sails and on the following morning [July 22] we

168. From the Breviary hymn *Ave Maris Stella,* sung at vespers on the
feasts of the Virgin. The scene described here probably took place on
Thursday, July 2, the feast of the Visitation of the Blessed Virgin Mary,
when this hymn would appropriately have been sung in the office.

came to Gothland. The bishop stood at the altar stone and gave thanks to the Lord, saying: "Our way led through fire and water, O Lord, yet in the end Thou has granted us relief.[169] Yes, Lord, Thou hast put us to the proof, tested us as men test silver in the fire; led us into a snare, and bowed our backs with trouble, while human masters rode us down.[170] Thou hast freed us, O Lord, from all our perils [171] and hast led us back to this firm rock." [172] The bishop greatly desired to come to the rock, which is Christ.[173] He abstained from the solemnities of the Mass only with many groans while he was at sea, though he took communion every other day between Sunday services. The Lord fulfilled his wish at last and sent him on that journey to Verona where, when he was seized by a mild illness, he commended his spirit to the Lord [Nov. 14 or 15]. His body was buried, in a marble tomb that had once belonged to some cardinal, in a monastery of the Augustinian order which is above a river. A citizen of Verona saw in a vision a column gleaming like a flash of lightning, which came across the Alps and settled itself to rest there. Others testified that they had seen similar angelic visions at his tomb. This is no wonder, for he was a steadfast, constant man who could not be budged from his longing for Christ, either in prosperity or in adversity. Nor would he ever let his order of silence be broken until after Matins and Prime, not even when Riga was once in flames and everything burned up and he was routed from his house, nor again when he was in the midst of the enemy at sea, nor on a third occasion when he was seriously injured by a watchman while he was saying his prayers on the wall at night. God, therefore, gave him the firm and stable place he desired upon the rock. His soul is with Christ and may his memory remain as a blessing!

169. Ps. 65:12.
170. Ps. 65:10, 11.
171. Cf. *Rituale Romanum, Ordo Commendationis Animae.*
172. Cf. *Breviaruim Romanum, Officium in Octava Dedicationis Ecclesiae, Resp. ad Lect. v.*
173. Cf. I Cor. 10:4.

(7) In the year of the Lord's incarnation 1215, a council was celebrated [Nov. 11–30] in the Roman church with Pope Innocent presiding in the presence of four hundred patriarchs, cardinals, and bishops and eight hundred abbots. Bishop Albert of Livonia and the bishop of Esthonia were among them. The bishop reported the troubles, the wars, and the affairs of the Livonian church to the supreme pontiff and to all the bishops. They all rejoiced together over the conversion of the heathen and likewise over the wars and the manifold triumphs of the Christians.

The bishop spoke: "Holy Father," he said, "as you have not ceased to cherish the Holy Land of Jerusalem, the country of the Son, with your Holiness' care, so also you ought not abandon Livonia, the land of the Mother, which has hitherto been among the pagans and far from the cares of your consolation and is now again desolate. For the Son loves His Mother and, as He would not care to lose His own land, so, too, He would not care to endanger His Mother's land."

The supreme pontiff replied and said: "We shall always be careful to help with the paternal solicitude of our zeal the land of the Mother even as the land of the Son."

When the council was finished, the pope sent them back joyfully, having renewed their authority to preach and to enlist, for the remission of their sins, pilgrims who would go to Livonia with them to secure the new church against the assaults of the pagans. Rome makes laws, while Riga irrigates the nations. Peter Kakuwalde and Otto the priest had, meanwhile, been sent from Riga to moisten Saccalia and Ungannia from the holy font and to invite them to life everlasting.[174]

(8) The Rotalians, indeed, were still in revolt and still refused to accept the Christian laws. An expedition was sent against them. When the feast of the Lord's Nativity had passed, the Livonians and Letts were warned to be prepared

---

174. Henry again puns on the words *Riga* and *rigo: Roma dictat iura, Riga vero rigat gentes. Nam Petrus Kakuwalde et Otto sacerdos, a Riga missi, Saccalam et Ugauniam interim sacro fonte rigantes ad vitam eternam.*

to assemble in order to set out against the enemies of the
Christian name. The Germans and the Brothers of the Militia
joined them. Count Burchard and the pilgrims were also
there and as they all went together over the ice they came to
the first province of Esthonia [1216]. They divided the army
and pursued the fleeing Esthonians among all the roads and
villages. They killed those whom they caught and seized the
women, children, and flocks. They gathered at the fort of
Sontagana, besieged the Esthonians in it, and fought with
them for nine days. They put up a wooden tower and brought
it up close to the fort. The Livonians and Letts climbed up
on it together with the ballistarii and they killed many of the
Esthonians on top of the wall with lances and arrows. They
also wounded many and drove them from the defenses. Since
the Esthonians were extremely bold about leaping into the
fray, as if to give more scope to the ballistarii, they had many
wounded and many killed. At length, after many men were
killed and because of a shortage of food and water, they gave
up and sought peace. The Germans, however, said: "If you
are willing to put down your treacherous weapons and receive the true peace, which is Christ, in your fort, we will
gladly pardon you and receive you in the love of our brotherhood." When they heard this, they joyfully promised to receive the sacrament of baptism and the full law of Christianity.
On the eleventh day, therefore, Godfrid the priest was sent
to them in the fort. He blessed them and said: "Will you
renounce idolatry and believe in the one God of the Christians?" They all replied: "We will." He poured the water
and said: "Be ye therefore all baptized in the name of the
Father and of the Son and of the Holy Spirit." [175] When these
matters were completed, peace was given and, having received the sons of the elders as hostages, the army returned to
Livonia with all the loot, spoils, and captives. They blessed
God for the conversion of the heathen, Him Who is blessed
for ever.

175. Cf. *Rituale Romanum, Ordo Baptismi Adultorum.*

(9) After a pause of a few days, when they had regained their strength, the Rigans, Livonians, and Letts again gathered and, going over the ice of the sea, which was very firmly frozen because of the continued bitter cold, turned their army toward Oesel. Finding that the sea road was best, they divided their army and went around through all the roads and villages. They took many people, killed all the men, and led the women, children, and flocks away with them. They gathered at one of the forts and, fighting with those who were in it, killed and wounded some of them. Because the cold was too intense, they did not attempt to reduce the fort, but returned by their road on the ice with all their loot and captives. When some shouted that an army [176] was following and others ran hurriedly to the fire, certain ones of them failed and fell, frozen by the cold, and died. The others returned safe and sound.

(10) After the solemnity of the Lord's Resurrection [April 10] had passed, the Esthonians sent to King Vladimir of Polozk to come with a numerous army and besiege Riga. They promised that they would meanwhile hold down the Livonians and Letts with wars and that they would likewise close the port of Dünemünde. The advice of the traitors pleased the king, who was always seeking to ruin the Livonian church. He sent to Russia and Lithuania and gathered a great army of Russians and Lithuanians. After they had all gathered and were all prepared, as the king was about to enter his ship to go with them, all at once he fell down and expired, and died a sudden and unforeseen death.[177] His whole army dispersed and the men returned to their own lands.

(11) The members of the bishop's household and the Brothers of the Militia who were in Riga heard of the Esthonians' design and bought a cog and strengthened it all about, like a fort. They put fifty men in it with ballistas and armor

176. The chronicler here uses the Livonian word *malewa*.
177. . . . *mortuus est morte subitanea et improvisa*. . . . Cf. *Rituale Romanum, Litaniae Sanctorum*.

and they stationed it at the mouth of the Dvina River to guard the entrance of the harbor, lest the Oeselians come and block it up as before. Word came to the Oeselians that the king was dead and they also heard that ballistarii and armed men were guarding the Dvina harbor. They entered the Salis River and went up to Lake Astegerwe, where they despoiled the villages of the Letts, seizing the women and killing the men. Some of the Letts assembled and followed them, taking and killing some, and chasing the others to the boats. The church, which was awaiting the arrival of its bishop, was quiet for a few days.

[XX]

ᘏᘏ (1) It was the bishop's eighteenth year [1216]. He returned from the Roman court and was encouraged by King Frederick at Hagenau.[178] He returned to Livonia with Bishop Theodoric of Esthonia and with other faithful men, knights, and pilgrims. At Dünamünde he found his men guarding the port and they reported to him about their expeditions into Esthonia as well as about the death of the king and how they had been consoled in all their tribulations.[179] There was joy in the church, both over the arrival of the bishop and over the liberation from the Russians and other nations.

(2) After this the bishops met with the Brothers of the Militia to make a certain division of Esthonia; but, since the division did not last, I have thought it useless to describe it. Let me rather say that the Rigans, Livonians, and Letts assembled again with Master Volquin and his Brothers and the pilgrims, Theodoric and the bishop's men also, and went with the army, though peacefully, into Saccalia, which was now baptized. They summoned the elders of that province and,

178. Frederick II was at Hagenau in January and March of this year.
179. Cf. II Cor. 1:4.

upon their advice, they went on to the other Esthonians, the elders serving as guides. On the day of the Blessed Virgin's Assumption [Aug. 15], they entered the province of Harrien, which is in the midst of Esthonia. There every year all the people round about were accustomed to assemble at Raela to make decisions. When we arrived there, we divided our army among all the roads, villages, and provinces of that land. We burned and devastated everything, killed all the males, captured the women and children, and drove off their horses and many flocks. We assembled at last at the big village of Loal, which is on a stream in the midst of the land. Resting there for three days, we laid waste all the land round about and got up to the villages of the Revalians. On the fourth day they placed an ambush near a village, but nine of them were captured and some killed. The army returned with a great deal of loot and they brought back innumerable cattle and sheep. The Esthonians followed with a great army [180] and wished to attack them from behind, but the lots of their gods fell out otherwise. The Rigans returned with joy to Livonia and in brotherly love divided everything that they brought back.

(3) After this the Russians of Pskov were enraged with the Ungannians because they had accepted the baptism of the Latins and had refused theirs. The Russians threatened them with war and demanded taxes and tribute from them. The Ungannians consulted the Livonian bishop and the Brothers of the Militia about this and sought help in this matter. They did not refuse the Ungannians, but promised to live and die together with them and they assured them that as they had always been free of the Russians before their baptism, so they would be now. When the great King Vladimir of Pskov died there arose a new adversary of the Livonian church, Vladimir, who rose up with a large army of Russians from Pskov and came into Ungannia. He encamped at Mount Odenpäh and sent his army through all the villages and provinces round about. They burned and despoiled the land, killed many men,

180. The Livonian word *malewa* is again used here.

and took the women and children captive. A certain German, Isfrid the merchant, was there and, after losing everything, he fled to Riga and announced the news there. (4) The Rigan elders then met with the bishops and the Brothers of the Militia. Considering that a big war with the Russians was threatening, they made a certain division of the Esthonian provinces that had been subjugated and baptized by the Livonian church. They decided that one-third of all the tribute and profit which came from Esthonia should go to the Livonian church and the bishop of Riga, so that, as they had taken part in the labors and wars, they should also partake in the consolation. They decided that another third was to go to the bishop of Esthonia and the last third to the Brothers of the Militia for their labors and expense.

(5) The Ungannians again came to the bishops, seeking help against the Russians. The bishops sent their men with the Brothers of the Militia into Ungannia. They summoned all the Esthonians from their provinces and they settled on Mount Odenpäh, where they built and fortified a very strong fortress against both the Russians and the other peoples who were as yet unbaptized. The Russians came, as was their custom, into the lands of the Tholowa Letts to collect their levy. When they had collected it, they burned down Fort Beverin. Berthold, the master of the Militia at Wenden, saw that they were preparing for war, since they were burning down the forts of the Letts. He sent and took them and cast them into prison. When emissaries from the king of Novgorod came, however, he released the prisoners and sent them back with honor to Russia. The Ungannians, indeed, wished to avenge themselves on the Russians. They rose up with the bishop's men and the Brothers of the Militia and went into Russia toward Novgorod. They found that the land had not been secured by any forewarnings. On the feast of the Epiphany [Jan. 6, 1217], when the Russians are accustomed to occupy themselves more with their feasting and drinking, they divided their army among all the roads and villages. They killed many

people, took captive a great many women, and drove off many horses and flocks. They took much loot and, having avenged their injuries with fire and the sword, they returned rejoicing to Odenpäh with all the loot.

(6) After the feast of the Epiphany the Rigans sent to all the Livonians and Letts and they gathered a great army and went into Saccalia. They took the elders of that province as their guides, and the Ungannians came to them with their Germans, and they marched into Jerwan. They divided up their army among all the villages and provinces of that region and struck the land a great blow.[181] They spent six days in the village of Carethen, burning and devastating everything round about. The stronger horsemen went into Wierland and devastated that land in like fashion, killing the men and capturing the women and children. They returned with many spoils to Carethen. There the Jerwanian elders of that province came to them seeking peace, and that the army would leave their territory. They said to the elders: "If you wish a true peace, it will be necessary that you be made sons of the true Peacemaker, who is Christ, so that, after receiving His baptism, you may attain our eternal friendship." The Jerwanians rejoiced at hearing this and in order to achieve peace with the Rigans they promised both to uphold their baptism and to pay a levy to the Rigans forever. Some of them, accordingly, we baptized there and, after taking their sons as hostages, we returned to Livonia with all our loot, praising God for the conversion of that nation.

(7) After the Livonian army returned from Jerwan, the people of Novgorod at once assembled a great army of Russians during Lent [Feb.]. King Vladimir of Pskov and his subjects went with them and they sent messengers throughout all of Esthonia to ask the Esthonians to come to besiege the Germans and Ungannians at Odenpäh. Not only did the Oeselians and the people of Harrien come, but even the Saccalians, who had already been baptized. The latter hoped

181. Cf. Num. 11:33.

thereby to throw off both the yoke of the Germans and their baptism. They went to meet the Russians and with them they laid siege to the fort of Odenpäh. They fought against the Germans and those who were with them for seventeen days and they could not harm them, since the fort was extremely strong. The bishop's archers, who were in the fort, and the Brothers of the Militia wounded and killed many of the Russians with their ballistas. The Russians with their bows and arrows likewise wounded some of the men from the fort. The Russians went around through the provinces, captured many people, killed them, and threw their bodies into the water, which was at the foot of the mountain, so that the men in the castle could not use the water. They did all the harm they could, laying waste and burning everything in the land round about. When eventually, according to their usual methods, they tried to take the fortification on the mountain with their whole force, they were strongly repulsed by the Germans and Esthonians. They suffered thereby many casualties among their men. The bishops and the Brothers of the Militia, when they heard that their men were besieged, sent about three thousand men to their aid. Volquin, the master of the Militia, went with them. Berthold of Wenden and Theodoric, the bishop's brother, also went together with the Livonians, the Letts, and some pilgrims. They came to Lake Restjerw and met a boy who was coming from the fort. They took him as a guide and came to the fort at dawn. Leaving the Oeselians on the right, they advanced toward the Russians and fought with them. Seeing that the army was large and strong, they turned aside to the fort. For there were about twenty thousand of the Russians and Oeselians; being afraid of such a multitude they went into the fort. Some of the Brothers of the Militia, the strong men Constantine, Berthold, and Heylas, fell and also some of the bishop's household. All of the rest came safely into the fort. Because of the multitude of men and of horses there was a famine and a shortage of food and of hay in the fort and the horses ate each other's tails. There was likewise a

shortage of everything in the Russian army and, on the third
day after the fight, they spoke with the Germans.
(8) They made peace with them, but on condition that all
of the Germans leave the fort and return to Livonia [*ca.*
March 1]. King Vladimir called upon his son-in-law Theo-.
doric to come with him to Pskov to confirm the peace.
Theodoric trusted him and went down to him. The people of
Novgorod seized Theodoric immediately from the king's
hands and took him away as a captive with them. The Germans, having made peace, went down from the fort with the
Livonians and Letts, through the midst of the Russians and
Oeselians, and returned to Livonia. The Saccalians, meanwhile,
had entered the land of the Letts, had laid waste their villages,
had taken men captive from the Sedde, and had returned to
Saccalia. Unmindful of all the sacraments they had once received, they had no concern for the peace they had made with
the Germans and broke it.

[XXI]

(1) In Bishop Albert's nineteenth year [1217], the
Livonians did not rest from the wars.[182] The aforesaid venerable bishop sent his emissaries both to Novgorod and to Saccalia to confirm the peace made at Odenpäh and also to ask
them for his brother Theodoric. Since they were men bloated
with elation and excessively haughty in their pride, they cared
neither for the bishop's pleas nor for the peace with the Germans. They conspired with the Esthonians and formed plans
to crush the Germans and destroy the Livonian church.
Knowing this, the bishop went to Germany with the returning pilgrims. Livonia he left once more in the custody of the
Lord Jesus Christ and His Mother. He made known to every-

---

182. In hexameter verse: *Presulis Alberti nonusdecimus fuit annus
Et non a bellis siluit gens Lyvoniensis.*

one the misfortunes of war and losses of his people. He advised the brave and noble men to make themselves into a wall for the Lord's house,[183] to take the cross, and to make the pilgrimage to Livonia for the remission of their sins. Count Albert of Lauenburg heard of all the evils which the Russians and Esthonians were doing to the Livonian church. He took the cross for the remission of sins and he made his way to Livonia with his knights and vigorous and noble men. Abbot Bernard of Dünamünde and the pilgrims, though they were few, came with him. The count was received with great joy. The Lord had hitherto placed him in His quiver, like a chosen arrow,[184] so that at an opportune time He could send him to Livonia to free His church from the enemy.

(2) After he came to Riga, the Esthonians sent many gifts to the Russians, asking them to come with an army to destroy the Livonian church. But Mstislav, the great king of Novgorod, had gone at that time to fight against the king of Hungary for the kingdom of Galicia and had left a new king [185] upon his throne in Novgorod. The latter sent his messengers into Esthonia and promised that he would come with a great army together with King Vladimir and many other princes. The Esthonians rejoiced and they sent throughout Esthonia and gathered an extremely large and strong army. They encamped near the Pala in Saccalia. Their prince and elder, Lembit, called everyone from all the provinces and there came to them people from Rotalia and Harrien, from Wierland and Reval, from Jerwan and Saccalia. There were six thousand of them, all of whom waited fifteen days in Saccalia for the arrival of the king of the Russians. The Rigans heard of their gathering and they rose up and speedily hastened to them, wishing to get there before the Russians came [Sept.]. Count Albert went with them with his knights and servants, along with Volquin, the master of the Militia, and

183. Cf. Ezek. 13:5.
184. Cf. Isa. 49:2.
185. Sviatoslav.

his Brothers, Abbot Bernard of Dünamünde, John the provost, the Livonians and Letts, and the very faithful Caupo, who never neglected the Lord's battles and expeditions. These all came near to Saccalia, where there is a place for the army's prayers and discussion. There were about three thousand chosen men in the army. They decided that the Germans should take the middle course, placed the Livonians on the right, and gave the Letts the left side. They sent others to the villages and when they had taken certain men they learned from them the size of the enemy army and that it was now approaching and was ready to fight. Having heard this, they set out cautiously and in orderly fashion and at evening they came near the fort of Fellin, where they rested for the night [Sept. 21]. After celebrating solemn Masses there, they set out on the feast of St. Matthew the Apostle to meet the enemy. They discovered that the enemy had all gone off to some other place. They followed them immediately, when suddenly they saw the enemy coming out of the woods toward them, ready to fight. They approached the enemy and the Germans fought in the center, where the mass of the enemy was greater and braver. Some of the Germans on horseback and others on foot proceeded gradually in formation and made their way through the middle of the enemy and, breaking up their battle-line, turned them to flight.

(3) The Letts, who were fighting on the left side, also boldly attacked the enemy together with the Germans. The Saccalians, with Lembit and their other elders, were arrayed opposite them. Wounding many of the Letts and killing some of them, they fought boldly and resisted for a long time. But when they saw that the mid-section of their army was turned to flight by the Germans, they also turned back. The Letts pursued them and killed many of them and the rest fled. Veko, the brother of Roboam, recognized Lembit, pursued him, and killed him. Veko took his garments and the rest cut off his head and brought it back to Livonia with them. Other elders of Saccalia also fell there, Wattele, Maniwalde, and many

others. The Livonians, who were placed on the right, saw the Esthonian lances flying cruelly upon them and they swerved toward the Germans. With them they pursued the men who were fleeing. But the Esthonians who had advanced against them charged upon some of our men as they pursued in the rear. Our men manfully repulsed them and put them also to flight. After all the Esthonians had been put to flight, the Livonians, Letts, and Saxons pursued them and killed some of them in the woods. The number of the dead ran almost to a thousand—nay, they were innumerable, for in the woods and swamps they could not be counted. They took nearly two thousand horses from them and all their weapons and booty. On the following day they divided all the loot equally among themselves.

(4) Caupo, indeed, who had been run clear through by a lance, faithfully commemorating the Lord's passion, receiving the sacrament of the Lord's body, gave up the spirit in a sincere confession of the Christian religion, after he had first divided all his goods among the churches established in Livonia. Count Albert, the abbot, and all who were with them, mourned over him. His body was burned and the bones were taken away to Livonia and buried at Cubbesele.

(5) After the battle the army marched to the Pala, into Lembit's village, and remained there for three days. They sent the Livonians and Letts to raid and burn all the villages round about. Lembit's brother, Unnepewe, came to them with the others who remained, begging for a renewal of the former peace. The Germans said to them: "Because you have despised the sacrament of baptism which you received and have contaminated the faith of Christ with the counsels of the pagans and the Russians, therefore the Lord has dealt you a blow. Return therefore, faithfully now to Christ, and we will still receive you into the fellowship of our brotherly love." This pleased them. When hostages had been taken, peace was now given them a second time, so that they would faithfully keep all the laws of Christianity. When this had been done, the

army returned with all its spoils to Livonia. The men blessed the Lord, Who is blessed forever, for the glorious victory given to them by God. After Count Albert had returned from slaughtering the Saccalians, he wished to arrange another expedition to Oesel. He had a larger engine made and he encouraged all for this journey. But after an assembly of an army had been many times proclaimed that winter, the rain poured from the clouds, the ice in the sea melted, and, since Oesel is an island in the sea, they could not get there. In Lent [March 3, 1218], therefore, the Rigans, together with the Livonians and Letts, decided to go out against the other Esthonians. They came to the Salis, sent their scouts on ahead, and encountered the Oeselians. Immediately after the Oeselians recognized the army of the Rigans, they turned in flight. The Rigans with all their army followed them that whole day. On the following day they entered the maritime provinces situated around Oesel. After dividing up their army among all the roads and despoiling the land, they killed all the men whom they caught, took the women and children captive, drove many flocks off with them, took much loot, and set fire to the villages and houses. They gathered their army together and rested for a few days in the midst of the land. The elders from Hannehl and Cozzo and from all the provinces lying between Rotalia and Reval came to them seeking peace terms, so that the army would leave their territory. The Rigans spoke: "If you are willing," said they, "to be watered by the sacred font and to become sons with us of the true Peacemaker, Who is Christ, then we will make a true peace with you and we will receive you into our brotherhood." The Esthonians heard this and rejoiced. After giving hostages, they subjected themselves to the Livonian church, so as to receive the sacrament of baptism and pay the annual levy. Peace was given and the Rigans returned with much loot, praising God for the subjugation of this nation.

(6) After the second return of the Saccalians to the Christian faith, the Jerwanians also came for a second time and gave

themselves to the Rigan church in the presence of Count Albert and all the Rigan elders. They gave their boys as hostages so that they would receive the mystery of baptism and supply the Rigan church forever with the levy or measure of wheat which was instituted instead of the tithe. They returned to their own land, rejoicing in the tranquility of peace.

(7) The Oeselians rose up at this time and came to Metsepole with an army. There were about a thousand of them, drawn from among their best men, and they despoiled that entire province in Metsepole. After this they entered another parish in Ledegore and despoiled the land round about. They killed some men and took the women and children away with them. As they approached the priest's house, Godfrey the priest saw them coming. He immediately mounted his horse, fled from them, and rode around his parish, calling upon all the men to fight with the pagans. Throughout the whole night he sent word to the neighboring parishes, that they should come to the battle the next day. Vetseke came with his Livonians and also some of the bishop's servants from Fort Vredeland and they gathered together and pursued the Oeselians. There were only seven of the servants of the German bishop and the eighth was the priest Godfrey, who belted on his weapons for war and put on his breastplate, like a giant,[186] desiring to save his sheep from the jaws of the wolves.[187] They rushed valiantly upon the Oeselians from behind, killing some of them most bravely. But the Oeselians turned on them and resisted for a long time, wounding many of them. At last, after a long fight, the Oeselians took to flight. About a hundred of them fell, the rest fled. The bishop's servants and the Livonians pursued them across the Salis, along a level road next to the sea and seized about four hundred of their best horses. These they later divided among themselves, along with the loot, blessing the Lord, Who with a few men had gained such a victory from the enemy.

186. I Macc. 3:3.
187. Cf. Matt. 10:16; John 10:12.

[XXII]

⟨⟩⟨⟩ (1) The bishop's twentieth year [1218] came and the land of the Livonians did not rest from the wars.[188] In that year the aforesaid bishop of Riga, the bishop of Esthonia, and Abbot Bernard, who was consecrated in that same year as Bishop in Semgallia, with Count Albert, who was returning from Livonia, came to the king of Denmark and humbly asked him to send his naval forces to Esthonia in the following year, so that the Esthonians would be greatly humbled and would cease attacking the Livonian church with the Russians. When the king knew of the great war of the Russians and Esthonians against the Livonians, he promised that in the following year he would come with his army into Esthonia, both for the honor of the Blessed Virgin and for the remission of his sins. The bishops rejoiced. The venerable Albert of the Livonian church went again to collect pilgrims. He preached to them the remission of sins and sent them to Livonia that they might stand up for the house of the Lord on the day of battle [189] and might defend the new church from the attack of the pagans. The bishop put off his journey to Livonia this year so that he could come the next year, stronger and with more men. In his place he appointed the dean of Halberstadt, who went to Livonia with Henry Borewin, a nobleman from Wentland, and some other pilgrims, in order to complete his year of pilgrimage there.

(2) After the feast of the Assumption of the Blessed Virgin [Aug. 15], when the heat of summer was past, an expedition was announced against the people of Reval and Harrien, who up to this time had always been rebellious and more cruel than

---

188. In verse: *Annus bisdenus antistitis adveniebat
         Et non a bellis Lyvonum terra silebat.*
189. Cf. Ezek. 13:5.

the others. The Rigans assembled with the Livonians and the Letts. Henry Borewin and Master Volquin with his Brothers went with them and they came near Saccalia at the place where the army was accustomed to pray and take counsel. Count Albert ordered a bridge to be made there and there they decided that they were going to despoil the province of Reval. On the following day they crossed Saccalia and came near the fort of Fellin. There returned to them the scouts whom they had sent to call together the elders of that province, so that they could as usual be their guides. The scouts brought back with them the emissaries of the Russians and Oeselians, whom they had taken in the villages. The emissaries had been sent by the Russians in order to collect an army throughout Esthonia. When it had been collected, they were to bring it to the Russian army, so that they could go together into Livonia. They stood the emissaries in the midst of the people and sought to get word of their mission from them. They reported that an army of the great Russian kings was coming the next day into Ungannia and was going to go into Livonia. They said that they had been sent so that they could bring the Esthonian army to the Russians. When they had heard this, the Livonian army returned immediately on the same road by which it had come. On the following day they went by the road into Puidise towards Ungannia to meet the Russians. The Russians spent the whole day crossing the river which is called the Mother of Waters and they came toward the Livonians. Our scouts returned to us suddenly and said that the army of the Russians was approaching. We rose up quickly and arranged our army so that the Livonians and Letts would fight on foot and the Germans on their horses. When our army was in order we marched toward them. When we had reached them, those of our men who were first forthwith sped toward them and, fighting with them, turned them to flight. They pursued the Russians vigorously and captured the banner of the great king of Novgorod, as well as the banners of two other kings, and killed the men who carried them.

They fell here and there along the road and our whole army followed them until finally the Livonians and Letts, who were running on foot, dropped out. Each of them then mounted his horse and followed after the Russians. (3) The fleeing Russians, about two thousand in number, came to a little stream, crossed it, and halted. They gathered their whole army together and beat their drums and sounded their pipes. King Vladimir of Pskov and the king of Novgorod went around the army, encouraging them to fight. The Germans, after they had forced the Russians as far as the river, also halted, for they were unable, because of the multitude of the Russians, to cross over the river to them. The Germans gathered on a little knoll by the river, awaiting the arrival of their men who were following. They arranged their army a second time, so that some on foot, some on horses stood opposite the Russians. Whatever Livonians and Letts came up the little knoll by the river, where the battle lines were formed, when they saw the size of the Russian army, immediately drew back, as if struck in the face by a mace, turned their backs, and fled. Each one of them fled after the other one, seeing the Russian arrows coming at them. At length all of them joined the flight together. The Germans, of whom there were only two hundred, stood alone. But some of these also withdrew, so that barely a hundred remained and the whole weight of the battle was turned against them. The Russians began to cross the river and the Germans allowed them to do so until a few had come across. Then, all at once, they drove them as far as the river and killed some of them. Some others again crossed over the river to the Germans and again were driven back by them. A certain very powerful man from Novgorod crossed the river to explore. He circled the Livonians from a long way off. Theodoric of Kokenhusen encountered him, cut off his right hand, with which he held his sword, followed him, and struck him as he fled. Others killed others. Whoever crossed the river to the Germans was struck down. The Germans fought with them around the river in this manner from the ninth hour of the day until nearly sunset. The king of Novgorod, seeing about fifty of his men killed, forbade his army to cross over to the Germans thenceforth. The Russian army retired to their fires. The Germans returned singing on the road, all safe and unharmed,[190] save for one of Henry Borewin's knights, who fell, wounded by an arrow, and another, a Lett, a certain Veko, who fought alone with nine Russians for a long time with his back to a tree. He was finally wounded from behind, fell, and died. All the other Livonians and Letts returned without any wound. Many of them came again to the Germans, from the forests to which they had fled, as the Germans returned by the road. They rejoiced with them that so few out of such a multitude of Russians had escaped. They all praised the clemency of the Saviour, Who brought them back and freed them from the hands of the enemy, or rather, Who had allowed so few of them to kill about fifty Russians and carry off their weapons and loot. There were on the Russian side sixteen thousand armed men whom the great king of Novgorod had assembled for two years from all of Russia with the best weapons that were in Russia. (4) After three days the Russians followed them into Livonia. They first despoiled and burned certain Lettish villages and their churches near the Sedde. After this they gathered at the fort of Orell and stayed there for two days. On the third day they came into the court of Alabrand the priest, above Raupa, as Vladimir had once predicted to him.[191] They rested there for three days and burned all the churches round about, both those of the Livonians and those of the Idumeans. They pillaged all the provinces and villages, took the women and children captive, killed all the men whom they took, and burned the grain gathered in the fields all about. Gerceslav, the son of Vladimir, came with another army, besieged the Brothers of the Militia at Wenden, and fought with them for a day. On the following day, after crossing the Aa, he advanced to the king of Nov-

190. See n.37, above.
191. See p. 135 (XVIII, 2), above.

gorod and also to his father at Idumea. With them he pillaged and laid waste the land of the Letts, Idumeans, and Livonians, doing all the harm that he could. The Rigans, hearing of all the harm that the Russians were doing in Idumea, rose up again with Volquin, the master of the Militia, and Henry Borewin, the pilgrims, and their Livonians. They came to Treiden and summoned to them the men from the provinces round about, wishing to fight again with the Russians. They sent scouts, who quickly discovered a crowd of Russians in Immeculle; [192] these pursued them to Raupa. The Russians, indeed, returned to their men and notified them that an army of Germans was coming. (5) When they heard this, the Russians immediately left that place and, crossing the Aa, besieged the fort of the Wends and fought throughout the day with the Wends. The archers of the Brothers of the Militia came down from their fort, got through to the Wends, and with their ballistas killed many Russians and wounded a great many of them. Many of the gravely wounded nobles were carried off, half alive, on litters slung between two horses. The master of the Militia of Wenden had gone the day before with his Brothers to the assembly of the Germans. The whole Russian army, meanwhile, besieged their fort. For this reason the Brothers stealthily crossed through the midst of the enemy at night and returned to their fort. When it was morning the king of Novgorod, seeing that many of his nobles were wounded and others were killed, and considering that he could not take the fort of the Wends, though, indeed, it was one of Livonia's lesser castles, spoke peacefully to the Brothers of the Militia. They cared nothing for such a peace and drove the Russians away with ballistas. The Russians, fearing an attack from the Germans who were following, turned away from the fort. They went for a whole day, came to Tricatia, and speedily left the land. (6) When they came into Ungannia, they heard that an army of Lithuanians was in Russia and when they returned to Pskov they found that part of that city

192. The manor of Inzeem.

had been pillaged by the Lithuanians. (7) Some of the Letts then rose up and entered Russia with a few men. They despoiled villages, killed men, captured others, and bore off loot. They did all the harm they could, in revenge for their people. When these men returned, still others went and they left undone none of the damage that they could do.

(8) It had been the plan of the Oeselians to come with the Russians and the other Esthonians into Livonia to destroy the church. But because of the battle of the Germans and Russians, their plan was abandoned, so that the Saccalians did not come, nor the Oeselians, but only the people of Harrien, who, with some others, followed the Russians. They reached them at Wenden and likewise they again went away with them. The Oeselians, indeed, entered the Dvina by ship and, after capturing a few people on the islands, seized many flocks and killed a certain hermit who had come from Dünamünde and had chosen to lead an eremitical life on a neighboring island where he awaited the agony of his martyrdom. When his martyrdom had been consummated, he undoubtedly passed over happily into the communion of the saints. The Russians of Pskov sent messengers to Livonia, alleging that they were going to make peace with the Germans. But their counsels with the Esthonians were always evil and full of all kinds of deceit. (9) The Rigans, knowing this, sent to the Livonians and Letts and gathered an army to proceed against the Esthonians. About the beginning of Lent [Feb. 1219] they gathered at the Salis. Volquin, the master of the Militia, was there with Henry Borewin and the pilgrims and the Livonians and Letts. They went on the ice of the sea until they came to Sontagana. They took some guides from the fort there and marched throughout the night to the province of Reval. A very cold north wind met them. The cold was so rigorous that many of them lost the extremities of their limbs from the cold. Some had their noses, others their hands, and others their feet frozen. All of them, after they had returned to us at home, had the old skin drop off their faces and new skin grew in its place.

Some of them, indeed, later died. They divided their army into three battle lines. Vesike and the Livonians made up one battle line and took the road to the left. The Letts took the right, leaving the middle road to the Germans, as was their usual custom. Vesike, departing from his road, went with his Livonians ahead of the Germans on the middle road. At the beginning of day, before dawn, they burned down the first village that they found, in order to warm themselves. Seeing the fire, the Esthonians of the whole province immediately recognized the Livonian army and fled, each one to his hiding place. The Germans, following and finding the village burned before dawn, thought that their guide had strayed from the road, and they killed him there. When morning came, they went around through all the villages, burning them, killing the men, capturing others, and seizing many flocks and spoils. In the evening, they came to a village called Ladise [193] and rested there for the night. The next day they went on to another neighboring village called Culdale and took much loot. After three days they went away over the ice of the sea, which was nearby, taking all their captives and booty with them. There the Danes have now built their fortress in the area.[194] Returning slowly over the ice, we halted for ten days because of the captives and the booty, being on the lookout for the Oeselians or other Esthonians, if perchance they would follow to war upon us. When we came to the Salis, after dividing all the spoils among ourselves, we returned to Livonia joyfully, as victors rejoice when they divide their loot.[195]

193. The manor of Laitz.
194. Reval.
195. Cf. Isa. 9:3.

[XXIII]

⁀⁀⁀⁀ (1) The bishop's twenty-first year [1219] began and the land of the Livonians did not rest from the wars.[196] For in that same year many expeditions were made and war was renewed. When the aforesaid prelate returned from Germany, many pilgrims and nobles came with him. The chief of them was the duke of Saxony, Albert of Anhalt; also, Rudolph of Stotle, a burgrave, a certain young count, and a great many others who were ready to defend the church and to stand for the house of the Lord on the day of battle.[197]

(2) The king of Denmark also rose up at that same time with a great army. There came with him Andrew, the venerable archbishop of the church of Lund, and Bishop Nicholas,[198] and a third bishop, the king's chancellor.[199] There was also with them Bishop Theodoric of the Esthonians, who had once been consecrated at Riga, but had left the Livonian church and had attached himself to the king; also the Slavic prince Wenceslaus[200] with his men. They all brought their army to the province of Reval and encamped at Lyndanise, which had once been a fort of the people of Reval. They destroyed the old fort and began to build another new one. The people of Reval and Harrien gathered a great army against them and they sent their elders to the king with deceptively peaceful words. The king believed them, not knowing their guile. He gave them gifts and the bishops baptized them, sending them back joyfully. Then they returned to their people and three days later they came after dinner, in the evening, with all their

196. In verse: *Bisdenus primus antistitis institit annus,*
      Et non a bellis Lyvonum terra quievit.
197. Cf. Ezek. 13:5.
198. Bishop of Schleswig.
199. Bishop Peter of Roeskild.
200. Prince of Rügen Slavs.

army. They rushed upon the Danes in five places and fought with them without warning. Some of them thought that the king was in a tent, which was really that of Theodoric, the venerable bishop of the Esthonians, and they went in and killed him. Chasing the Danes in all directions, they killed many. Lord Wenceslaus was standing in a valley which is on the seaward slope of the mountain with his Slavs. Seeing the enemy approach, he quickly hurried toward them. He fought with them and turned them to flight, striking and killing as he chased them along the road. The other Esthonians, who were following the Danes, seeing the flight of those who had fought with the Slavs, halted and stopped pursuing the Danes. All of the Danes gathered with the king and some Germans who were with them and they went to meet the Esthonians and fought bravely with them. The Esthonians fled before them, and, after the whole multitude of them had turned to flight, the Danes, together with the Germans and Slavs, followed after them. A few men killed more than a thousand of their men and the rest fled. The king and the bishops returned thanks to God for the victory which God had given them over the pagans. They replaced Bishop Theodoric with his chaplain, Wescelo. When the fort was finished and his men had settled in it, the king returned to Denmark.[201] The bishops remained there with the king's men, who throughout that year fought with the people of Reval until at last they received the sacrament of baptism.

(3) After the return of the bishop with his pilgrims to Livonia, the Semgalls of Mesoten came to him asking for help against the Lithuanians. The bishop said: "If you are willing to be baptized and to accept the Christian laws, then we will give you help and receive you into the company of our fraternity." They said: "We dare not be baptized because of the ferocity of the other Semgalls and the Lithuanians, unless, by sending men to us, you will safeguard us in our fort from their attack. Your men can stay with us and administer the

201. King Waldemar II was in Alborg by Sept. 25.

sacrament of baptism to us and teach us the laws of the Christians." Their proposal pleased the bishop and the Rigans. The bishop sent his emissaries back with them to secure the assent of those who were at home. They came again and again with the same request. Then the bishop, at length, rose up with the duke of Saxony, certain other pilgrims, and the provost of Blessed Mary and went with his men into Semgallia. Abiding peacefully next to the fort of Mesoten, he summoned to him the Semgalls of that same province. As they had promised, they faithfully obeyed. All of them assembled, accepted the doctrine of the gospel, and about three hundred men were baptized, in addition to their women and children, and there was joy over their conversion. After this the bishop, at their request, placed his men, together with their own men and some pilgrims, in Fort Mesoten and he sent others to bring what was necessary from Riga by boat. The bishop, indeed, returned with the duke and the others to Riga.

(4) Then Vesthard, the elder of the other Semgalls of the neighboring province, which is called Thervetene, hearing of the conversion of the people of Mesoten, collected an army from all of his territories (the peace having been broken) and came to the fort. For a whole day he fought with the Germans. His people brought up piles of wood and set them afire, but though they fought very strenuously they were unable to take the fort. Vesthard's sister's son was killed by an arrow. When he saw this, Vesthard was grief-stricken and immediately he turned away from the fort with his army. He heard that other Germans were coming by boat on the Misse River and he quickly went to meet them. He intercepted them in a narrow place where the river was only moderately deep. He caught thirty or a few more of their men and killed them. The rest fled and returned to Riga. Among them was Segehard, a priest of the Cistercian order, who had been sent to the fort from Dünamünde to serve Bishop Bernard, to whose bishopric that place had been annexed. Segehard sat on the river bank and, seeing the pagans coming, he placed the sleeve of his

hood over his head as he awaited the savagery of the pagans. Commending his spirit to the Lord, he was struck down with the others, whose souls undoubtedly will rejoice with Christ in the company of the martyrs. Their business was holy, for they, when called, came to baptize the pagans and to plant the Lord's vineyard [202]—and planted it with their blood. Their souls, therefore, are coequal with the saints in heaven. The Germans who were in the fort heard of the slaughter of their men and, not having the necessary supplies for the year and also considering the ferocity of the Semgalls, Lithuanians, and Kurs against the Christian name, they rose up with all their men, left the fort, and went to Riga. The baptized Semgalls now fell away, unmindful of their reception of the sacraments, and joined with the other Semgalls. They conspired with them and the Lithuanians and joined together against the Rigans, the Livonians, and all Christians. They all gathered together in that same fort, both those who were still pagan and those who were baptized, and they entrenched the fort and built up its fortifications most powerfully. They went on an expedition against the Livonians of Holm and began to kill and despoil them. The Livonians also entered their territories and did like harm to them. The bishop and Duke Albert of Saxony heard of the slaughter of their men and all the evils which the Semgalls were doing. They sent to all the Livonians and Letts, ordering them to be ready so that, if the Lord would allow a prosperous journey,[203] they would take vengeance on the heathen.

(5) Meanwhile the Letts of Kokenhusen and certain other Letts of the Brothers of the Militia, Meluke and Warigribbe, not unmindful of all the harm which the Russians from Pskov and Novgorod had perpetrated in Livonia the previous year, went into Russia. They despoiled the villages, killed the men, captured the women, and turned all the land around Pskov

202. Cf. Isa. 5:7.
203. . . . si quando Dominus prosperum concederet iter. . . . Cf. Rituale Romanum, Itinerarium Clericorum, Resp.; also Ps. 67:20.

into a desert. As these men returned, others went and did similar damage and they brought back much loot all the time. They left their plows [204] and settled in the land of the Russians. They ambushed them on the plains and in the forests and villages and seized and killed them. They gave the Russians no peace and took away their horses, flocks, and women. Towards autumn the Russians from Pskov collected an army and came into the land of the Letts. They despoiled all their villages and settled in the territories of Meluke and Warigribbe, despoiling everything they had and burning the grain. None of the harm that the Russians could do was omitted. The master of the Militia in Wenden sent to all the Letts to come to expel the Russians from the land.

(6) But when the Russians had left, it seemed to the Letts that they were gaining little [205] from persecuting the Russians. They turned their army toward Saccalia and, taking the Saccalians with them, they crossed the Pala and entered Jerwan and struck that land a great blow.[206] They killed the men, captured the women, and carried off the horses and flocks and many spoils. They alleged that their victims had come to help the people of Reval against the Danes. The elders of that same province of Jerwan came to Rudolph, the master of the Militia there, saying that they had already made peace with the Rigans in the presence of Count Albert and that they were going to receive their baptism. They asked him to leave their territories with his army. Rudolph took their boys as hostages and renewed the peace with them. Since the whole law had once been accepted by them, they promised that henceforth they would keep the Christian faith and laws. They suggested to the Brothers of the Militia that they should return quickly and go with them into Wierland with an army, so that they

204. The measure of land, not the agricultural implement, is meant here. See n.22, above.

205. . . . *modicum se lucrum reportare.* . . . Cf. Pope Gregory I, *Homilia 9 in Evangelio*, cited in *Breviarium Romanum, Commune Confessoris Pontificis, Lect. ix.*

206. Cf. Num. 11:33 *et alibi.*

could carry that yoke of Christianity even into those provinces. The Brothers made a promise to them and returned with all their loot to Livonia.

(7) After the Jerwan expedition the Brothers of the Militia from Wenden summoned the bishop's men, Gerhard the magistrate, all of the Livonians and Letts, and the young count of the bishop's household, together with the other Rigans and went into Saccalia. They took with them the Saccalians and even the Ungannians and marched into Jerwan. They chose guides for themselves from among the Jerwanians and they spent the whole night entering Wierland, a very beautiful and fertile land and fair with level fields. The Jerwanians, both cavalry and infantry, followed them and the people of Wierland had not heard that the Livonian army was coming. The people were all in their villages and houses; when day broke, the invaders divided the army among all the provinces: they gave some to the Jerwanians to despoil, some to the Ungannians, and others to the Livs and Letts. They found all the people throughout the whole of Wierland in their villages. They struck them, great and small, and did not spare any males whom they found. They captured the women and children, drove off the horses and many flocks, and took many spoils. The Germans made the large village of Torma their meeting place. The Livonians and Letts chose Awispä as their base of operations.[207] The Saccalians encamped in the province of Reval. The Jerwanians rested in their own provinces. The Ungannians pillaged a province called Pudiviru, which bordered on their own territory, and encamped there. For five days they most grievously beat down the whole land and killed many thousands of people. At length the elders of the provinces, who had escaped by flight, came to us, humbly begging for peace. Rudolph, the master of the Militia, said: "Do you people, who have so often disturbed our peace with your wars, want peace now? No peace will be given you—except

207. Here the chronicler uses the Livonian word *maya* ("house," "home").

the peace of that true Peacemaker; Who has made both one,[208] joining and pacifying heaven and earth; Who, the King desired by all the nations,[209] descended from heaven, their hope, their Saviour; Who commanded His disciples, saying, 'Go, teach all nations, baptizing them.' [210] If, therefore, you wish to be baptized and to worship with us the one God of the Christians, we will give you that true peace which He gave to us, which He left to His worshippers when He ascended, and we will receive you forever into the company of our brotherhood." This speech pleased them and they promised at once that they would faithfully accept all the laws of Christianity and the Rigan baptism. There was among them one Thabelin, who had once been baptized by our people in Gothland, and another, Kyriawan, who begged us to give him the good God, saying that up to now he had had the bad god. For this same man had, up to that time been most unhappy in all his dealings. But, after he had been baptized by us, he became a most happy man, as he later confessed to us, and complete prosperity came to him with baptism. So at his urgent request we promised him there that God would be propitious to him and would give him sufficient temporal goods in this life, and also eternal life in the future. He believed us and we catechized him immediately. Rudolph, the master of the Militia, stood as godfather for him. While we were on the point of anointing him with the holy oil,[211] a great clamor arose and a rushing of our army through all the streets and everyone ran to arms, crying that a great host [212] of pagans was coming against us. We immediately put down the holy chrism and the other holy articles, therefore, and hurried to the ministry of shields and swords. We hastened onto the field, putting our battle lines in order

208. Cf. Ephes. 2:14 and *Breviarium Romanum, Officium Pretiosissimi Sanguinis Domini Nostri Jesu Christi* (July 1), *Resp. ad Lect. iii.*
209. Aggaeus 2:8.
210. Matt. 28:19.
211. Cf. *Rituale Romanum, Ordo Baptismi Adultorum.*
212. Here, again, the Livonian term *malewa* is used.

against our adversaries, and the elders of the Wierlanders stood with us. A great multitude of what we thought were enemies approached us. They were the Saccalians, our allies, who were returning to us with all their loot. We returned, therefore, and completed the baptism, but we put off baptizing the others until their proper time. Peace was given and, after taking hostages from the five provinces of Wierland, we went back to Livonia with the captives and all the spoils, bringing praise to God for the conversion of the heathen. Five elders from the five provinces of Wierland followed us to Riga with their gifts. They accepted the mystery of holy baptism and gave themselves and all of Wierland to Blessed Mary and the Livonian church. They made peace and went back, rejoicing, to Wierland.

(8) After the feast of the Lord's Nativity, the elders of the Livonian church assembled and announced a campaign against the apostate people assembled in Mesoten. But they were held back by south winds and rain. After the solemnity of the Purification of the Blessed Virgin [Feb. 2, 1220] had been celebrated, therefore, they assembled a second time, gathering a great army from Livonia and Lettia. With them there was, first and foremost, the venerable bishop of Livonia, with the duke of Saxony and all the pilgrims and the master of the Militia with his Brothers. Having four thousand Germans and another four thousand Livonians and Letts, they proceeded into Holm, bringing with them a great machine and other smaller ones, together with still other instruments for besieging the fort. They went throughout the night and, arranging the army near the Misse, they marched to the fort. They seized the village which was thereabouts and took off spoils and besieged the fort, making war upon it for many days. Some of them built a tower, others put up the paterells, others used the ballistas, others built hedgehogs [213] and began to dig at the rampart from below. Still others carried up wood,

213. *Ericeos:* military instruments consisting of beams studded with sharp spikes, used to keep off assailants.

filled the moat with it, and pushed the tower across it, while others began to dig beneath its shelter. Many of the Semgalls in the fort were hit by stones and were wounded by arrows, while many were killed by the lances of the Livonians and Letts from the tower. The rebel mob did not cease fighting back at this. At last the larger machine was put up and great rocks were cast at the fort. The men in the fort, seeing the size of the rocks, conceived a great terror. The duke took charge of the machine, shot the first stone, and crushed the enemy's balcony and the men in it. He shot a second one and dislodged the planks and the logs of the rampart. He discharged a third one and pierced and shattered three large logs in the rampart and struck some men. After seeing this, the people in the fort fled from the ramparts and sought safer places. But since they had no refuge, they asked for quarter so that they could come down and make their plea to the bishop. Peace was given, a path was opened up for them, and Made and Gayle came down with the others. They were told that they must give up the fort and everything in it in order to keep their lives. These terms displeased them. They returned to the fort and the fight waxed fiercer than before. All the devices of war were introduced. The knights protected themselves with their armor and went up the ramparts together with the duke. They wanted to take the summit of the fort, but they were still pushed back by those half-alive men in the fort. After this, much wood was piled up in heaps and set on fire and the treacherous knaves were smitten by every means until, at last, in exhaustion, on the following morning, they gave up. Coming down from the ramparts, one by one, they gave themselves up to our army and bent their necks. About noon, after the number of those who had come down totaled about two hundred, lo, suddenly Vesthard and a great mob of his Semgalls and Lithuanians came spying out of the woods, wishing to make war upon us. At once we arrayed our battle lines against them and placed the infantry around the fort. Some dolts (whose number is infinite) from among our people came and seized the elders who had come down from the fort. While our lords, who had gone off to fight the pagans in the field,[214] knew nothing of it, they killed a hundred and more of the captives. Viewald, the elder of Ascheraden, went up closer to the enemy and called them to come to fight with the Germans in the field. But they said: "We accepted a payment from the Semgalls, so that we would come and look upon your army. Now that we have seen your army we shall return to our own land, for we do not wish to break the peace we made with you." When the Lithuanians had departed, the Germans returned to the fort and found the elders slain. Those who had remained in the fort, seeing their elders killed, thenceforth dared not leave. The fight began anew, arrows flew, the lances of the Livonians and Letts from the tower killed many of them. Fires were kindled. The undermined rampart and the palisades now fell to the ground. When the enemy saw that they had no further defenses as a refuge, they prayed humbly throughout the night that the security of peace be guaranteed to them, so that when they came down from the fort they might keep their lives. The bishop, with the duke and all the multitude, pitied them. He sent the sign of the holy cross into the fort. They believed the Germans and promised that thenceforth they would never violate the sacrament of holy baptism. They came down from the fort with their women and children and went away to their villages. The army went up into the fort and plundered the money and all the goods, horses, and flocks. The Livonians and Letts left nothing there. They took everything and, having burned the fort, they returned with all their plunder to Livonia. They gave thanks to God for the vengeance wreaked upon that lying people, who had forgotten their word, had cast off the faith of Christ, had mocked the grace of baptism, and had not feared to be contaminated again by their pagan rites.

(9) When the Rigans had returned from Semgallia, they remembered all the evils which the Oeselians and the people

214. . . . *in campum abierant.* Cf. I Macc. 16:5.

of Harrien had frequently inflicted on the Livonian church. Both they and their horses rested for two weeks. Then they again gathered a great army of Livonians, Letts, and Germans. Duke Albert of Saxony, their chief dignitary, was with them and Master Volquin with his Brothers, and Theodoric the bishop's brother, with the rest of the church's men. They gathered near Saccalia, at the army's place for prayer and counsel. After celebrating solemn Masses, they marched to the Pala. There they summoned the Saccalians and Ungannians, as well as the Jerwanians, and they chose guides from among them for themselves. They divided their whole army into three squadrons. They cast lots and the Livonians got the left-hand road, the Esthonians got the road to the right by lot. The Germans with the Letts took the middle road, as was their usual custom. Rising in the morning before dawn, we marched by the middle road into Nurmegunde and when the sun rose there appeared before our faces many fires and much smoke in the land of the Jerwanians. The Jerwanians had often been overcome by the Livonian church. Their sons were hostages in Livonia and they were prepared both to pay the annual levy and to receive baptism. So the Oeselians had gathered a great army and sought the will of their gods by casting lots as to whether they should fight the Danes in Reval or re-enter the province of the Jerwanians. The lot had fallen upon the Jerwanians. God had sent them on the same day that we came. They had divided their army on that same morning among all the villages, burning and despoiling them. Some of our men, namely Duke Albert and his knights and Master Volquin with his Brothers, had seen their flames and smoke. They donned their armor and marched into Jerwan to meet the enemy. Finding all the villages burned and despoiled, they hastened more quickly after the enemy and met some of the Jerwanians who had escaped from the foe by fleeing. Each of them reported the same thing, saying: "The Oeselians have struck our land an exceedingly great blow [215] and I alone have

215. Cf. Num. 11:33.

escaped to tell you." [216] When we had heard that it was the enemy of Christ's name, we hurried toward them and after the ninth hour we caught four of them who were burning a village. After killing them and taking their horses, we hurried after the others. With the Letts, who were quicker at pursuing them, we went to a village called Carethen, which was their base of operations [217] and their place of assembly. When we came toward the village we saw their whole multitude coming suddenly toward us in order to fight in the field. They approached us, clamoring in a loud voice and striking their shields, and those who remained in the village followed after them. They ran, seeing the small numbers of our men, and threw their lances upon us. The Letts and those who were with us (those, that is, who had come first; they were still very few) cried out and ran likewise toward the foe, throwing their lances at them. Our road was narrow because the snow was frozen and each man followed after the other. The Germans, therefore, who were following a long way behind us, had not yet come and their delay was serious for those of us in the front. Trusting, therefore, in the Lord, we put the Letts on the left. The Germans as they came one by one along the road took their stand on the right. We rejoiced very much when we saw the banner of the Brothers of the Militia approaching and the duke with his great banner following. The duke, seeing the smallness of our numbers and the multitude of the enemy, said: "Are these Christ's enemies?" Someone said: "They are." And he said: "Now let us attack them." Immediately they rushed toward the enemy together with the Brothers of the Militia and the other Germans and Letts. They ran through the midst of the enemy, killing them to the right and to the left. The enemy fell away from them on every side, just as hay falls to the ground before the mower. They thrust the enemy back to the village and pursued them as they fled through the streets and houses and dragged them out

216. Job 1:15, 16, 17, 19.
217. The Livonian word *maya* is used here; see n.207, above.

and slaughtered them. The enemy went up on top of the houses and on top of the wood piles, defending themselves. The army seized them and slew them all with the edge of the sword: they would spare no one. The Jerwanian women, whom the Oeselians had taken captive, rushed out and struck the already-stricken Oeselians with clubs, saying: "May the God of the Christians smite you!" The Germans pursued them from the village into the field, killing them through the fields up to their sacred grove, stained their holy woods with the blood of many of their slain men. The Letts followed around the village and met some fugitives, whom they scattered here and there. They killed them, took away their horses, and carried off their spoils. They returned to the site of the battle and took horses, clothing, and much booty, but returned the captives with the women and children to the Jerwanians. But the Germans and Letts divided the horses and all the other loot equally among themselves, blessing the Lord Who had worked such a glorious victory over the pagans by the hand of a few men. There were about five hundred dead on the field of battle and many others fell on the plains, the roads, and elsewhere. Two of our men fell and two of the Letts: the brother of Russin and the brother of Drivinalde of Astigerwe, the young count from the bishop's household and one of the duke's knights. May their memory be blessed and may their souls rest in Christ. Since the Livonians had gone by another road to the left and the Esthonians had turned off to the right, they did not come to the battle, and so they took no part in the division of the spoils. They went by their road straight through the night into Harrien. When morning dawned they divided their army among all the villages, slew the men, took the women captive, and collected much loot. The Germans with the Letts followed them and on the following day they did similar damage. They located their assembly in the village of Lorne, which is in the midst of the land. The Livonians placed their base elsewhere and the Saccalians encamped near Reval. Contrary to the command of

the elders, they crossed over and despoiled the province of
Reval, which already had the promise of the Danes.[218] The
people from Warbole sent to us asking for terms of peace and
for us to leave their territories. Master Volquin spoke: "If you
are willing," said he, "to worship with us the one true God, to
be moistened by the font of holy baptism,[219] and to give your
sons as hostages, we will make a perpetual peace with you."
This proposal pleased the Warbolians and they gave hostages.

(10) Our knights sent their messengers also to the archbishop, the venerable Lord Andrew, to the other Danish
bishops, and to the king's men who were in the fort of Reval.
They immediately sent the king's men to us, thanking God
and us for attacking the pagans, both the ones from Oesel and
those from Harrien. They added, furthermore, that all of
Esthonia belonged to the king of Denmark, since it had been
given to him by the bishops of Livonia. They asked that the
hostages of the Warbolians be turned over to them. Master
Volquin, declaring that he was quite unaware of the gift of
Esthonia to the king of Denmark, recounted how in the
presence of the Saxon duke and everyone who was gathered
there with them, all of Esthonia had been subjected to the
Christian faith by the Rigans under the banner of the Blessed
Virgin, save only for the province of Reval and the island of
Oesel. And he added: "We are returning, indeed, the hostages
of the province of Harrien to their fathers, wishing thereby
freely to honor the king of Denmark, but under this condition, that the rights of the men of Riga shall not be at all
diminished thereby." Then, leaving there the hostages of
that province, we returned to Livonia with our loot. The
Livonians' loot was exceedingly great, for they had besieged
the underground caves of the people of Harrien, to which
these people were always accustomed to flee. They set fires
and made smoke at the mouths of the caves, suffocating them

218. I.e., the Danes had promised to keep peace and to safeguard the
province.
219. Cf. *Rituale Romanum, Ordo Baptismi Adultorum, Oratio.*

day and night, and they smothered all of the people, both men and women. They then dragged them out of the caves, some expiring, some unconscious, others dead, and killed them and took others captive. They took away all their belongings, money, clothing, and many spoils. The suffocated people of both sexes from all of the caves amounted to about a thousand souls. The Livonians returned after this with the Germans, blessing God because He had indeed humbled the proud hearts of the people of Harrien to the Christian faith.

(11) In the same year, when Theodoric, the venerable bishop of the Esths, died—his throat was slit in Reval by swords of the impious, so that, as we believe, he passed into the company of the martyrs—Bishop Albert of Livonia appointed in Theodoric's place his brother Hermann, the no less venerable abbot of St. Paul's in Bremen. Bishop Albert sent messengers through Kurland and Samland into Germany to announce this to him. Hermann went, therefore, to the archbishop of Magdeburg [220] and by him was consecrated bishop of Esthonia. When the king of Denmark heard of this, he kept him from going to Livonia for a few years. For this reason, the bishop came to the king and promised to receive his bishopric from the king and to adhere faithfully to him.

[XXIV]

⁀ⵯ⁀ⵯ (1) It was now the bishop's twenty-second year [1220] and the land of the Livonians rested a bit.[221] The same bishop, in his ever-anxious care for all the churches,[222] was careful to send preachers into Esthonia. He sent Alabrand the priest and Louis into Saccalia. They baptized a great many

220. Archbishop Albert I.
221. This heading is, again, in verse:
    Annus bisdecimus antistitis atque secundus
    Iam fuit, et modicum Lyvonum terra quievit.
222. Cf. II Cor. 11:28.

people from Jerwan and the other provinces and returned again to Livonia. The bishop sent messengers into Russia and spoke peaceful words to the people of Novgorod and, in the meantime, he did not delay sending other priests into Esthonia. The first of them was Peter Kakuwalde from Finland and Henry, the minister of the Letts from the Sedde.[223] They went together into Esthonia, crossed Ungannia, which was now baptized, until they came to the river which is called the Mother of Waters at Dorpat. Starting from the river they sowed the seed of Christian doctrine and watered the villages lying round about from the holy font of regeneration. After they had celebrated the holy mysteries of baptism in Love-cote[224] and the other villages, they went on to Sadegerwe[225] and, having gathered the people there, they baptized about three hundred. After this they went around to the other villages and did likewise. They came to Waiga, instructed the men of that province in the holy mysteries, and baptized them all. At length in Riale, the furthest of their forts, they gathered the men and imparted the doctrine of the gospel to them. After baptizing five hundred of both sexes there, they went into Wierland. The Wierlanders of the first province, called Purdiviru, received them and everyone from fourteen villages was baptized by them, including Tabelin, their elder, who was later hanged by the Danes because he had received baptism from the Rigans and had placed his son as a hostage with the Brothers of the Militia. The rest of the Wierlanders from the other provinces dared not receive the Rigan priests because of the threats of the Danes, but summoned the Danes, as they were so near, and they were baptized by them. The Wierlanders believed that the Christians had one God, both for the Danes and the Germans, and one faith and one baptism. They thought that no discord would come of it and so they accepted, unconcernedly, the baptism of their Danish

223. Presumably the author of this chronicle.
224. The village of Lofkatten, east of Dorpat.
225. Sadjerw, a manor north of Dorpat.

neighbors. The Rigans, however, held that Wierland was theirs, since it had been subjected to the Christian faith by their men, and sent the aforesaid priests to baptize there.

(2) But the Danes desired to take over this neighboring land for themselves and sent their priests, as it were, into a foreign harvest. They baptized some villages and sent their men to the others to which they could not come so quickly, ordering great wooden crosses to be made in all the villages. They sent the rustics with holy water and ordered them to baptize the women and children. They tried thereby to anticipate the Rigan priests and sought in this manner to put the land into the hands of the king of the Danes. Peter and Henry, realizing this, went into Jerwan and, after they had baptized a great many men in the first villages there, they heard that Walter, the priest of the Danes, was coming there. They went out to meet him, saying that this land was in the power of the Rigans. They said that this vineyard had been planted by the zeal of the pilgrims and the labor of the Rigans through the Blessed Virgin's banner. They went after this into the fort of the Danes with the priest and made the same statement to the venerable Archbishop Andrew of Lund. But the archbishop said that all of Esthonia, whether conquered by the Rigans or not yet subjugated, belonged to the Danish king, having been made over to him by the bishops of Riga. Sending messengers to Riga the archbishop ordered them not to pluck the hanging clusters of grapes, nor to send their priests to preach in the corners of Esthonia. The bishop of Riga, the venerable Albert, wrote back to him and said that the vineyard of the Esthonian church had been planted by his people for many years before the time of the Danes' coming. It had been cultivated by the blood of many men and by the many sufferings of war and his priests had appeared, not in the corners of Esthonia, but in the middle of Jerwan and, indeed even in Wierland and in the very face of the archbishop himself. The king of the Danes, having learned of this, was rather angered at the bishop of Riga, yet he summoned him and the

Brothers of the Militia to his presence. The bishop did not come, but hastened to the supreme pontiff on this same matter. The Brothers of the Militia, Rudolph of Wenden and the others, came to the king. The king gave them Saccalia and Ungannia, which had already been subjugated and baptized by the Rigans, together with the adjacent provinces, as their one-third of Livonia, excluding the bishop of Riga and his newly-consecrated brother, Hermann. Word of this came to Riga, and Bishop Bernard and the other Rigans took it ill. The Rigans met with the Brothers of the Militia and in a friendly way they established a three-part division of Esthonia and allotted to the bishops, as hitherto and henceforth, their parts, leaving the Brothers their third. The Danes, after they had baptized the whole province of Reval, also sent their priests to the people of Harrien. After baptizing them, the Danes incited them to go to the Jerwanians with an army, so that, seized by fear, they would depart from the rule of the Rigans and accept Danish rule and baptism. The people of Harrien went with their armies nine times into the land of the Jerwanians during that same summer. They despoiled the Jerwanians and killed and captured a great many of them. They even struck and wounded the Danish priest himself, among others, until at last many of the Jerwanians chose Danish rule and baptism. Likewise the Wierlanders, first defeated by the Rigans, were terrified by the threats of the Danes and accepted their dictation and their rule. The archbishop, therefore, consecrated a new bishop [226] for Wierland and Jerwan and gave the provinces of the people of Harrien to the bishop of Reval.

Meanwhile King John of Sweden with his duke [227] and bishops, having collected a great army, came into Rotalia, hoping to acquire dominion over some parts of Esthonia. The king established himself at the fort of Leal, where Bishop Hermann, the brother of the bishop of Livonia, was. Bishop

226. Bishop Ostrad.
227. Duke Charles of East Gothland.

Hermann had been confirmed by the pope because that province had formerly been conquered by the Rigans and initiated in the rudiments of the faith. The Swedes went around through the province, teaching and baptizing people and building churches. They came to the Danes in Reval and conferred with them. The Rigans also sent messengers to the Swedes to say that these provinces had been subjected to the Christian faith by their men. They also warned the Swedes not to trust too much in the treacherous words of the Esthonians and to take a little care of themselves. The king, after placing his men in the fort—Leal, that is—returned with Duke Charles and the bishop [228] to Sweden. Since the Swedes were in the middle, with the Livonians on one side and the Danes on the other, they began to have but small fear of the pagans. It happened one day at the first light of dawn that the Oeselians came from the sea with a large army. They besieged these Swedes, fought with them, and set fire to their fort [Aug. 8, 1220]. The Swedes went out and struggled with them, but they were unable to resist such a multitude. The Swedes fell, killed by the Oeselians. The fort was captured, the duke fell, and the bishop, slain by fire and sword, entered (as we believe) the company of the martyrs. The Danes came a little while later, collected their corpses, and, with sorrow, consigned them to the grave. The Rigans, likewise, hearing of the slaughter of the Swedes, mourned and groaned for them for many days. About five hundred were slain, though a few of them escaped by flight and made their way to a Danish fort. All of the rest perished by the edge of the sword. May their memory be blessed and their souls rest with Christ.[229]

(4) The bishop of Livonia crossed the sea and came to Lübeck. When he learned of the plots of the Danish king, he secretly left the city with the help of his faithful friends. Hurriedly he came to the Roman court, to the supreme pontiff,[230]

228. Bishop Charles of Linkoping, the nephew of Duke Charles of East Gothland.

229. Cf. Ecclus. 65:1.

230. Pope Honorius III (1216–27).

who mercifully and paternally listened to his petitions. The king of Denmark sent his emissaries to oppose the bishop. They disturbed the business of the Livonian church at the Roman court not in the least and they helped themselves still less. The bishop of Livonia went to the Emperor Frederick, then newly elevated to the Empire,[231] and sought aid and counsel from him against the grievous disturbances both of the Danish king and of the Russians or of pagans, besides, since Livonia and all its subject provinces always held the Empire in respect. The emperor, however, was occupied with the various and deep affairs of the Empire and gave the bishop but little consolation. The emperor had promised to visit the Holy Land of Jerusalem and, anxious about that, he denied aid to the bishop. Yet he warned and instructed him to keep peace both with the Danes and with the Russians until the new plantation was firmly established. After that he could build a structure over it. Since the bishop got no relief either from the supreme pontiff or from the emperor, he returned to Germany. It seemed better to him, on the advice of good men, to go to the Danish king rather than to endanger the Livonian church. For the king of the Danes forbade the citizens of Lübeck to offer their ships to pilgrims to Livonia until he could bring the bishop around to his point of view. The same venerable bishop, therefore, went at last with his brother, Bishop Hermann, to the king of Denmark. He committed both Livonia and Esthonia to the king's power, provided that the prelates of his convents, as well as his men, all the Rigans, and the Livonians and Letts would give their consent to these terms. There died at this time [March 27, 1221] the queen,[232] the Danish king's wife, in childbirth. Someone said that the new church, which daily was to give birth to spiritual offspring and which was at that time given over to the power of this king, would undoubtedly be endangered for the period of his reign. And he was telling the truth, as will appear below.

231. Frederick II was crowned emperor on Nov. 22, 1220.
232. Queen Berengaria.

(5) Meanwhile, as others fought for rule over the lands, the priest of the Letts from the Sedde [233] went again into Esthonia, taking along with him another priest, Theodoric, who was then newly ordained. They crossed through Saccalia, came to the Pala, and, beginning from that river they moistened from the holy font of baptism the neighboring province, which is called Nurmegunde. They stopped in each of the larger villages, called the people together, and imparted to them the teaching of the gospel. They went around for seven days and baptized three or four hundred people of both sexes each day. They went after this into Jerwan and came to the farthest province which was not baptized in the direction of Wierland, a province called Loppegunde. They celebrated the mystery of holy baptism in each of the larger villages, until they came to a village called Kettis, where they did the same. The Danes afterwards built a church there, as they did in many other villages baptized by us. They came at last to a village called Reinewer and sent to summon people from the other villages. A rustic, who was their elder, said: "We are already all baptized." When they asked him by whose baptism they had been baptized, he replied: "Since we were in the village of Ialgsama when a priest of the Danes performed the sacrament of baptism there, he baptized some of our men and gave us holy water. We returned to our own villages [234] and each of us sprinkled our families, wives and children, with that same water. What more should we do? [235] Since we have been baptized once, we will not receive it again." When the priests heard this, they smiled a bit and, shaking the dust from their feet at them,[236] they hurried to the other villages. They baptized three villages within Wierland. There was there a mountain and a most lovely forest in which, the natives say,

233. Henry of Livonia, the author.

234. . . . *reversi sumus ad proprias villas.* . . . Cf. *Rituale Romanum, Itinerarium Clericorum, Antiphona.*

235. The text here reads: . . . *et nobis ultra quem faciemus?* The translation given seems the most likely meaning of a rather cryptic statement.

236. Cf. Acts 13:51.

the great god of the Oeselians, called Tharapita, was born, and from which he flew to Oesel. The other priest went and cut down the images and likenesses which had been made there of their gods. The natives wondered greatly that blood did not flow and they believed the more in the priest's sermons. Having finished seven days of baptizing in that province, therefore, the priests returned to another province, called Mocha, and they likewise spent a week there. They went around to all the villages and every day they baptized three or five hundred people of both sexes until, when the baptism was finished, even in these parts they had wiped out the pagan rites. From that province they proceeded into Waiga. On the road they found many villages which had not yet been visited by any priests and, having baptized all the men, women, and children there, they went on around Lake Worcegerwe [237] and came into Waiga. Since Waiga had already been baptized, they returned to the province called Iogentagania and visited each of the villages which still remained unbaptized, namely Igeteveri,[238] Wetpole,[239] and Wasala,[240] and many others. They baptized all their men, women, and children. At the end of the week, when they had consummated the mysteries of holy baptism in those parts, they returned joyously to the Mother of Waters and, having fulfilled the work of piety and doctrine toward the unbaptized on both sides alike of the river, they returned at length to Odenpäh. They committed the vineyard they had planted and watered from the holy font to God, who would make it grow.

(6) After a little while Theodoric the priest again returned to his baptized people in Jerwan and Wierland and lived there with them. The Danes heard of this, seized him and his servant, took away their horses and everything that they had, and sent them back, despoiled, to Livonia. The brothers of the

237. Lake Wirzjärw.
238. The village of Iggafer.
239. Perhaps the estate of Fehtenhof, south of Iggafer.
240. The estate of Wassula, southeast of Fehtenhof.

bishop of Riga [241] sent Salomon the priest into Rotalia after the slaughter of the Swedes. Salomon was received by them in a kindly fashion and they promised that they would always gladly be subject to the Rigan church and would never accept either the baptism or the rule of the Danes. They collected the levy from all their territories, as formerly they were always accustomed to do, and sent it to the Rigans by the hand of this priest. The Danes came, seized everything, and sent the priest back, despoiled, into Livonia. Hartwig, a young priest of the Brothers of the Militia, also went into Ungannia, lived there with his Brothers, and baptized everyone whom he found unbaptized. Likewise the priest who hitherto had been with the Letts [242] went into Ungannia and came to Walgatabalwe, in the direction of Pskov. By celebrating the sacrament of baptism in every furthest little village, he opened the Christian faith to them. When he had finished baptizing, he returned to Livonia. At that time baptism was completed throughout Esthonia and many people were baptized in all its regions and provinces, so that some priests baptized a thousand, many others baptized five thousand, and certain of them baptized ten thousand and more among the thousands of Esthonians. The church rejoiced in the tranquility of peace and the whole people together praised the Lord, Who, after many wars, had at last converted the hearts of the pagans from idolatry to the worship of their God, Who is blessed through the ages.

(7) At that same time, indeed, the Christians from the land of Jerusalem had taken Damietta, a city of Egypt. They lived

241. Bishop Albert's two brothers and also two of his three half-brothers were men of prominence in his Livonian state. One brother, Rothmar, was a Brother of the Militia and provost of Dorpat; the other brother, Hermann, was first abbot of St. Paul's monastery at Bremen and later became bishop of Dorpat in Esthonia. Of Bishop Albert's half-brothers, one, Englebert, became prior of the chapter at Riga, and another, Theodoric, married King Vladimir's daughter, while the third, Johann, remained in Saxony as squire of the manor of Appeldorn. See the genealogical chart appended to the *Annales Stadenses* in *MGH, SS,* XVI, 374.

242. Most probably this was the author, Henry of Livonia.

in it and the church of God had victory and triumphs over the pagans everywhere throughout the world, though with us it was not for long. For in the year immediately following [1221] the Oeselians came with a great army after Easter and besieged the Danes at Reval. They fought with them for fourteen days and, lighting many fires, they hoped to take them in that fashion. The Danes at last left the fort to fight with the Oeselians and they were again pushed back into the fort by their enemy. The Oeselians saw four cogs coming over the sea and feared that the king of the Danes was coming with his army. They left the Danish fort, went to their ships, and returned to Oesel. The Danes forthwith sent and took the elders of the province of Reval, of Harrien, and also of Kurland and hanged them all, whoever had been on the side of the Oeselians in besieging the Danish fort or had shared in their evil counsels. The Danes imposed on the rest of the people a tribute double or triple that which they had previously been accustomed to give and they took many heavy reparations from them. For this reason the Esthonians began to entertain a greater hatred of the Danes and they were always looking for deceitful designs and base strategems against them, to see if somehow they could drive them out of their territories.

[XXV]

〰〰 (1) It was the twenty-third year [1221] of Bishop Albert's consecration, and the land of the Livonians rested for a few days.[243] When Count Adolf of Dassel went to Germany the venerable bishop of Riga returned with some more—though few—pilgrims. Among them was Bodo of Homburg,[244] a nobleman, with other knights and clerics. Upon the

---

243. This last phrase forms a verse line:
        Et siluit paucis Lyvonum terra diebus.
244. Homburg near Eimbeck.

return of the bishop, the Rigans learned that not only Esthonia but even Livonia had been delivered into the power of the king of Denmark. Everyone was very much disturbed and all alike cried out with one voice. The prelates of the convents, the men of the church, the citizens, the merchants, the Livonians and Letts, all protested, saying that hitherto they had fought the Lord's battle against the pagans for the honor of our Lord Jesus Christ and His beloved Mother, not for the honor of the king of Denmark, and that they would rather forsake the land itself than obey the king. Word of this came to the ears of the venerable archbishop of the church of Lund, who had been tested in no small way by the persecutions of the pagans during the siege of the fort of Reval. The archbishop recognized that he greatly needed the help of the Rigans and he sent messengers to the bishop of Riga, promising that he would restore Livonia to its original liberty. The bishop went with the master of the Militia and his men to the archbishop in Reval and they received gifts and consolation. The archbishop promised them that he would take all care to restore Livonia's liberty once more, if only the Germans and Danes would rejoice at being one in peace and one at war against the pagans and the Russians.

In Saccalia and Ungannia, indeed, they gave all royal and secular rights [245] to the Brothers of the Militia and committed the spiritual rights to the bishop. They returned joyfully to Livonia.

(2) After their return there came a certain knight, Gottschalk, a messenger of the king of Denmark, sent by the king to take over the magistracy of that city [246] for the king. Everyone throughout all of Livonia, the Livonians, Letts, and Germans, opposed him, so much so that even the merchants denied him a pilot for his ship either to come from Gothland to Livonia or to go from Livonia to Gothland. Gottschalk went away discomfited from Livonia and came onto the wide and

245. . . . *regalia cuncta simul et secularia iura.* . . .
246. Riga.

spacious sea. He was going without a pilot in his ship and was tossed about by a contrary wind. He had come to Livonia, perhaps, against the will of Him Who rules the winds,[247] and the winds, therefore, rose not unjustly against him. The sun of justice [248] did not shine upon him, because he had offended Mary, His Mother, Who is called the Star of the Sea,[249] and for this reason She would not show him the right way. In such fashion, the knight, driven out of Livonia, returned to Denmark and renounced thenceforth the royal magistracy in the land of the Blessed Virgin Mary. Thus, even thus, the Star of the Sea always guards Livonia. Thus, even thus, the Lady of the world and the Empress of all lands always protects Her special land. Thus, even thus, the Queen of Heaven [250] rules over earthly kings. Did She not rule when She afflicted the many kings who were fighting against Livonia? Did She not afflict them when She struck with sudden death the great King Vladimir of Pskov as he was coming into Livonia with his army? Did She not immediately deprive of his kingdom the great king of Novgorod who despoiled Livonia for the first time, and did She not cause him to be driven out shamefully by his citizens? Did She not kill through the Tatars the other king of Novgorod who devastated Livonia for the second time? Did She not sufficiently humiliate King Vsevolod of Gerzika, who despoiled the Rigans with fire and the sword? Did She not later destroy with a cruel death at Dorpat (as will be related below) King Vetseke, who once killed the bishop's men at Kokenhusen? Might I not speak of the Swedes, who entered the Rotalian provinces which were subject to the banner of the Blessed Virgin—for were they not slaughtered by the Oeselians? Did She not, if one may say so, trouble the king of the Danes with a long and marvelous

247. Cf. Matt. 8:27.
248. Cf. Mal. 4:2, and the Mass for the Nativity of the Blessed Virgin (Sept. 8): . . . *ex te ortus est sol justitiae.* . . .
249. Cf. the Breviary hymn *Ave Maris Stella.*
250. Cf. the Breviary antiphon *Regina Coeli.*

captivity in the hands of a few people, when he wished to trouble Livonia with his rule? Did She not kill Svelgate and many other princes and elders of the Letts through her Livonian servants? Did She not cause Ako, once the prince of the treacherous Letts at Holm, and many others, to fall dead at the hands of the Rigans? Did She not lay to rest Russin, the elder of the Letts in the fort of Dobrel? Did not all the elders of Treiden, who were called traitors, fall and die in the time of the pestilence? Did not all the elders of Oesel as well as of the provinces of Rotalia fall dead before the Rigans at Treiden? Did not Lembit, Vytames, and their other treacherous elders in Saccalia fall dead before the Rigans? And all those who remained and persisted in their treachery—did they not all perish? Behold how the Mother of God, so gentle to Her people who serve Her faithfully in Livonia, always defended them from all their enemies and how harsh She is with those who invade Her land or who try to hinder the faith and honor of Her Son in that land! See how many kings, and how mighty, She has afflicted! See how many princes and elders of treacherous pagans She has wiped off the earth and how often She has given Her people victory over the enemy! Up to this time, indeed, She has always defended Her banner in Livonia, both preceding it and following it, and She has made it triumph over the enemy.[251] And what kings whether of pagans or of Danes or of other nations, have fought against Livonia and have not perished? Consider and see, you princes of the Russians, or the pagans, or the Danes, or you elders of whatever people. Fear this gentle Mother of Mercy. Adore this Mother of God and give satisfaction to Her, Who takes such cruel revenge upon Her enemies. Do not wish henceforth to attack Her land, so that to you She may be a mother,

251. Cf. the Breviary office of St. John Capistrano (March 28); the office of John Capistrano, of course, dates only from the eighteenth century, but the relevant phrase used there and in this chronicle has been found by Arbusow in medieval liturgical texts; see *Deutsches Archiv*, VIII, 119–20.

Who has hitherto been an enemy to Her enemies, She Who has always more afflicted those who afflict Her people [252] in Livonia. Give heed and see,[253] you who hold dominion and magistracies in Her land. Do not unduly oppress the poor, I mean the poor Livonians and Letts, or any other converts, the servants of the Blessed Virgin, who have hitherto borne the name of Christ Her Son [254] to the other peoples and who still bear it with us. Give deep, fearful consideration and recall to your minds' eyes [255] the cruel death of some who were harsh to their subjects. The Blessed Virgin does not, indeed, delight in the great tribute which converts are accustomed to give, nor is She appeased by the money taken from them by various exactions, nor does She wish to impose upon them a heavy burden, but one which is sweet and easily borne. Her Son says: "My yoke is sweet and My burden light." [256] He simply demands of them that they believe in His name, that they acknowledge Him to be the one true God with the Father, and, believing, may have life in His name,[257] Who is blessed world without end. Amen.

(3) The citizens of Riga assembled at that time with the merchants, Livonians, and Letts at Treiden and they banded together with oaths and common spirit both against the king of Denmark and against all their other adversaries. The Brothers of the Militia sent their servants and captured some of the Livonian elders in Segewold and cast them into chains. They thereby overthrew the counsel of the others. The Russians of Pskov renounced the peace agreement which had been made at Odenpäh and they followed at once with a large army. The king of Novgorod, who was immediately killed by

252. *Breviarium Romanum, Officium in Dominicam IV, Quadragesimae,* Resp. ad Lect. viii; cf. Exod. 23:22.

253. *Ibid., Officium in Sabbato Sancto, Resp, ad Lect. v.* See also Lam. 1:12.

254. Cf. Acts 9:15.

255. Cf. Pope Gregory I, *Homilia 18 in Evangelio,* cited in *Breviarium Romanum, Officium in Dominica Passionis, Lect. viii.*

256. Matt. 11:30.

257. John 20:31.

the Tatars in the following year, was in command of the army.
There were twelve thousand Russians in that army and they
came both from Novgorod and from the other cities of Russia against the Christians who were in Livonia. They came
into the land of the Letts and awaited the Lithuanians for two
weeks, devastating everything in the vicinity. After this they
approached Wenden. The Brothers of the Militia and the
Wends went out to meet them at the gate. They did not wish
to oppose the multitude, so they burned the village and turned
away to their fort. The Russians, indeed, left the fort, crossed
the Aa, and came to Treiden. They pillaged the whole land,
burning all the villages and churches and the crops which were
already gathered in the fields. Capturing and killing men,
they did much evil in the land. The Lithuanians came by the
same road past Wenden, followed the Russians, crossed the
Aa and joined them. The Lithuanians carried out the harm
which the Russians had failed to do. The master of the
Brothers of the Militia left Riga with his men and Bodo the
knight with some pilgrims. Only a few others followed because of the discord in the land. The master of the Militia
went with his men and the others who were following him to
the Aa. They held the Russians back from the banks so that
they could not cross over into the Brothers' territories. Certain of the Livonians crossed the river and pursued a crowd
of Lithuanians who were coming with their captives and spoils
from Coiwemunde. The Livonians killed about twenty of
them and the others escaped by fleeing to the Russians. The
Livonians found another crowd of Russians in the village of
Cogelse.[258] They likewise killed seven of them, while some fled
and returned to their people, and others escaped by hiding in
the forests. The Russians said: "It is not good for us to be
here, for the Livonians and Germans are gathering all around
us." They rose up in the middle of the night and began to
leave the land. They spent the following night in Ykewalda,
burning and plundering the province round about. On the

258. The estate of Kolizen, northeast of Treiden.

third night they did similar harm at Imera and then hurried
into Ungannia, where they likewise devastated that land for
four days and then returned to Russia. The Lithuanians, out
of fear of the Germans, dared not be separated from the Russians and went with them to Pskov, where they remained with
them for a whole month, so that afterwards they could securely return to their land.

(4) The Brothers of the Militia with the others who had
followed them to Sedde returned thinking that they would
meet the Lithuanians by the Dvina. Together with the members of the bishop's household from Kokenhusen, they laid an
ambush and waited three weeks for them. But the Brothers of
the Militia became bored and returned to Riga. Theodoric the
knight from Kokenhusen, together with the other knights,
the servants of the bishop, and a few Letts, went on a journey
toward Pskov and spent seven days looking for the Lithuanians. At length they found traces of them and immediately
hurried to them. Since there were only fifteen Germans and
more Letts, so that in all they were one less than ninety, and
since there were six hundred of the pagans, the Germans and
Letts were afraid indeed of their multitude, but they placed
all their hope in the Lord and boldly approached them. The
Lithuanians, seeing that the Germans and Letts were coming
toward them, arranged their army facing them and placed
two hundred of their best horsemen to one side, so that they
could pursue the Germans when they fled. All the others came
in a great crowd to meet the Germans, and the Germans, because of the fewness of their numbers, were unable to fight
them. But He, Who once made one man pursue a thousand
and two men put ten thousand to flight,[259] was fighting. Confiding in Him, they raised their banner, approached, and began
the battle. Men fell at first on one side and on the other in
equal numbers. Since the road was narrow, because of the
nearby forest, the Germans went first into the battle and all
the Letts followed, shouting as they had been taught in the

259. Cf. Deut. 32:30.

German language to seize, ravage, and kill. The Lithuanians were extremely frightened by the noise and thought that many men were following the Germans. They turned in flight and the strongest of them fell, along with about a hundred of the others. The rest threw away their weapons and fled through the woods. The Germans collected all of their spoils, and what they could not carry with them they burned in a fire. They caught about four hundred of the enemy's horses and brought them with them, praising Him Who fought for them. Three of the Germans, however, were slain there. May their souls rest in peace with Christ. Amen. Since it was now winter, the Lithuanians who escaped through the woods, because of the difficulty of crossing the Dvina, either drowned in the Dvina or hanged themselves in the woods, that they might not return to their own land. For they had despoiled the Blessed Virgin's land and Her Son returned vengeance against them. To Him be praise throughout the ages.

(5) The Rigan merchants also went into Rotalia with their wares, and the Danes came and seized them, saying that this was the land of their king. The Danes bound them and brought them with them to Reval. The bishop of Riga and the master of the Militia sent to ask them to send them back, but they would not. After this it was announced to the Danes that the Rigans were coming with an army, and they sent back the merchants at once. The Rigans did not go into Esthonia, but went with the Livonians and Letts into Ungannia. They summoned the Saccalians and Ungannians and went into Russia, to their enemies who had despoiled Livonia. They left Pskov behind, entered the kingdom of Novgorod, and plundered the whole land round about. They burned houses and villages, took many people captive, and killed others. The Letts came to a church which was not far from the city of Novgorod, took away the icons, bells, thuribles, and such things, and returned to the army with many spoils. After taking revenge upon their enemies, the whole army returned joyfully without anyone being wounded. Each man returned

to his home and the shame cast by the Russians on the Livonian church ceased. The Letts, also, and the Saccalians and Ungannians continually entered Russia, killed many people there, took captive many of both sexes, and carried away many spoils. The Letts of Kokenhusen likewise entered Russia with the Germans and all the time brought back much loot and many captives.

The Brothers of the Militia with their servants were at the same time in all the forts, both of Ungannia and of Saccalia, administering magistracies, gathering tribute, and saving the bishop his share. They built up all the forts and fortified them most strongly. They dug cisterns within and filled the forts full of weapons and ballistas. They collected the Esthonians into the forts out of fear of the Russians and remained there with them. (6) The Ungannians, however, went with an army in the very deep snow about mid-winter. They passed by Wierland, crossed the Narva, pillaged the neighboring land, and brought back captives and loot. When they had returned, the Saccalians went by the same route, crossed the Narva, and marched by a most distant road into the land called Ingaria,[260] which belongs to the kingdom of Novgorod. They found that land full of men and forewarned by no rumors. They struck the Ingarians an extremely great blow, killing the men and many people and capturing many of both sexes. They slaughtered sheep and cattle and many flocks which they could not take away with them. They returned with much loot and Esthonia and Livonia were filled with Russian captives. For all the harm which the Russians had brought upon the Livonians, they received double or triple that year.

260. Ingermanenland.

[XXVI]

(1) It was now the prelate's twenty-fourth year [1222], and the land did not yet rest in tranquil peace.[261] In that same year[262] the Tatars (who are said by some to be Parthians and who do not eat bread, but feed on the raw flesh of their flocks) were in the land of the Valvus pagans. The Tatars warred upon them and defeated them and slew them all with the edge of the sword and others fled to the Russians, seeking aid from them. Word went out through all of Russia that they should fight with the Tatars, and the kings of all Russia went out against the Tatars. The Russians were not strong enough to fight with them and fled before them. Mstislav, the great king of Kiev, fell,[263] together with forty thousand men who stood by him. The other King Mstislav,[264] of Galicia, escaped by flight. About fifty of the other kings fell in the same battle. The Tatars pursued the Russians for six days and killed more than a hundred thousand men, whose numbers God alone knows; the rest fled. The king of Smolensk, the king of Polozk, and certain other Russian kings sent their emissaries to Riga seeking terms of peace. Peace was renewed throughout all the areas as it had prevailed in earlier times.

(2) The king of Denmark, too, after collecting a great army, came with Count Albert to Oesel and began to build

261. In verse: *Bisdecimus quartus iam presulis affuit annus,*
     Et nondum terra tranquilla pace quievit.

262. 1223 is meant here.

263. Mstislav III of Kiev and two other princes were captured alive by the Tatars in the Battle of the Kalka. They were stretched on the ground and covered with boards upon which the Tatar chiefs sat for a victory banquet. The princes were smothered.—See George Vernadsky, *Kievan Russia* (New Haven, 1948), p. 238.

264. Mstislav the Daring.

a stone fort. The Danes went out to fight against the Oeselians and, alone, they were not strong enough. But Count Albert and his men came to their aid, turned the Oeselians to flight, and killed many of them, while the rest fled. The venerable bishop of Riga also came with the master of the Militia and his Brothers and with certain Livonians and others who had been sent from Livonia to the king of Denmark in Oesel. The king rejoiced at their arrival. He spoke to them about the gift by which Livonia had been given to him. They would not agree with him, but rather all unanimously dissented, as they had been instructed by all the people living in Livonia. They besought him to desist from troubling Livonia and to allow the land of the Blessed Virgin to remain free. After taking counsel with his prudent men, therefore, the king at length restored Livonia and everything pertaining to Livonia to the bishop with complete liberty. He abandoned the royal rights [265] in Saccalia and Ungannia to the Brothers of the Militia and all spiritual rights [266] to the bishop. He added that they should render perpetual fealty to himself and that they should not refuse their aid to his men, both against the Russians and against the other pagans. They promised their aid faithfully and forever, both to him and to his men. They therefore left Theodoric the bishop's brother and certain Brothers of the Militia in the new fort there at the king's request and returned to Livonia. The king, indeed, after speedily finishing the wall of the fort and after placing men in it, returned to Denmark.

(3) The Oeselians assembled from all the villages and provinces and besieged that fort. They sent to the Esthonians on the coast to come to their aid. Some of the Oeselians went into Warbole to study the use of the paterell or the machine which the Danes had given to the people of Warbole as their subjects. They returned to Oesel and began to build paterells and machines. They taught others and each of them made his

265. . . . *regalia iura.* . . .
266. . . . *spiritualia.* . . .

own machine. All of them came together with seventeen paterells; they shot many great stones continually for five days and they gave no rest to the men who were in the fort. The latter had no houses and buildings, nor was there a shelter or refuge within the unfinished fort, and many of them were injured. But many of the Oeselians fell, wounded by the ballistarii. The Oeselians did not, however, cease attacking the fort for that reason. After many days of fighting, the Oeselians spoke thus to the men in the fort: "Since you in this fort know that you cannot be saved at all from our continued attack, we urge and beseech you that, after making peace with us, you all leave the fort, safe and unharmed, and relinquish the fort and all our land to us." The men who were fighting under the open sky, lacking houses, in need of everything, accepted these terms of peace. They went out of the fort, brought their belongings with them to the ships, and gave up the fort and the land to the Oeselians. The Oeselians also kept seven of the Danes and Theodoric, the brother of the bishop of Riga, as hostages there for the confirmation of the peace. All of the rest returned to the Danes in Reval.

(4) The Oeselians then destroyed the fort on all sides, leaving not a stone upon a stone,[267] and they sent this message throughout all of Esthonia, that they had taken the fort of the Danish king and had expelled the Christians from their territory. They encouraged the Esthonians in all the provinces to cast the yoke of the Danes from themselves and expunge the Christian name from the land, saying that it was easy to storm a fort of the Danes. The Oeselians taught them to build machines and paterells and other instruments of war, and evils arose in the land.

(5) So when the Oeselians and the people of Harrien had perfected their wicked devices and plots against the Danes and against the Christian name, they all assembled with the Esthonians from the coast in the fort of Warbole and killed some of the Danes and their priests who lived with them. They sent

267. Cf. Matt. 24:2; Luke 19:14.

messengers into Wierland, saying that the people there should
do likewise. The people of Wierland and the Jerwanians,
since they were simple people and more humble than the other
Esthonians, did not presume to do such a thing. They led
out their priests and sent them back unhurt to the fort of the
Danes.

The Saccalians, indeed, who lived together with the Brothers
of the Militia in the fort of Fellin, were unable to disguise any
longer the evil thoughts in their hearts against the Brothers.
They all ran with their swords, lances, and shields, seized some
of the Brothers, their servants, and the German merchants
and killed them. On the Sunday [268] [Jan. 29, 1223] when the
gospel is read: "When Jesus entered into the ship, behold a
great tempest arose in the sea," [269] as Theodoric the priest
celebrated the solemnity of the Mass and the other Brothers
stood around in the church, a great disturbance and commo-
tion indeed took place. For after killing the Brothers, the
servants, and all the Germans outside, the Saccalians gathered
at the church. They sought to make blood, not prayers, flow.
They did not desire the sacrament of the Masses, but rather
wanted to disturb the rest of Jesus Christ. They brought with
them, in fact, the iniquity of Cain.[270] They occupied and
surrounded the door of the church and encircled the unarmed Brothers with their weapons. In order to get them out
more easily, they treacherously gave the Brothers their hands
and promised them peace. Maurice, their magistrate, who was
too ready to believe the infidels, went out to them first. At
once they rushed upon him and killed him. The rest, therefore, were terrified by their certain knowledge and prepared
to defend themselves. After a long delay, peace was at last
sworn to and the Brothers went out, one by one, to the Saccalians. The traitors at once seized them, cast them into
shackles and chains, and pillaged their money, horses, and all

268. The fourth Sunday after the Epiphany.
269. Matt. 8:23, 24.
270. Cf. Gen. 4:1–15.

their goods, which they divided among themselves. They threw the bodies of the slain into the fields, to be gnawed at by the dogs, as it is written, "They have thrown the corpses of Thy servants to feed the birds of heaven; the flesh of Thy saints for the beasts of the earth; their blood has flowed like water, and there was none to bury the dead." [271] Certain of them went to another fort which was by the Pala and there ordered similar things to be done. On the road they killed their priest and others.

(6) After this the Saccalians went into Jerwan. There they seized the magistrate, Hebbus, and brought him with the other Danes back to their fort and tormented him and the others with a cruel martyrdom. They tore out their viscera and plucked out Hebbus' heart from his bosom while he was still alive. They roasted it in the fire, divided it among themselves, and ate it, so that they would be made strong against the Christians. They gave the bodies of the Danes to the dogs to gnaw and to the birds of the air.

(7) When they had finished their abominable work, the elders of Fellin sent on that same day to Odenpäh to urge the people there to do likewise. They sent the bloody swords with which they killed the Germans, together with their horses and clothing, to the people of Dorpat as a sign. All of them rejoiced and accepted the message. They rushed upon the Brothers of the Militia and put them in chains. They slew John, who was their magistrate, and all their servants. They struck many of the merchants with swords and the rest escaped by hiding. They afterwards threw the latter in chains. They plundered all the goods of the Brothers of the Militia, the merchants, and the other Germans and divided the goods among themselves. They left the bodies of the slain unburied on the plains. May their souls rest in peace with Christ. In Dorpat at the same time they placed the priest Hartwig, a colleague of the Brothers of the Militia, upon an extremely fat ox, for he was equally fat. They brought him out of the

271. Ps. 78:2, 3.

fort and by lot they sought the will of their gods as to which of them, namely the priest or the ox, they should choose as their victim. The lot fell upon the ox and he was sacrificed in a moment. According to the will of the gods, they allowed the priest to live, though he had received a large wound, which later healed.

(8) Then word went out through all of Esthonia and Oesel to fight against the Danes and the Germans. They cast the Christian name out of all their territories. They called upon the Russians both from Novgorod and Pskov to help them. They made peace with the Russians and placed some of them in Dorpat, some in Fellin, and others in other forts to fight against the Germans and Latins and all the Christians. They divided with them the horses, money, and all the belongings of the Brothers of the Militia, as well as of the merchants and everything that they had plundered. They fortified their strongholds most firmly. They built paterells in all their forts, teaching one another the ballistarian art, and they divided among themselves a great many ballistas, which they had seized from the Brothers of the Militia. They took back their wives, who had been sent away during the Christian period. They disinterred the bodies of their dead, who had been buried in cemeteries, and cremated them according to their original pagan custom. They washed themselves, their houses, and their forts with brooms and water, trying thus to erase the sacrament of baptism in their territory.

(9) The Saccalians sent messengers to Riga and said that they would like to reestablish peace, but that they would never hereafter accept the Christian faith so long as a boy a year old or a cubit high remained in the land. They demanded their boys who were hostages and promised that for each of their hostages they would return one of the merchants and Brothers of the Militia whom they had, still alive, in chains. This was done.

(10) There was at that same time a Christian merchant in the house of an Esthonian in Saccalia and when all the Ger-

mans in the land were being killed, this Esthonian rushed upon his guest and murdered him. After this had happened, the wife of the murderer gave birth to a son. This son had upon his body fresh wounds in all the spots in which the father had wounded and slain the innocent man, and the wounds were similar in every way to the wounds of the murdered man. They later healed, and the scars appear to this day. Many people saw this and were astonished, bearing witness to and proving God's vengeance, for the murderer was slain at once by the Christian army.

(11) Wars were then begun afresh in all the regions of Esthonia. The Oeselians, the maritime people, and the people of Warbole, together with the people of Jerwan and Wierland, besieged the Danes in Reval for a long time, until the Lord freed them. The men in the fort were extremely weary and after a long time the Germans and Danes went out to the enemy and carried the war to them. God turned the Esthonians to flight and many of them fell, killed by the Christians, and the rest fled. The Christians bore off their cattle, horses, and many spoils, praising the Lord Who, in this instance, had liberated them from such evils.

(12) The Letts saw all the evils which the Esthonians planned to do in Livonia and at once they began to undertake a war with the Esthonians. Rameke went with his men and Warigerbe went with other Letts into Ungannia. They ravaged villages, captured and killed men, and took many spoils. When these men returned, others went again and did similar harm. The Esthonians likewise pursued the Letts into Lettia and perpetrated similar evils.

(13) After this, the Brothers of the Militia, too, went into Ungannia and by pillaging and burning several villages, they did similar harm to the Esthonians. When they returned to Riga, they recalled the bishop's men and also all the Germans, so that the latter would grant them help against the ferocity of the Esthonians. But these all said, as if with one mouth: "If you are willing to give up to the bishop of Riga and to the

church of Blessed Mary their one-third of Esthonia and to
restore freely to Bishop Hermann his one-third and to be
content with your own third part, we will willingly offer you
aid." They promised that thenceforth they would relinquish
to the bishops their thirds. All of the men of the church,
therefore, rose up immediately, summoned an army from their
Livonians and Letts, and went into Saccalia. They appeared
at dawn next to the fort of Fellin and the Esthonians went
out and fought with them up to the third hour. They then
turned away from the Esthonians, divided up their army
among all the villages, and despoiled the land. They captured
and killed those whom they found and the whole army assembled and returned to Livonia. At the fort which is on the
Pala, they fought for three days with the enemy. Some of
them crossed the Pala, despoiling and burning all of Nurmegunde. There they killed a great many men and, coming to
their own men, they returned with the whole army to Livonia.
They beheaded all the men whom they had brought along as
prisoners, in order to take vengeance upon those lying and unfaithful nations. They divided the spoils and together they
praised Him Who is always blessed.

[XXVII]

(1) It was the bishop's twenty-fifth year [1223], and
the church still did not rest from the wars. When Bishop
Bernard, the first bishop of the Semgalls, returned from Germany with many pilgrims, the Saccalians and Ungannians
with the people of the neighboring provinces collected a large
army. They came to the Sedde, despoiled the land of the
Letts, and killed many of the Letts. They took the women
captive, divided up their army throughout the province, and
struck the land a great blow. Some went to Tricatia, some to
Rosula, some to Metsepole, and some to Treiden. They found

a great many men and women in all the villages and killed
many of them. They took others captive, took away many
spoils, and consigned all the villages and churches to the fire.
After this they fixed Loddiger as the assembly place for their
army with all their plunder. Rameko with a few other Letts
was following behind the Esthonians at Orellen and, by some
chance, came to Waremar, the prince of the Russians in Fellin,
and killed him, together with many other Russians and Esthonians. They took away the weapons and many spoils and returned to Wenden.

In Riga the word became known about all the evils which
had been brought upon the Livonians and Letts and everyone
wept and mourned for their colleagues who had been killed.
With no delay, they at once threw down their bread, bags,
and cloth. The knights and infantry, the Brothers of the Militia and the pilgrims, the merchants and the Livonians, all went
to Treiden. They sent scouts and discovered that the enemy
had now left Loddiger. They followed the enemy night and
day. All of the infantry and a great many of the others were
worn out by the excessive work and returned to Riga. But
those who were constant of heart about taking vengeance
upon the nations and about setting themselves up as a wall for
the Lord's house did not go back. Among them were John,
the provost of the church of Blessed Mary, Daniel the priest,
and Volquin, the master of the Brothers of the Militia. These
men encouraged the rest by inspiring and admonishing them
to show themselves steadfast and strong in fighting the Lord's
battle against those apostates and presumptuous men. There
came to them the Brothers of the Militia from Segewold and
Wenden and a great multitude of Livonians and Letts. They
followed the enemy along the road which goes to the Aa, but
the enemy had gone by another road which leads to the
church next to the Sedde. They stabled their horses in the
church at night and wrought their other enormities there.
They plundered and burned the crops, houses, and everything
that belonged to the priest. In the morning they marched to

the Sedde. It happened that when one part of the army had crossed the Sedde bridge, some of the Christians suddenly came along by a side road. They rushed through the midst of the enemy army, carrying the war to them and the Esthonians met them very fiercely. But He Who formerly terrified the Philistines so that they fled before David, terrified them. The Germans joined battle with them and the Esthonians turned tail and fled before the Christians. The Christians pursued them, scattering and driving them along the road by which they came, and killed a great many of them. They chased them in complete rout to the bridge and killed some along the road. They fought with them at the bridge, where Theodoric, a Brother of the Militia, a strong and devoted man, fell, wounded by a lance. The rest crossed the bridge and went up to the enemy. But the latter left all their loot and horses, killed some prisoners, and fled by foot to the forests. Six hundred and more of them were killed. Some of them perished in the woods, other drowned in the Aa, and others shamefully returned to their land and announced the news at home. But the Christians—Germans, Livonians, and Letts—made off with their spoils. They divided the horses and cattle equally among themselves and restored their captive brethren, both men and women, to their original liberty. Together they praised and blessed Him Who, not solely in this instance, but at all times, fought for them in Livonia and always gave a glorious victory over the apostate peoples.

(2) After the Esthonians, who had fallen away from the faith of Jesus Christ, had been beaten at the Sedde, Bishop Bernard sent throughout Livonia and Lettia, summoning everyone, the men of the church, the Brothers of the Militia, the Livonians and Letts, so that they would all come to fight against the Esthonians. They all faithfully obeyed him. They all assembled at once and the pilgrims and merchants were there. Some of them went by ship on the Aa, some went on foot, some went with their horses. Eight thousand of them came to the place for prayer and counsel. After celebrating

the solemnities of prayer and counsel, they hurried into Esthonia, to the fort of Fellin, which had been taken by the Germans ten years before and had been subjected to Christianity.[272] Now [Aug. 1] they attacked the fort a second time.
They put up paterells and smaller machines; they built a tall
and very strong wooden tower, which they pushed up to the
moat so that they would be able to dig at the fort from below. They were very much hindered by the ballistarii of the
men in the fort; for the latter had a great many of the ballistas
of the Brothers of the Militia which they used against the
ballistas of the Christians and they had built paterells and
machines against the Christians' machines. They fought
against one another for many days. The siege of the fort began on the feast of Peter's Chains in August and they were
exhausted and gave themselves up on the feast of the Assumption of the Blessed Virgin [Aug. 15]. Since the heat was, indeed, exceedingly great and there was a multitude of beasts
and men in the fort, and they were perishing from hunger
and thirst, there was a great pestilence because of the excessively great stench of those who had died in the fort and the
men began to get sick and die. The rest who remained were
not strong enough to defend themselves and gave themselves,
still alive, and all their belongings into the Christians' hands,
especially since they saw that the fort was again set on fire by
the Christians and they had protected themselves and the fort
by the greatest labor. After they had made peace with the
Christians, therefore, they left the fort and accepted again the
yoke of Christian discipline. They promised that they would
never thereafter violate the sacrament of the faith by apostatiz-
ing and that they would make satisfaction for what they had
done. The Brothers of the Militia and all the Germans spared
them, although they had lost both their lives and all their
goods. After taking the fort the army hanged all of the Russians who were in the fort and who had come to aid the
apostates. This was done to the terror of the other Russians.

272. See above, p. 105 (XV, 1).

When peace had been restored in all matters, the Christians
went to the fort and took away everything in it. They turned
out the horses and flocks, which they divided equally among
themselves, and they allowed the men to depart for their villages. After they had divided the spoils, the Christians proceeded to another fort which is at the Pala and they made war
likewise upon the people there. The people in the fort feared
that their fort would be taken and that they would suffer
pestilence and deaths, such as had occurred in the earlier fort,
and similar hardships. They gave themselves up as quickly as
possible into the hands of the Christians and begged only for
their lives and freedom. All of their goods they turned over
into the army's hands. The Christians allowed them their lives
and their freedom and sent them to their villages. The Christians took away all of the many spoils, the horses, sheep, and
cattle and everything that was in the fort. Together they
praised God for the recovery of the two forts and the subjugation once again of that perverse people. They returned
with great joy to Livonia.

(3) The Saccalian elders had been sent into Russia with
money and many gifts to call out, if they could, the Russian
kings to help them against all the Germans and Latins. The
king of Suzdal [273] sent his brother [274] with a numerous army to
help the people of Novgorod. The people of Novgorod joined
him, as did the king of Pskov with his citizens, and the army
numbered about twenty thousand men. They came into Ungannia near Dorpat, and the people of Dorpat sent them large
gifts. They also delivered into the hands of the king the
Brothers of the Militia and the Germans whom they held
as prisoners, as well as horses and ballistas and many other
things, and they asked for help against the Latins. The king
placed his men in the fort so that he would have control in

273. Grand Prince George of Suzdal. The city of Suzdal, at this time the
capital of Suzdalia, lies southeast of Rostov, northeast of Vladimir, and some
two hundred miles west of Nizhnii Novgorod.
274. Iaroslav.

Ungannia and throughout all of Esthonia. The king went on
to Odenpäh and acted similarly there. After this he turned
his army toward Puidise in Livonia and the Ungannians followed him, making his army larger. The Oeselians came out
to meet him and asked him to turn his army against the Danes
in Reval, so that, when the Danes had been beaten, they
could more easily invade Livonia. They said that in Riga
there were many pilgrims who were prepared to attack them.
The king listened to them and returned by another route with
his army into Saccalia. When he discovered that all of Saccalia had now been subjugated by the Germans, that two forts
had been taken, and that his Russians at Fellin had been
hanged, the king was greatly angered and visited his wrath
upon the Saccalians. He struck the land a great blow and
determined to kill all those who had escaped from the Germans and from the great pestilence which had been in the
land. Some escaped by flight into the forests. The king proceeded into Jerwan with his great army and summoned the
Jerwanians, the Wierlanders, and the Warbolians, with the
Oeselians. With all of them the king besieged the fort of the
Danes at Lyndanise. He fought with the Danes for four weeks
and was unable to take them or their fort, because there were
many ballistarii in the fort, who killed many Russians and
Esthonians. Because of this the king of Suzdal was at length
confounded and with all his army he returned to Russia.
This army was, however, very great and strong and it tried
to take the fort of the Danes, using the skills of the Germans,
but it was unable to do so. After destroying and plundering
the province round about, the Russians at last returned to their
country.

(4) The Brothers of the Militia and the other Germans
had meanwhile laid siege to the fort of Dorpat with a few men,
and they fought with the men in the fort for five days. Since
they could not overcome such a strong fort with a few men,
they plundered the territory round about and returned to
Livonia with all their booty. The Brothers of the Militia again

collected an army and entered Esthonia. They struck the people of Jerwan a great blow because the latter were always starting wars with the Danes. The Brothers killed and captured many of them and carried off many spoils. The Jerwanians came to them at Kettis and promised perpetual fidelity to the Germans and to all Christians. The Brothers left their territory at once, therefore, and returned to their own land with all their loot.

(5) After this the people of Novgorod sent King Vetseke, who had once slain the bishop of Riga's men at Kokenhusen. The people of Novgorod gave him money and two hundred men and gave him authority over Dorpat and the other provinces which he could subject to himself. This king came with his men to Dorpat, and the people in the fort received him with joy, that they might be made stronger against the Germans. They gave him tribute from the provinces lying round about. He sent his army against whoever would not pay tribute to him and he laid waste all the lands which rebelled against him, from Waiga to Wierland, from Wierland to Jerwan and to Saccalia. He did all the evil that he could to the Christians.

(6) When the solemnity of the Lord's birth had been celebrated, the Rigans planned to besiege the fort of Dorpat. They assembled with the Brothers of the Militia, the pilgrims, the Livonians, and the Letts at Astigerwe, and they had a large army. They recollected their long-continuing quarrel with the Danes, against whom all the adjacent lands and peoples had now fought for a long time, and they gave up the journey to Dorpat. They went with all their army into Harrien and besieged the fort of Loal. They fought with them for two weeks, building machines, paterells, and a very strong wooden tower, which they pushed up near the fort, so that they could dig at the fort from below and fight more readily with the enemy from the top. The Danes heard this and rejoiced. They came and gave thanks to the Rigans because they had pitied the Danes and come to help them. After this, indeed, many

men were killed by the ballistarii and hit by the operators of
the machines and the rest began to fall seriously ill and die.
The sappers, moreover, were now approaching the top of
the fortifications, so that the people in the fort thought that
they and the earthworks together would now tumble down to
the bottom. For this reason they at last besought the army to
give them their lives and their freedom. The army allowed
them to live and burned the fort. The Germans took all the
horses, cattle, flocks, goods, money, clothing, and everything
that was in the fort and divided them equally with the Livonians and Letts. They gave the men back to the Danes, however, and sent them back free to their villages. The Germans,
meanwhile, sent some men from their army to three other
lesser forts lying round about and threatened war upon them
unless they gave themselves up. These three neighboring forts
gave themselves up to the Rigans and sent them tribute and a
great many *waipas* [275] in that same expedition. The army of
the Rigans returned to Jerwan and certain of them went to
plunder the province. The Jerwanians and Wierlanders came
to them and begged for peace, promising that they would not
thenceforth violate the sacraments of the Christian faith. The
Rigans again made peace with them and received them in
grace, taking hostages from them. The Danes afterwards
troubled them and made war upon them a great deal because
they had received peace and the yoke of Christianity from
the Rigans. The Rigan army returned joyfully to Livonia,
praising Jesus Christ, Who always led them out and led them
back safe and sound on all their expeditions. Messengers from
the Russian kings were in Riga, meanwhile, awaiting the outcome of events and greatly marveling, for the Rigans never
returned empty, without victory, just as the arrow of Jonathan never turned back nor did his shield fall in battle, and
the sword of Saul returned not empty,[276] while the great and
strong armies of the Russian kings were never strong enough

275. The Esthonian word *waip* means a type of crude cloth.
276. II Kings 1:22.

not their own.

to subjugate to the Christian faith a single fort through their attacks.

Suggest that conversion needs violence

[XXVIII]

(1) It was the twenty-sixth year [1224] of Bishop Albert's consecration, and the church did not yet rest from the wars. For King Vetseke and the people of Dorpat troubled all the land around about and the Letts and Livonians went against them frequently with a few men, but they were unable to harm them. After Easter [April 14] the Brothers of the Militia again collected an army, besieged Dorpat, and fought for five days with them, but could not take the fort because of the smallness of their force. They plundered the country round about and returned with their spoils to Livonia.

The venerable Bishop Albert, meanwhile, returned from Germany with many pilgrims and his whole retinue. There came with him his brother, the no less venerable Bishop Hermann, who had long ago been elected and consecrated bishop in Esthonia and who had now been kept from his bishopric for many years by the king of Denmark. But after the king of Denmark was taken prisoner by the Germans in Saxony,[277] the bishop of Riga and this brother of his went to the king to seek his will and approval. It pleased the king that Hermann should go to Livonia and from Livonia to his bishopric in Esthonia. When they came to Riga they were received with great joy by the Rigans and by everyone who was in Livonia. They all rejoiced together and praised God because, after many evils and sad wars, nearly all of Esthonia was once again taken over and secured, save for the one fort of Dorpat, concerning which the divine vengeance held back.

(2) The Brothers of the Militia assembled with the bishops,

277. King Waldemar II was captured on May 7, 1223, and confined in Dannenberg Castle in Saxony.

the men of the church, and all the Rigans on the matter of the
division of the provinces of Esthonia which belonged to Riga.
They gave Bishop Hermann Ungannia with its provinces and
the Brothers of the Militia by lot drew Saccalia for their part.
They allotted to the church of Blessed Mary in Riga and to the
bishop of Riga the maritime provinces and seven *kilegunds*.[278]
When the maritime people heard that they belonged to the
Rigan church they were overjoyed and they paid up in full
the tribute for two years, which they had neglected because of
the attack of the Danes. The Ungannians also rejoiced over
the rule of Bishop Hermann, who was in Odenpäh. King
Vetseke and his people of Dorpat, however, hindered them,
for he was like a snare and a great devil for the Saccalians and
the other nearby Esthonians.

(3) The bishops had sent messengers to the king in Dorpat,
asking him to forsake those rebels who were in the fort, who
had violated the sacraments of their baptism, who had cast off
the faith of Jesus Christ and returned to their paganism, who
had expelled the Brothers of the Militia, their brethren and
lords, from their territory, slaying some and capturing others,
and who daily despoiled and devastated all the neighboring
provinces which had come to the faith of Jesus Christ. The
king did not wish to forsake them, for the people of Novgorod
and the Russian kings had given him the fort and the nearby
lands by a perpetual gift and they had promised him freedom
from German attacks. All of the criminals from the neighboring provinces and from Saccalia assembled in that fort with
that king. These men were traitors, the murderers of their
brethren, of the Brothers of the Militia and the merchants, the
inventors of evil schemes against the Livonian church. Their
prince and lord was this king, for he was the old root of all
evils [279] in Livonia. He had broken the peace of the true
Peacemaker and had killed in ambush all the Christian men
who were faithful to Him and who had been sent by the

278. *Kihhelkund* is an Esthonian word meaning "parish."
279. Cf. I Tim. 6:10.

Rigans to help in an attack upon the Lithuanians, and he had pillaged all their goods. All of these people, therefore, placed their trust in his very strong fort. They despised the peace of the Christians and sought daily to do evil to the Christians. This fort was, indeed, stronger than all the forts of Esthonia, since the Brothers of the Militia had formerly strengthened it with great labor and expense and had filled it with their weapons and ballistas, all of which the traitors had taken. The king, moreover, had with him there a great many of his Russian archers. They got ready, in addition, paterells according to the Oeselians' method and other instruments of war.

(4) The church of the Esthonians was thus exposed at that time to the many misfortunes of war and was like the woman in labor, who has great sorrow and anguish until she gives birth.[280] In pursuit of her offspring there comes a dragon,[281] namely that Behemoth who drinks up a river and still trusts that the Jordan will flow into his mouth.[282] The church could in no way be freed from the misfortunes of the wars (for she was still weak and an infant), save by the Livonian church, which had always been her true and original mother by the labor of conquest and had also given birth to her by the washing of regeneration[283] in the faith of Jesus Christ. Many mothers, indeed, claimed this daughter falsely and always drew her to them by their lies. One of these was the Russian mother, always sterile and barren,[284] for she always attempted to subject lands to herself, not with the hope of regeneration in the faith of Jesus Christ, but with the hope of loot and tribute.

(5) In order for the Livonian church to free her daughter, the Esthonian church, which she conceived by Jesus Christ, from present evils, the venerable bishop of Riga sent and summoned the Brothers of the Militia, as well as the men of

280. Cf. John 16:21.
281. Cf. Apoc. 12:13.
282. Cf. Job 40:10, 18.
283. Titus 3:5.
284. Cf. Exod. 23:26.

the church, the pilgrims, merchants, citizens of Riga, and all
the Livonians and Letts. He proclaimed an expedition to all
those belonging to the Livonian church. They all faithfully
obeyed him and assembled with their army at Lake Rasti-
gerwe [285] and called to them the venerable bishop of Riga
and his no less venerable brother, Bishop Hermann, with all
their men, priests, and knights. When the mysteries of counsel and prayer had taken place there, they sent on ahead the
best and strongest men from the army so that, crossing Ungannia during night and day, they might be able on the following
morning to take by surprise the fort of Dorpat. They again
split up their army, assigned some to attack the fort, and sent
others into Wierland to despoil those who were still rebellious. After three days they brought back an abundance of
sheep, cattle, and the rest of the things that were necessary
for the army. The bishops, indeed, followed with the pilgrims and all the multitude and they came to the fort on the
feast of the Assumption of the Blessed Virgin [Aug. 15]. On
that very same day in the previous year the fort of Fellin had
been taken. They covered the fields with tents and made war
upon the people in the fort. They constructed paterells and
lesser machines, prepared a great many instruments of war,
and put up a *propugnaculum*, or very strong wooden tower.
In eight days they constructed this from large, tall trees. They
made it as high as the fort and pushed it over the moat, close
to the fort. They began at once to dig at the earth from below.
Half of the army was assigned to dig night and day, so that
some dug and others hauled away the loose dirt. When morning came a large part of the earthworks crumbled away from
the battlement and they soon placed the wooden tower closer
to the fort. Mediators, meanwhile, were sent to the king,
priests and knights, honorable men, who promised him a free
route, so that he could leave with his men and horses and all
his belongings, if only he would go away from the fort and
abandon that apostate people. But the king, expecting to be

285. Lake Restjerw.

relieved by the people of Novgorod, stated very firmly that
he would by no means give up the fort. The Russians came,
meanwhile, and pillaged the province. Rumors were brought
to the tents. The Germans prepared at once and came, wishing to meet the Russians. They took to the fields and left the
others at the siege of the fort. When the Russians did not
come, they again returned to the attack upon the fort. They
wounded many men atop the fort with the arrows of the ballistas, killed others with the missiles of the machines, and with
the paterells they shot glowing irons or pots of fire into the
fort. They struck the people of the fort with many kinds of
terror, because some were preparing instruments, which they
called hedgehogs [286] and swine,[287] others were bringing up
piles of wood, others setting fire to them. In this way they
fought for many days. Those who were in the fort likewise
constructed machines and paterells against the Christians' machines and countered their arrows with their own archers and
ballistarii. The Christians did not stop digging by day and
night and the tower came up closer to the fort. No rest was
allowed to the weary.[288] They fought by day and shouted and
played by night. The Livonians and Letts made a clamor by
pounding their swords and shields together. The Germans
with their drums, pipes, and other musical instruments, the
Russians with their instruments and their shouting, stayed
awake every night. All of the Christians, therefore, gathered
and sought counsel from God. Among them was Duke Frederick, Duke Fredhelm, and the noble and wealthy magistrate
of the pilgrims. The latter said: "We ought to storm this fort
violently by going over the walls and to take revenge upon
the evildoers to the terror of the others. For in all the forts
hitherto taken by the Livonians, the enemy have always kept
their lives and freedom, and the rest, therefore, have not been

286. See above, n.213.

287. A "swine" was a moveable hut or cover, like a mantelet, used especially in siege warfare to protect the attackers from the missiles of their
enemies.

288. Cf. Job 3:17.

made afraid thereby. Now, therefore, we should glorify with great honors whoever of our men will first enter the fort by scaling the wall and we should give him the horses and the best captive there is in the fort, except for the king, whom we shall raise above all the others by hanging him from the highest limb." This advice pleased everyone. They made vows to the Lord and to the Blessed Virgin and they began the fight immediately at dawn after the solemn celebration of Masses. They made piles of wood, but all their work was foiled, because the time for God's vengeance had not yet come. At the ninth hour, therefore, the Esthonians in the fort lit great fires. They opened a big hole in the fortifications and from this they put out wheels filled with fire and directed them toward the tower and threw great piles of wood on top of it. The brave Christians in arms, however, broke up the fires, destroyed the wheels, stamped out all the force of the flames, and defended their tower. Other men from the army, meanwhile, gathered wood and set fire to the bridge.[289] All of the Russians ran together to the gate to oppose them. (6) John of Appeldorn, the brother of the bishop and an outstanding knight, took fire in his hand and began first to climb up the ramparts. Peter his servant immediately became the second to do so. With no delay they swiftly came to the bulwark. The other men of the army saw this and they all ran and followed them. What more? Each man hurried to go up first so that he might exalt the glory and praise of Jesus Christ and His Mother Mary and so that he might himself receive praise and a reward for his labor. He went up—which man went over first, I know not, God knows [290]—and the whole multitude followed him. Each man helped his partner up into the fort and others went into the hole through which the people of the fort had thrust out the wheels of fire. The first man

289. . . . *pontem incendunt.* . . . Presumably this must refer to a draw-bridge, unless of course, there is a defect in the text and *pontem* has been read for *portam.*

290. Cf. II Cor. 12:2, 3.

prepared a place for those who followed. With swords and lances they put the Esthonians to flight from the fortifications. After many Germans had already come into the fort, the Letts and some of the Livonians followed them. They began at once to kill the people, both the men and some women. They did not spare them, so that the number amounted to a thousand. The Russians, indeed, defended themselves for a very long time. At last they were beaten and fled up into the fortification. They were dragged out of there and all of them were killed: about two hundred, together with their king. The other men of the army also surrounded the fort on all sides, allowing no one to flee. Whoever came down from the fort, after eluding those who were inside, fell into the hands of those who were outside. Of all the men who were in the fort, only one remained alive. He was a vassal of the great king of Suzdal who had been sent by his lord with the other Russians to that same fort. The Brothers of the Militia later dressed him up and sent him back to Novgorod and Suzdal on a good horse so that he could announce to his lords the news of what had happened. After all the men had been killed there was great rejoicing among the Christians and they played upon the drums, pipes, and musical instruments because they had taken vengeance upon the malefactors and had killed all the traitors from Livonia and Esthonia who had gathered there. After this they took all the weapons of the Russians, the clothes, horses, and all the booty that was in the fort, and the remaining women and children, and burned the fort. They returned at once on the following day with great joy to Livonia, praising God in heaven for the victory He had brought them, since He is good and His mercy endures forever.[291] The people of Novgorod had come, indeed, with a great army to Pskov, wishing to free the fort from the German siege. When they heard that the fort was already taken and their men killed, they returned to their city with violent sorrow and indignation.

291. Cf. Ps. 105:1.

(7) The Oeselians also freed Theodoric the bishop's brother from captivity and sent him back to Livonia. The maritime Esthonians also came to Riga, returned to their obedience to the bishop, and paid up in full a double tribute which, because of the Danes, they had overlooked for two years. They promised perpetual fidelity to the church of Riga and they returned to the Christian faith. The people of Warbole likewise brought tribute and gifts and gave themselves up in all matters to the Rigans. The Rigans, however, made no definite agreement about them and only accepted without doubt the seven maritime provinces which they had always held by every right. The Rigans lacked none of the legal rights in the maritime provinces, which they had always possessed by right of conquest, which they had brought to the Christian faith and baptism, which had given them tribute and hostages. They had never delivered the hostages from these maritime provinces to the king of Denmark. The Wierlanders and the Jerwanians, too, heard of the capture of Dorpat, came to Riga, and brought horses and gifts to the lords.

(8) Bishop Hermann went with his men into Ungannia and began to build up the fort at Odenpäh. He placed in the fort noble men and honorable knights, Engelbert, his relative [292] from Thysenhusen, Theodoric, his brother, Helmold of Luneburg, a prudent and noble man, and John of Dolen and gave each of them a province, or *kilegund*,[293] in fee. He took in a great many other Germans to live in this same fort, so that they could defend the land and the fort from the enemy and could teach their Esthonian subjects the Christian faith. The Esthonians, however, inasmuch as they had previously been traitors, were not allowed to live with the Germans in the fort. The same bishop also called upon the priests to come with him into Ungannia and gave churches to them as benefices and

292. The text reads: . . . *generum suum* . . . , meaning literally "his son-in-law."
293. See above, n.278.

endowed them with a grain supply and sufficient fields. He instructed the Esthonians and taught them properly about the tithe, which was always ordained by God. They accepted it and began to pay it annually thenceforth. The bishop thus arranged to pay what was promised and to give the necessary things to his priests and vassals. He installed Rothmar, his brother, as provost, appointed a place for his monastery in Dorpat, and assigned him twenty-four villages with sufficient income and fields. He arranged for regular canons there and designated it as his cathedral church.

(9) The Brothers of the Militia went into Saccalia, took possession of the fort of Fellin, and began to build it up very strongly. They placed priests in the churches and assigned them sufficient revenue both in grain and fields and they received the tithe from the Livonians. They collected, moreover, full satisfaction for everything that had been taken from them and for all the damage done to them, both in Ungannia and in Saccalia. They also divided up Waiga. They turned over half of it to Ungannia and took the other half, together with Saccalia, Nurmegunde, and Mocha, for themselves. The Russians, both from Novgorod and from Pskov sent messengers to Riga, asking for peace. The Rigans received them, made peace with them, and restored to them the tribute which they had always had in Tholowa. The bishop of Riga divided the Letts of Tholowa with his Brothers of the Militia. The bishop took two-thirds of them and left the other third to the Brothers of the Militia.

[XXIX]

(1) It was the bishop's twenty-seventh year [1225], and now the land of the Livonians reposed in the tranquility of peace.[294] For after the very strong fort of Dorpat was

---

294. Henry casts this last statement in a hexameter line:
 Lyvonum terra tranquilla pace silebat.

captured and all of the Esthonians and Russians, together with the king, were killed, a fear of the Rigans and the Germans fell upon all the neighboring lands and upon all the peoples round about. They all sent their messengers with gifts to Riga: the Russians, the maritime Esthonians, the Oeselians, the Semgalls, the Kurs, as well as the Lithuanians. All of them sought peace and the alliance of the Rigans, for they feared lest the Rigans do unto them what they had done to the people of Dorpat. The Rigans received them and gave peace to all who asked for it from them and the land reposed in their sight.[295] The Esthonians left their forts and rebuilt their burned-out villages and churches. The Livonians and Letts, too, did likewise. They came out of the hiding places in the forests in which they had hidden now for many years in time of war and each man returned to his village and his fields.[296] They plowed and sowed in great security, such as they had not had for the previous forty years, for both before the preaching of God's word and after their baptism, the Lithuanians and other peoples had never given them any rest or security. Now, therefore, they rested, rejoicing in their fields and their labors, and there was no one who terrified them. With fuller understanding of the Christian faith they confessed Jesus Christ, the Son of God, Who, after the difficulties of war, after the killing of many people, after the pestilences, and after many evils, at last had mercy upon the rest of His people and gave them peace and security. The whole people rested after following the Lord [297] and blessed Him Who is blessed forever.

(2) In that same year the venerable bishop of Riga sent his priest Maurice to the Roman court to ask the apostolic see for a legate to Livonia. The supreme pontiff agreed and sent the venerable bishop of Modena,[298] the chancellor of his

295. Cf. I Macc. 1:3.
296. Cf. John 7:53.
297. I Kings 7:2.
298. Bishop William of Modena was named apostolic legate to Livonia on December 31, 1224.

palace, with that same priest back to Livonia. He came to the
Dvina with his household, pilgrims, and his whole retinue.
The Rigans went out to meet him, received him, and with
great joy led him into the city. He rejoiced with them and
extolled Jesus Christ because he found that God's vineyard
was so gloriously planted, that the church was watered with
the blood of so many of the faithful, and that it had grown so
much and so far that its branches extended for a ten-day
journey,[299] as far as Reval, or, in another direction, it spread
out equally far to Pskov, or, along the Dvina, as far as Gerzika,
and now had five separate bishoprics with their bishops. He
sent his messengers at once back to the Roman court and
wrote to the supreme pontiff about the true state of affairs.

(3) The legate being anxious about the new converts, frequently called together the Livonians and others who were in
the city, both men and women. He diligently ministered the
Word of God and joyfully gave many indulgences. After this,
desiring to see the Livonians and the others, the Lithuanians
and Esthonians, he journeyed to Treiden, and there were
with him the venerable bishop of Riga, John the provost of
the church of Blessed Mary, and a great many other wise and
discreet men. Coming first to Cubbesele, he celebrated solemn
Masses for the Livonians there and preached the word of
salvation so that he could strengthen them in the Catholic
faith. From there on he did the same in Vitisele[300] and in Loddiger. He afterwards did likewise in Metsepole, Idumea, and
Lettia. He sowed the seed of the gospels to all, taught them
to bear good fruit,[301] and zealously elucidated the Christian
faith. He proceeded then into Ungannia and found there the
church of the faithful, both Germans and Esthonians. He
found that the new inhabitants were living in the fort of
Odenpäh and that the fort was firmly built. He blessed the
Lord because he found a monastery of the faithful in Esthonia.

299. Cf. Ezek. 17:7.
300. Perhaps this was the estate of Idsel.
301. Cf. Matt. 7:17; 12:33.

He admonished the Esthonians, by instructing them in the faith of Jesus Christ, and the Germans, by exhorting them faithfully. They were to live together in a friendly way, they were not to stir up evil for each other, the Germans were not to impose any harsh, unbearable burden upon the shoulders of the converts, but rather the sweet and light yoke of the Lord, and they were always to teach the sacraments of the faith. He blessed them and went on into Saccalia. There in the first parish, which he found by Lake Worcegerwe, he most devotedly admonished the newly-converted Esthonians and taught them never to stray from the faith of our Lord Jesus Christ. He proceeded thence to the fort of Fellin, which belongs to the Brothers of the Militia and which they had already built up very solidly at that time. They went out joyfully to meet the legate of the apostolic see and received him into the fort. They told him of all the evils that they had suffered there from the Esthonians because of the Christian faith. He summoned the Esthonians, both men and women, into their churches and went to them. He admonished them by faithfully ministering the word of exhortation [302] henceforth not to presume to do such evil or to violate the sacraments of the faith. The devout man likewise impressed the warnings of sacred doctrine upon the Brothers of the Militia there. He taught them that they should not be harsh to their subjects, these stupid Esthonians, either in taking the tithes or in any other matter whatever, lest through such conditions they should again be forced to return to paganism. Messengers from the Danes of Reval also came to him there. They welcomed him with joy and told him about their wars and tribulations. Likewise messengers from the maritime Esthonians, who were always fighting with the Danes, came to him and offered him their lands and provinces, as they were always offering them to the Rigans, if only he would defend them from the Danes and Oeselians. He received them. He returned

---

302. Cf. Pope Gregory I, *Homilia 17 in Evangelio,* quoted in *Breviarium Romanum, Officium Commune Evangelistarum, Lect. viii.*

after this to the land of the Letts and the Letts from the whole
province which is called Tholowa came to him at Tricatia.
The legate joyfully preached the Word of God to them and
explained all the sacraments of the faith. He went from there
to Wenden, where he was received with the greatest devotion
by the Brothers of the Militia and the other Germans who
lived there. He found there a very great multitude of Wends
and Letts. In the morning, when all the Letts had joyfully
gathered, he preached to them the joyous doctrine of the
Lord Jesus Christ. Frequently he made mention of the passion
of that same Lord Jesus and, happy as they were, gladdened
them greatly.[303] He commended their faith and constancy because they had first received the Christian faith voluntarily
and without being disturbed by any wars, and later had never
violated the oaths of baptism, in the manner of the Livonians
and Letts. He praised highly their humility and patience, for
they had gladly borne the name of our Lord Jesus Christ to
the Esthonians and other peoples, and had sent many of their
people, slain for the Christian faith, into the company of the
martyrs as we believe. He did not deny the Wends the faithful admonition of his teaching, nor did he fail to bid their
lords, the Brothers of the Militia, to live faithfully with their
subjects and always to impose upon them a light yoke.[304] After
this he provided similar lessons of piety in Segewold. With
all care he admonished the Livonians henceforth not to neglect their baptismal oaths and return to paganism. He always
took special care to warn the Brothers of the Militia and the
other Germans in other provinces that they should teach the
Christian faith to the Livonians and Letts and other converts,

303. Henry plays here upon the words *Lettus* ("Lett"), and *laetus* ("joy-
ful"): *Unde mane facto, congregatis Letthis universis cum letitia letam eis
domini Iesu Christi doctrinam predicavit, et sepius passionem eiusdem domini
Iesu commemorans, letos eosdem quam plurimum letificavit.* . . .

304. Arndt's text here reads: . . . *quantumvis subditis suis leve semper
iugum imponentes fideliter cohabitarent, attentius iniunxit. Quantumvis*
makes no sense here and probably *quatinus* is meant—this, indeed, is given as
the reading of a seventeenth-century manuscript copy of the chronicle in
the Reval Gymnasium.

that they should impose the delightful burden of Jesus Christ upon their shoulders, and that they should be sparing toward them, both in the matter of tithes and in everything, lest if too heavily burdened they should return to infidelity. When he had finished all these things, he returned to Riga [Aug.]. (4) The Germans, Livonians, and Letts came to him there, seeking judgment in various matters. He replied to each one according to his case and complaint and settled the cases and lawsuits of many people.

The Russians of Novgorod and others from other cities also heard that the legate of the apostolic see was in Riga and they sent their messengers to him to ask from him a confirmation of the peace already made by the Germans. He heard their petitions in this matter, strengthened their faith with many exhortations, and sent them all back to their land with joy. Vesthard, the prince of the Semgalls, was also called and came to him. The legate invited him to the faith of Jesus Christ with many discussions and long sermons, but the prince, in the hardness of his infidelity,[305] did not understand the words of salvation. He would not yet receive baptism, but again promised to do so in the future, and allowed a preacher of the lord legate to come with him into Semgallia. People came, therefore, from all the lands round about to see the legate of the Roman court. Among them was Vsevolod, the king of Gerzika, Count Burchard, the Danish bishops from Reval, the Oeselians, and also the maritime Esthonians, who offered themselves for the legate's defense and promised that they would receive priests and the whole Christian law, if only he would free them from the attacks of the Danes. The legate promised them all freedom and sent his messengers to the Danes and the Oeselians, so that they would set aside the wars, accept his peace, and be obedient to his commands.

(5) The legate desired to see still other converts. He visited

---

305. . . . . *infidelitatis sue duritia.* . . . Cf. Pope Gregory I, *Homilia 29 in Evangelio*, quoted in *Breviarium Romanum, Officium in Ascensione Domini, Lect. viii.*

the Livonians in Holm, celebrated solemn Masses there, and
sowed the seed of holy doctrine. He went on to Uexküll,
where he recalled the memory of the first holy bishops and
strengthened those Livonians in God's service. From there he
went on to Lennewarden and Ascheraden, where he no less
recalled the Livonians from idolatry and diligently taught
them the worship of the one God. In Kokenhusen, at last, he
likewise faithfully impressed the lessons of holy teaching on
the Germans, Russians, Letts, and Selonians who lived there
together. He always admonished the Germans not to hurt
their subjects by excessive exactions or undue harshness. They
were to bring in Christian customs and abolish pagan rites by
assiduously teaching the faith of Christ, and to teach and
instruct [306] them both by their words and by their good examples.

(6) After the legate of the apostolic see had returned to
Riga, the Germans in Odenpäh rose up in the autumn with
all their retinue and at the call of the elders of Wierland they
came into Wierland. They took over the forts of Wierland
and expelled the Danes, saying that this land had first been
made subject to the Christian faith by the Livonians with the
banner of the Blessed Virgin. They began to rule in all the
provinces and forts of Wierland. When he knew of this, the
legate summoned those Germans to himself and by ecclesiastical censure forced them to transfer that land to the protection of the supreme pontiff. He immediately sent messengers
to the Danes in Reval and likewise forced them to transfer to
his hands that land as well as the other lands over which the
Germans were quarreling with the Danes. The Danes dared
not kick against the goad. They promised that they would
faithfully obey the Roman court and transferred Wierland,
Jerwan, Harrien, and the maritime provinces to the hands
of the lord legate's messengers. They sent sealed letters to

306. The text here reads: . . . *et tam exemplis eorum bonis quam verbis eos
instruere docerent. Instruere* here is impossible to construe; probably *in-
struendo* is meant.

Riga to confirm this donation. When this had been done the legate sent his men, pilgrims, and priests into Wierland. He removed all the Germans and Danes and held those lands in his own power.

(7) After the feast of the Epiphany [Jan. 6, 1226], when traveling is better in those cold countries on account of the snow and the ice, the lord legate, with clerics and servants, taking with him also Bishop Lambert of the Semgalls, John the provost of the church of Riga, citizens of Riga, some Brothers of the Militia, and many others, crossed through Livonia, came to the province of the Letts, and went from the Letts into Saccalia, although he was very weak in body. He rested for two days in Fellin and afterwards went to Jerwan. All of the Jerwanians went out to meet him in the village of Carethen and with joy he preached the Word of God to them. He instructed them in the Catholic faith, collected them in the hands of the supreme pontiff, and went on to the first fort of Wierland, which is called Agelinde. He was gladly and gloriously received there and called the whole multitude of people to him. He expounded the salutary precepts of eternal life and revealed to them the name of Jesus Christ. He proceeded from there to Tharwanpe, where he did likewise. The Danes came there, as they had been called. First peace was made between the Danes and the Germans and then with the Esthonians of all the provinces. After this the legate went into the province of Tabellinus, where all the elders of Wierland came to him and heard Christian doctrine and faith from him. He received them all into the hands of the supreme pontiff and he appointed from among them elders and judges for all their provinces. He then returned to Tharwanpe. From there he went to the Danish fort at Reval and even there he was joyfully received by the Danes and Swedes and all who lived there. After this he began to demand from them the boys who were held as hostages from Wierland. The Danes did not wish to deliver the hostages into his hands, but at length they were forced to give them up when they were struck by an

ecclesiastical censure. The legate sent these hostages back to their parents in Wierland. The people of Warbjala accepted the peace of the Roman lord legate and came to him in Reval. On the urgent petition of the Danes, the legate gave the people of Warbjala and the other people of Harrien back to the Danes. The *kilegund* [307] which is called the maritime, together with the whole maritime province, Wierland, and Jerwan, he took into the power of the supreme Roman pontiff. The Esthonians of Reval together with the Danes gathered before him and the legate devotedly ministered the words of eternal salvation to them and faithfully admonished them that thenceforth, living together in good will, they should avoid thoughts of infidelity. When he had finished all of these matters, he sent his priests into the maritime province and returned through Saccalia to Riga. These priests, namely Peter Kakuwalde and his colleague, another priest, went into Sontagana and the maritime peoples received them with joy. The people heard the Word of God from them and the men, women, and children who were as yet unbaptized were baptized by them in Sontagana as well as in Maianpathe and Paehalle. After this the priests returned to Livonia, rejoicing and praising God for the propagation of the faith.

(8) The legate of the apostolic see returned to Riga [308] and the bishops, priests, clerics, Brothers of the Militia, vassals of the church, and citizens of Riga came to him. In the presence of all these people he celebrated a solemn council during Lent,[309] according to the provisions of Innocent,[310] to refresh their memories and institute certain new measures that seemed necessary for the newly-planted church. After everything was done and finished that could be done by him and after in-

---

307. See above, n.278.

308. He was back in Riga on March 15, 1226.

309. Ash Wednesday fell this year on March 4, Easter on April 19.

310. Pope Innocent III is, of course, meant. The reference is to the system of regular diocesan synods and visitations prescribed under Pope Innocent's direction by the Fourth Lateran Council in 1215. See *Decretales Gregorii IX*, 3, 35, 7, *In singulis* (ed. Friedberg, II, 600–601).

dulgences had been given, the legate said farewell to everyone, blessed them, and returned to the ships, commending Livonia to Mary, the Blessed Mother of God, and to Her beloved Son, our Lord Jesus Christ, to Whom is honor and glory, world without end. Amen.

I remember it and rejoice in remembering it.[311] You, Virgin Mary, Mother of God, know the rest. Do You have mercy on me! [312]

(9) Many and glorious things happened in Livonia at the time when the heathen were converted to the faith of Jesus Christ, which cannot all be written down or recalled to the memory, lest it be wearisome to the readers. But these few little things have been written in praise of our Lord Jesus Christ,[313] Who wishes His faith and His name to be carried to all nations.[314] Through Him and with His coöperation and approval, these things were done. He and His beloved Mother (to Whose honor, together with Her Son, our Lord Jesus Christ, all these newly converted lands are credited) [315] always allowed His people in Livonia such great and glorious victories as these over the pagans. These victories were always won with only a few men, rather than with a multitude. Lest the praise owed to Him for such glorious deeds should in later times fall into oblivion through the negligence of the lazy, it has pleased a humble man, at the urging of his lords and companions, to put these things down in writing and to leave them to posterity, so that they may give praise to God and place their hope in Him,[316] and that they may not forget God's work and may seek His commandments.[317] Nothing has

311. Cf. *Aeneid*, I, 203.
312. In verse: *Et memini et meminisse iuvat. Scis cetera mater*
        Virgo Maria Dei. Tu miserere mei.
313. Cf. John 20:30–31.
314. Cf. Acts 9:15.
315. Cf. Arnold of Lubeck, *Chronica Slavorum*, V, 30 (*MGH, SS, XXI*, 211).
316. Cf. Ps. 72:28.
317. Cf. Ps. 118:45.

been put in this account except what we have seen almost entirely with our own eyes. What we have not seen with our own eyes, we have learned from those who saw it and who were there. We have not written this for praise or for the reward of temporal advantage. Rather, we wrote for the remission of our faults and in praise of our Lord Jesus Christ and the Blessed Virgin Mary, the Mother of the Lord, Who with the Father and the Holy Spirit, always was, is now, and shall be blessed, world without end. Amen.

[XXX]

(1) The prelate's twenty-eighth year [1226] followed, and this year the church was calm with a just peace.[318] As the legate of the apostolic see left Livonia, he remained for a long time by his ships near the sea, awaiting the gift of the winds.[319] Suddenly he saw the Oeselians returning from Sweden with their spoils and a great many captives. The Oeselians were accustomed to visit many hardships and villainies upon their captives, both the young women and virgins, at all times, by violating them and taking them as wives, each taking two or three or more of them. They allowed themselves these unlawful actions, though it is not right that Christ be joined with Belial,[320] or is it suitable for a pagan to be joined to a Christian. The Oeselians were even accustomed to sell the women to the Kurs and other pagans. When the lord legate learned of all the evils which they did in Sweden, of the churches that were burned, the priests who were slain, the

318. The heading is again in verse:
  Bisdenus octavus sequitur huius presulis annus,
  Hic erat ecclesia pace silente pia.
Henry's verse-making has faltered badly here: his lines do not scan and the verse is hard to construe sensibly.
  319. The legate is known to have been at Dünamünde from April 28 to May 23, and on July 6 he was at Wisby on the Island of Gothland.—Bunge, *Urkundenbuch*, I, 116; III, 18.
  320. II Cor. 6:15.

sacraments that were administered and violated, and similar misfortunes, he sorrowed with the captives and prayed to the Lord that revenge be taken upon the evildoers. He came to Gothland and sowed the Word of God [July] and displayed the sign of the holy cross for the remission of sins to all who bore the Christian name, that they might take revenge upon the perverse Oeselians.[321] The Germans obeyed and took the cross. The Gothlanders refused. The Danes did not hear the Word of God. Only the German merchants wanted the heavenly merchandise for themselves. They got horses, prepared weapons, and came to Riga. The Rigans rejoiced and went out to meet them as they arrived. The baptized Livonians, Letts, and Esthonians also rejoiced that they might carry the Christian name to the unbaptized Oeselians.

(2) In this year Master John, a companion of the lord legate,[322] held in trust the lands over which there was a quarrel between the Germans and Danes, namely Wierland, Jerwan, and Rotalia. After the peace had been broken, the same Master John began to war with the Danes. The Danes, indeed, plundered and burned Rotalia, took many spoils; but the master's servants pursued them, killing fifty of them and besieging fifty in the fort of Maianpathe. But after three days they had mercy upon them because they were Christians and sent them away. The legate, indeed, sent a great many Germans into Wierland to aid this same John against the savagery both of the Danes and of the Oeselians. The Rigans heard of their war, sent messengers, and made peace with the Danes, so that they would be better able to fight against the Oeselians and to spread the faith among the tribes.

(3) When the feasts of the Lord's birth and Epiphany [Jan. 6, 1227] were over, snow covered the land and ice covered the waves; for the surface of the deep was solidified and the waters were as hard as stone.[323] Ice was formed and it made a better path over both land and sea. When a path was

321. In other words, the legate preached a Crusade against the Oeselians.
322. John was the chaplain of Bishop William of Modena.
323. Job 38:30.

made over the sea, the Rigans desired at once to water the
Oeselian people, who lived on an island of the sea, with the
moisture of their baptism.[324] They announced an expedition
and summoned everyone to the river which is called the
Mother of Waters. When the feast of Fabian and Sebastian
[Jan. 20] was past, all the Germans, Rigans, and Livonians,
with the Letts and Esthonians from all their provinces, assembled. They followed the venerable lord bishop of Riga,
who was accompanied by the bishop of the Semgalls and
Master Volquin with his Brothers and the pilgrims, bringing
their weapons and food with them. After celebrating solemn
Masses, they proceeded on the ice toward Oesel. The army
was large and strong, comprising nearly twenty thousand
men, who marched in their ordered formations, each formation with its own banners. As they trod on the ice with their
horses and vehicles they made a noise like a great peal of
thunder, with the clashing of arms,[325] the shaking of the
vehicles, and the movement and sound of men and horses
falling and getting up again here and there over the ice, which
was as smooth as glass because of the south winds and the rain
water which had fallen at that time and the cold that followed.
They crossed the sea with great labor until at last they joyfully came to the Oeselian coast.

(4) They came on the ninth day to the fort of Mona,[326]
proposing to spend only one night there. They fought with
the people in the fort and the latter, afraid of the approach
of war and of the missiles of the ballistas, retreated into their
houses in the fort. At night they sent words full of deceit to
the bishop and the rest of the elders of the army. They said
that they would accept the faith of Christ and the peace of
the Christians, so that, when the army had gone on, they could
inflict the damage and losses of war upon those who followed.

324. Another play on words: . . . *Rigenses, sacri baptismi sui irrigatione
gentes illas Osilianas, que habitant in insula maris, irrigare cupientes.* . . .

325. Cf. I Macc. 6:41.

326. Mona is an island northeast of Oesel and separated from the larger
island by a narrow strait.

The bishop and the other elders were willing to accept the conditions and give them peace, but their deceits and wickednesses made them hesitate, for there is no wisdom or advice that can be matched against the Lord.[327] The people of the fort did not want to give up their wicked habits, they still thirsted to drink Christian blood, they desired to do other evil things, and their vile minds were not worthy of the gift of holy baptism. They placed their trust in the strength of their fort, they did not wish peace, and they said wicked things. They deserved to be killed, rather than to be baptized. Since it happened that they did not want peace, peace fled from them and only revenge came. The Germans, therefore, first attacked the rampart and hoped to scale the fort, but they were repelled by the defenders and were wounded by the stones and lances that were thrown. The Germans were forced, therefore, to fight with skill as well as arms. They built machines, shot stones into the fort with their paterells, against the paterells of the enemy, and made a "swine," [328] under which they dug at the fort until they came to the center of the rampart. Then, after the swine was removed, they put a strong wooden tower in its place. The ballistarii and the strong armed men climbed upon the tower and sent their spears, javelins, and lances upon the Oeselians and the fortification. They hurled rocks and missiles outside at them. After the sixth day had dawned, the first, that is, after the feast of the Purification [Feb. 3], lest that day of purification be defiled with the blood of the slain, the fight was intensified at the crack of dawn. With a curved piece of iron, or iron hook, they now took hold of, and one by one they dragged down, the huge logs by which the walls were held up, so that some part of the fortification now fell to the ground. The Christian army rejoiced, shouted, and implored God. The enemy also cried out, rejoicing in their Tharapita.[329] They called upon

327. Cf. Prov. 21:30.
328. See above, n.287.
329. The Oeselian god; see above, p. 194 (XXIV, 5).

their sacred grove, the Christians upon Jesus. In His name and in praise of Him they went up bravely and reached the top of the rampart, but they were very strongly repulsed by the enemy. The first man who went up was overwhelmed with the threats of many lances and the blows of many stones; for surely only God kept him unwounded among so many raging enemies. As he went up, he was immediately thrust back by the enemy horde. He climbed up again and again and was repulsed by the enemy each time that he tried to reach the top, until at last that same German, beating off the hostile spears with his long sword, was lifted up, as if by an angel of God. He got up on top of the battlements, above the heads of the enemy, and, lest he be wounded by the lances of the enemy, he placed his shield beneath his feet. He stood alone upon his shield and fought with the enemy [330] until God sent a second and a third man. The third man, alas, was pushed and fell back from the height. The two of them, nevertheless, defended themselves against the multitude of the enemy. Five of the Oeselians climbed up against them, behind their backs, mounted likewise to the top of the fortification, and threw their lances at them. The first of the enemy was struck by a lance, a German smote him with his sword, and he perished; [331] the others turned to flight. Other Germans followed and climbed up bravely to come to the aid of the first ones. Though they were very fiercely repelled by the savagery of the enemy, and many of them were hit and wounded, and others were killed, they had confidence, nevertheless, in the Lord; with great labor they drove back the enemy multitude and at last they reached the top of the battlements. The ascent was, however, extremely difficult, because the hill was high and icy, the wall was on top of the hill, and it was made of stones as smooth as ice, so that there were no footholds. Some

330. A hexameter line:
     . . . *stansque super clypeum solus pugnavit ad hostes.* . . .
331. Another verse line: . . . *Theutonus ense ferit, ille cadendo perit.* . . .

of them, however, got there by a ladder, some by clinging to a rope (or, rather, they were lifted up by an angel of the Lord). They pressed upon the enemy on all sides and the latter turned their backs and fled. The Christians' voice of rejoicing and salvation! [332] A voice in Rama! Lamentation and great mourning [333] of the pagans over their confusion and ruin. The Germans entered the fort and killed the people. They could not spare the Oeselian pagans: some they killed, others they captured.[334] The Livonians and Letts surrounded the fort and allowed none to escape. When the enemy was defeated, the victors rejoiced and sang praise to God. He Who always defended David from the Philistines freed His people and gave them victory over the enemy. They took the town, seized the loot, plundered the goods and fine possessions, drove away the horses and flocks, and burned what was left with fire. Fire devoured the Oeselians' fort, but the Christians rejoiced and snatched up the loot.

(5) When the fort of Mona had been reduced to ashes, the army hurried to another fort, called Waldia,[335] in the midst of Oesel. Waldia is the strongest city among all those of the Oeselians. The army encamped there, preparing the instruments of war; paterells, namely, a large machine, huge fir trees and turpentine trees to make a tower against the wall of the fort. The Livonians, Letts, and Esthonians, together with some Germans, went around to all the provinces and took away the horses, the choice cattle, many spoils, much grain, and similar things. They burned down the villages with fire. The people of Waldia could not withstand the stone missiles, because of the multitude of people who were in the fort. Likewise they could not bear up under the missiles of the ballistarii.

332. Ps. 117:15.
333. Cf. Jer. 31:15; Matt. 2:18.
334. In verse: *Parcere paganis non possunt Osilianis*
             Nam trucidant alios et capiunt alios.
335. The modern Woldia.

They took notice, also, of the instruments which had been prepared and with which the fort could easily be taken. They conceived a fear of God and begged for peace. They were dismayed by the slaying of the people of Mona and they gave themselves up humbly. They spoke peaceful words and begged that the sacrament of holy baptism be given to them. This was a joy to the Christians. They sang praise to the Lord and gave peace to the people. They demanded the sons of the better people as hostages. The Oeselians of Waldia became sons of obedience,[336] though they were once sons of pride. He who was once a wolf was now converted into a lamb. He who was formerly a persecutor of the Christians now became their brother, accepted peace, did not refuse to give hostages, faithfully begged for the grace of baptism, was not afraid to pay perpetual tribute.

The sons of the nobles were given up. The venerable bishop of Riga joyfully and devotedly catechized the first of them and watered him from the holy font. Other priests poured water on the other hostages. The priests were led with joy into the town in order to preach Christ and to throw out Tharapita, the god of the Oeselians. They consecrated a fountain in the middle of the fort, filled a jar, and, after catechism, baptized first the elders and upper-class men and then the other men, women, and boys. From morning to evening the men, women, and children crowded very closely around, shouting: "Hurry and baptize me," so that even these priests, of whom there were sometimes five, sometimes six, were worn out with the work of baptizing. The priests, therefore, baptized with the greatest devotion many thousands of people, whom they saw rush with the greatest joy to the sacrament of baptism; and they, too, rejoiced, hoping that the work would count for the remission of their sins. What they could not accomplish on that day, they completed on the next day and the third day. When these rites had been cele-

336. Cf. I Pet. 1:14.

brated in the town of Waldia, messengers came, sent from all
the towns and *kilegunds*[337] of Oesel, seeking peace and begging for the sacrament of baptism. The army rejoiced and,
when the hostages had been received, peace and fraternal love
were given. They were told to restore the captive Swedes to
freedom. They obeyed and promised to free them. They
brought priests with them to their forts to preach Christ,
throw out Tharapita and the other pagan gods, and wash the
people with holy baptism. So the priests, with great joy, baptized all the people of both sexes in all the forts of Oesel. The
priests wept from joy because, by the bath of regeneration,[338]
they were producing so many thousands of spiritual children
for the Lord and a beloved new spouse for God from among
the heathen. They watered the nation by the font, and their
faces by tears.[339]

(6) Thus does Riga always water the nations. Thus did she
now water Oesel in the middle of the sea. By washing she
purges sin[340] and grants the kingdom of the skies. She fur-
nishes both the higher and the lower irrigation.[341] These gifts
of God are our delight. The glory of God, of our Lord Jesus
Christ, and of the Blessed Virgin Mary gives such joy to His
Rigan servants on Oesel! To vanquish rebels, to baptize those
who come voluntarily and humbly, to receive hostages and
tribute, to free all the Christian captives, to return with victory—what kings have hitherto been unable to do, the Blessed
Virgin quickly and easily accomplishes through Her Rigan
servants to the honor of Her name. When this is finished,

337. See above, n.278.
338. Cf. Titus 3:5; *Rituale Romanum, Ordo Baptismi Adultorum.*
339. Cf. Ovid, *Metamorphoses*, 11:419. The sentence makes a verse line:
    Gentes fonte rigant, fletibus ora rigant.
340. Cf. the postcommunion verse of the Mass for the vigil of the Epiphany (January 5).
341. Cf. above, p. 37 (IV, 5). These three sentences form three more
verse lines: *Sic maris in medio nunc rigat Osiliam.*
          Per lavacrum purgans vitium, dans regna polorum.
          Altius irriguum donat et inferius.

when it is done, when all the people are baptized, when Tharapita is thrown out, when Pharaoh is drowned,[342] when the captives are freed, return with joy, O Rigans! Brilliantly triumphal victory always follows you. Glory be to the Lord, praise to God beyond the stars.[343]

342. Exod. 14:23–29.
343. Cf. Isa. 14:13. These two sentences make a verse couplet:
Vos semper sequitur victoria clara triumphi,
Gloria sit Domino, laus super astra Deo.

FINIS

Index

Aa, river, 61, 70, 94, 101, 102, 103, 108, 110, 111, 112, 127, 133, 138, 169, 170, 201, 213, 214
Absolon, archbishop of Lund, 35
Adia, river, 141
Adolf, count of Dassel, 196
Advocatus. See Magistrate
Agelinde, fort, 235
Ako, Livonian prince of Holm, 59, 60, 199
Alabrand, priest: builds church at Cubbesele, 65; becomes magistrate, 67; sent to Ungannia, 74–75; sent as emissary to Ungannia, 93–94; mediates quarrel, 125; reprimands Livonians, 129–30; cautions Prince Vladimir, 135; sent to Saccalia, 187–88; mentioned, 40, 134, 169
Albert, count of Lauenburg, 161, 163–66, 206
Albert I, archbishop of Magdeburg, 187
Albert of Anhalt, duke of Saxony: comes to Livonia, 173; on expedition to Semgallia, 175; operates siege machines, 181; mentioned, 176–77, 180, 183
Albert Sluc. *See* Sluc, Albert
Albert von Buxhövden, bishop of Riga: named bishop of Uexküll, 7; date of consecration, 7 n9; first journey to Livonia, 7–8; journeys to recruit pilgrims, 8; consecrated bishop, 35; secures recruits, 35; present at coronation of King Philip, 35; in Denmark, 35; journey to Livonia (1200), 36; returns to Livonia with pilgrims (1201), 38; makes peace with Kurs, 39; journey to Germany (1202), 39; translates bishopric to Riga, 40; return to Livonia (1203), 41; sanctions attack on Esthonians, 42; trip to Germany (1204), 45; return to Livonia (1205), 50; bids farewell to pilgrims, 55; negotiations with King Vladimir of Polozk, 56; receives head of Livonian prince, 60; trip to Germany (1206), 62; seeks recruits in Germany, 68; receives Livonia as imperial fief, 68; return to Livonia (1207), 68; agreement on division of Livonia, 69–70; mediates between Kokenhusen and Lennewarden, 76; recruits pilgrims in Germany (1208),

Viewold, elder of Ascheraden, 182

Viezo, Livonian of Uexküll, 26

Viliendi, fort. *See* Fellin

Vitisele, village, 230

Vladimir, prince of Polozk: receives tribute from Livonians, 26; plots attack on Riga, 54–55; sends embassy to Riga, 55; invades Ungannia, 95; prepares to attack Riga, 154; death, 154

Vladimir Mstislavich, prince of Pskov: expelled from Pskov, 120; with Bishop Albert, 120; magistrate of Letts, 131; misconduct, 133; returns to Russia, 133; comes back to Livonia, 134; goes to Russia, 135; kidnaps Theodoric, Bishop Albert's brother, 160; mentioned, 77, 122, 123, 134, 135, 156, 158, 161, 168, 169, 198

Volchard of Harpstedt, 44

Volquin, master of the Brothers of the Militia: becomes master, 89; journey to Rome (1211), 108–9; routs Lithuanians, 134; in campaign against Oesel, 240–45; mentioned, 155, 161, 167, 170–71, 183, 186, 213

Vredeland, castle, 134–35, 165

Vsevolod Mstislavich, prince of Gerzika: lament over burning of his city, 92; ransoms wife, 92; becomes vassal of Bishop Albert, 92–93; secret coöperation with Lithuanians, 93; attacked, 141–42; confers with papal legate, 233; mentioned, 90, 133, 136, 198

Vytames, elder of Saccalia, 199

Wade, Livonian of Holm, 27

Waiga, Esthonian province, 118, 146, 188, 194, 218, 228

Waip, 219

Waldeke, Livonian of Holm, 27

Waldemar II, king of Denmark (1202–41): comes to Livonia (1219), 173; detains Bishop Hermann of Esthonia, 187; wife dies (1221), 192; invades Oesel (1222), 205–6; renounces claims to Saccalia and Ungannia, 206; taken prisoner by Saxons (1223), 220 n277; mentioned, 35, 192

Waldia, Oeselian fort, 243–44

Walgatabalwe, village, 195

Walter, Danish priest, 189

Walter of Hammersleben, 87

Wane, son-in-law of Caupo, 101

Warbjala. *See* Warbole

Warbole, province, 119, 186, 206–7, 211, 217, 227, 236

Wardeke, Lett, 85

Waremar, Russian prince, 213

Waribule, son of Thalibald, 133

Waridote, elder of Autine, 83, 84, 86

Warigerbe. *See* Warigribbe

Warigribbe, 176–77, 211

Wasala, village, 194

Watmal, 29

Wattele, elder of Saccalia, 162

Wenceslaus, prince of Rügen, 173–74

Wenden, fort, 83, 89, 93–94, 99–101, 105, 107, 115–17, 123, 131, 133–34, 144–46, 157, 169–71, 177–78, 201, 213, 232

Wendendorf, 111

Wends, 66, 93, 100, 170, 201, 232

Wenno, Brother of the Militia, 85

Wentland, 166

Wescelo, chaplain of king of Denmark, 174

Westphalia, 50

Wetpole, village, 194

Wickbert, Brother of the Militia, 88–89

Wierland: devastated, 30; attacked by Livonians (1219),